The CFA Franc Zone

"Veterans of Africa's development usually say that the countries in the CFA zone face the same challenges as the rest of the continent. It is just that they face them all at once, have little analysis of the causes, and cannot talk about their currency arrangement. That is about right. This book is a pioneer attempt at filling the knowledge gap that has, for far too long, prevented governments—and the army of donors, financiers, and academics who support them—from articulating an agenda that unleashes the economic potential of a region the world has left behind. From poverty to migration, from governance to extractives, and from business climate to climate change, it is all here. And to the delight of macroeconomists, Zafar looks at the CFA regime right in the eye: is it a vestige of colonial times or is it still the right exchange rate policy when institutions are weak and trade shocks are frequent? His answers are path-breaking and kick off a debate that is as fascinating as it is overdue."

—Marcelo Giugale, *Professor at Georgetown University and former Director of the World Bank's Department of Financial Advisory and Banking Services*

"When monetary unions were first established in Africa, there were reasons to believe that they might reduce transaction costs by integrating economies of member countries and promoting market efficiency, both of which should have led to better economic performance in the member countries. This book shows us how CFA Franc zones have failed to promote strong economic growth. It presents the glaring problems of institutional design in two CFA Franc Zones in Francophone Africa. It exposes how political interests, both in Africa and France, trumped the functioning of monetary and fiscal institutions."

—Serdar Yilmaz, *Lead Public Sector Specialist, World Bank*

"Exchange rate management is among the most important policy instruments for use by a country in its quest for rapid economic growth and external balance. Yet for over 75 years, the 14 countries of the CFA zone in Africa did not have this choice, having kept the same exchange rate and monetary arrangements with their colonial power, France. Very few studies have been pursued on this issue; it is as if the world has largely passed by these countries. Zafar fills this important knowledge gap by carefully dissecting the CFA zone, reviewing its history and analyzing the effects of the fixed exchange rate regime on these economies. He makes a substantive contribution to the current policy debate by evaluating the development outcome of this currency arrangement from different economic and political perspectives. This is a fascinating and must-read book for policy makers and anyone interested in Africa development."

—Hinh T. Dinh, *Senior Fellow, Policy Center for the New South, Rabat, Morocco and Senior Research Fellow, Indiana University, Bloomington, Indiana, USA*

Ali Zafar

The CFA Franc Zone

Economic Development and the Post-Covid Recovery

palgrave
macmillan

Ali Zafar
Falls Church
VA, USA

ISBN 978-3-030-71005-7 ISBN 978-3-030-71006-4 (eBook)
https://doi.org/10.1007/978-3-030-71006-4

This Palgrave Macmillan imprint is published by the registered company Springer Nature Switzerland AG
The registered company address is: Gewerbestrasse 11, 6330 Cham, Switzerland

Preface

This book is the result of a long personal and professional journey. As a macroeconomist, my job working with many international organizations and agencies allowed me to travel to many parts of the world. It has been a blessing to see so many places and interact with so many people. Early in my career, my brother, a genuine development practitioner, advised me that if I genuinely wanted to work in the field of economic development, I should not be spending too much time hobnobbing in big cities and in conferences with the industry leaders but should be out in low-income countries talking to practitioners, entrepreneurs, and civil society representatives. He said how can one understand people's problems in poor countries unless one talks to them close up and hears their stories. It was valuable advice as it allowed me a unique vantage point into some of the development issues.

In the early part of my career, I arrived in the Republic of Congo in April 2001. It was my first trip to Sub-Saharan Africa. The Republic of Congo is deep in the heart of the African tropics and not far from the equator. It was emerging from a crisis and a difficult civil conflict. The airport has been damaged in the war, and the city was filled with military. The lush forests and humid environment made it a tropic environment. The tension in the air was palpable, and one felt in a Conradian universe.

Only when I was there did I learn the existence of the CFA zone. There were 14 countries in West and Central Africa that were tied to France and that had a fixed exchange rate and monetary arrangement with France since 1945. They were pegged to the French franc and then the euro for more than 70 years. Given the change in the world, I was surprised to discover an institutional system and exchange rate regime that had survived the Cold War, the fall of the Berlin Wall, the financial crisis, and much more. Over the years, I traveled in most of the CFA countries and got to learn their histories and cultures—from the landlocked cotton-producing triad of Burkina, Mali, and Niger to the coastal power of Cote d'Ivoire, to the conflict-plagued Central African Republic, from the charming Senegal to the oil-rich Gabon. The West is agricultural, with the Sahelian countries, sitting at the nexus of poverty and famine, while the Central zone is oil rich and vulnerable to the vagaries of the oil market. While the countries are so diverse, there are several things that bind them together—culture, language, tradition. However, none of the countries has become a prosperous, wealthy, and equitable country.

As my career path changed and I traveled a lot to Asia, especially China and Bangladesh, and the Middle East, but I never forgot the CFA zone and my rich experiences there. It always remained at the back of my mind. It was an area of promise and potential. Some of the greatest people I met have been in the CFA zone. I started learning from the experience of countries like Vietnam, Malaysia, Mauritius, and others. There were ways for countries to grow and to end poverty. No one had done so with an overvalued currency and with an institutional and exchange rate regime that dated back to the 1940s. No one had done without empowering agriculture. Most had done it with a strong manufacturing sector, with the exceptions of maybe the Vatican, India, and Singapore. I thought that what worked in one part of the world may also have a chance in another part of the world, while including adjustments to the local context.

Once I did a memorable road trip from Ouagadougou, Burkina, deep in the Sahel, to Ghana with my colleague Valerie. It was a long trip that took about 16 hours, between border crossings, administrative checkpoints, and improper roads. The most interesting part of the trip was traveling through northern Ghana and seeing a level of economic dynamism, local markets, and rural transformation that was not common in the CFA zone. I set out to explore how Anglophone Africa and Francophone Africa were similar and how in some sense were they so different. Anglophone Africa seems more dynamic, more entrepreneurial, more business and investment-friendly. Less dirigiste. And of course, the British had less desire to keep a strong colonial link as did the French.

Visiting countries like Mauritius, Rwanda, Ghana, and Ethiopia, one got a sense of growth and possibility, in a way that one did not experience in the CFA zone, whether in the oil-rich countries of CEMAC or the landlocked Sahel, or even Senegal and Cameroon, which were two of the more promising members of the CFA zone. Something was going on and I felt that it was important to try to understand it. Despite low inflation and better fiscal management than the 1990s, the CFA countries seemed to be stuck in development terms. There were general African problems, such as transport costs, lack of agricultural technology, skills gaps, and vulnerability to shocks. But there were a particular set of problems particular to the CFA. I was perplexed why a lovely country like Senegal would have a similar per capita income in the 2000s and 2010s as it had at independence in 1960. The one partial exception in the CFA zone has been Cote d'Ivoire, which has had stronger economic growth after years of conflict and which is the driver of growth in Francophone West Africa, but which unfortunately still has high poverty rates.

The CFA is one of the most interesting but understudied parts of the world. It has also been affected by stubborn poverty, despite some progress in some of the countries. The mystery of the CFA zone deepened when I learned that it was a taboo topic and that no one really discussed the merits and demerits of the existing system. The topic was considered sensitive. I found it strange that one could not have a balanced discussion about it, even among many Francophone Africans. There is an interesting world of geopolitical interests, French power, and African elites. The more I explored, the more I discovered. A world within the world so to speak. The only discussions were either from the defenders of the system, who argued that the system was fine but could benefit from tweaking to those who wanted to tear it down without fully understanding it and proposing an alternative. I felt that there are workable solutions that could benefit all parties—a win-win for France and Africa both.

Three things happened that accelerated the book. First, in December 2019, French President Emmanuel Macron and Cote d'Ivoire President Alassane Ouattara signed a deal to officially end the CFA in West Africa and to begin the reform of the zone. It was a momentous decision by two leaders who were trying to modernize the CFA arrangement and put the relationship between France and its ex-colonies on a more egalitarian footing. It was an act of political courage from these two leaders against powerful commercial interests and organized bureaucracies. They succeeded in breaking the taboo that has enveloped discussions on the zone and opening up a greater dialogue.

Second, COVID-19 happened. Even though the CFA zone was not the epicenter, the ripple effects of the virus impacted the global economy. Both developed and developing countries have felt the economic shock inflicted by the covid pandemic. Beginning in early 2020, it has caused more than three million global deaths and led to prolonged economic crises resulting in a great world recession—the most severe one since the Great Depression. Gone were the days when a country could be isolated from the global system. When a greater power coughs, other powers sneeze. The pandemic threatened to amplify the shocks that many countries faced, and it required a strong policy response. The CFA countries perhaps are not ready to deal with the shocks, due to the rigidity of their exchange rate system. As one macroeconomist wryly quipped, it is hard to run a marathon with a refrigerator on one's back.

Third, I spent time in Asia, particularly China, Bangladesh, and Vietnam and spoke to many central bankers, development practitioners, and policymakers about competitiveness. Here was a real-world lab of successful economic policy. In the 1970s, no one had imagined that these economies would take off economically. Back in the 1950s, development economists thought Africa would rise and Asian countries, especially Korea and China, had few prospects. The Asian economies benefited from good leadership and policy reform. Their policymakers merged private sector and public sector in a creative symbiosis. And they all had competitive currencies and freedom to make decisions. China's extraordinary success of becoming the world's manufacturing hub and become an export powerhouse was partly due to their ability to keep the currency competitive and even undervalued for significant periods. Why cannot the Francophone African countries have the same freedom I thought? Why cannot Francophone African policymakers have tools to fight shocks? It did not violate any of the Ten Commandments to delink from the euro, which seemed to me a very expensive currency. After all, the South Asian countries disconnected from the British pound so long ago. Why was the 1940s mindset still prevailing in a world of open ideas and information?

For many people, exchange rate is not a dinner table conversation. But the ramifications of exchange rate affect the lives of many people. The exchange rate provides the pricing framework under which global trade happens. It is the DNA of international trade. Not many people talk about it, but it matters. The exchange rate is the most important price in international trade and affects how a country competes with its neighbors. It affects whether a nation manufactures or produces food or whether it imports. If the currency becomes overvalued, your exports are considered too expensive by foreigners. One cannot talk meaningfully about reducing poverty in a country without talking of having a competitive exchange rate. Management of oil revenues, fiscal policies to deal with famines, and export promotion policies are all linked to the exchange rate in one way or another. Money matters, and incentives to export and import matter.

The more I thought about it, the more I realized that it was important to tell the story and try to connect the dots. A senior government official once told me that everyone knew the system was anachronistic, but that no one knew what would replace it. There was a critical need to modernize the system and to think of a new institutional architecture, especially for the fragile countries of the Sahel, who are facing a confluence of shocks.

The book was written for several reasons. First, I wanted to make aware to both an Anglophone audience and a Francophone one the interesting parts of the developing world and propose a plan for a revised macroeconomic, structural, and exchange rate framework to address post-COVID-19 recovery. Second, given the importance of the topic and its impact on so many people, I wanted to present an empirical analysis of the system and inject a technical assessment of a topic, based on my own analysis and a growing academic literature. Third, I also feel that discussing a reform that could have a potentially significant effect on global poverty would be interesting to a wider audience. Fourth, the idea was to bring international experience and examples to bear on the CFA zone.

Finally, the book is also meant to be part of a bigger conversation on African economies and jobs for African youth in the future. In trips to places like Bangui (Central African Republic), Douala (Cameroon), Bamako (Mali), Niamey (Niger), Ouagadougou (Burkina), and Dakar (Senegal), I met many farmers, entrepreneurs, and youth who had apprehensions of their future and expressed unhappiness at the economic system. I felt that the conversation should be expanded both globally and in Africa because many lives are still trapped in difficult poverty, with not a clear future ahead. This book is my small contribution to this debate. This is a personal book as well as an academic book. It is driven by the hope that the CFA zone will become a development success story, and that the international community help support this process.

Falls Church, VA, USA

Ali Zafar

Acknowledgments

This book has been a long time in the making. It has been motivated by my research, travels, and personal observations, as well as countless conversations with colleagues and government officials over nearly two decades. Francophone Africa is still an area of the world poorly understood outside of the region and select policy circles. The region is rich and diverse in history, culture, and natural resources, yet bonded by its colonial heritage and common currency, formally known as the CFA zone. The story of the CFA zone—its history and political economy, along with the costs and benefits of managing development under this framework—has not been fully told, in part due to inconsistent interest, but also because the topic is still perceived as taboo for many policymakers. Since the 1940s the CFA has been pegged to European currencies—first the French Franc, and since 1999 to the Euro—limiting macroeconomic policy options for its member countries. The zone is governed by a set of arrangements, whereby the 14 countries deposit 50% of their reserves in an Operations Account in the French Treasury in return for a convertibility guarantee. While the CFA zone has lower inflation than other countries, it is falling behind most developing countries in the world, including many other parts of Africa, in terms of per capita growth, competitiveness, governance, human development, and poverty reduction. Its currency is structurally overvalued, hurting exports and penalizing the rural economy. The fixed exchange rate hinders response to shocks and prevents an independent monetary policy.

As the challenges of economic development compound in face of the global pandemic and the effects of climate change, the time is ripe to expand the discussion around the CFA zone in order to strengthen African economic growth and the fight against poverty. As West Africa is planning to move to a common currency, it is an opportune time for a modernization of an outdated CFA franc system and a strengthening of African sovereignty. Handling the post-COVID-19 recovery in the short and medium term will require a full arsenal of weapons—replacement of the euro peg with a more market-based and flexible exchange rate regime, fiscal stimulus, fiscal transfers within the zone, especially to landlocked countries, to deal with asymmetric shocks, and countercyclical monetary policy—that are vitally necessary in the CFA zone. These countries have to sequence macro reforms to address the myriad challenges.

This book raises sensitive policy issues and attempts to explore them in a straightforward manner, and it is my sincere hope that it catalyzes thoughtful and productive dialogue. As sole author, the opinions and recommendations expressed herein are my own; however, I am grateful for the support, guidance, and technical feedback of many people who challenged my ideas and helped shape my thinking on this topic over the years including, in no particular order, Shanta Devarajan, Marcelo Giugale, Hinh T. Dinh, Darryl McLeod, Emmanuel Pinto Moreira, Theresa Osborne, Helene Purcell, Cadman Mills, Salomon Samen, El Mechry El Koudouss, Cyrus Talati, Errol Graham, Hippolyte Fofack, Lawrence Hinkle, Volker Treichel, Sebastian Dessus, Alessandro Nicita, David Cal McWilliam, Philip English, Blanca Moreno Dodson, Keiko Kubota, Miria Pigato, Vasco Molini, Paolo Zacchia, Raju Singh, and Valerie Nussenblatt. Many others have also provided input but have asked to remain anonymous given that they continue to play important roles in policymaking. In certain instances, I have drawn upon the work of others to advance an argument that deserves consideration in this context. Finally, I owe a particular note of thanks to my wife and my family for their unflagging encouragement, support, and patience with my extended travel over the years.

Contents

List of Figures

List of Tables

List of Boxes

PART I

Anatomy of the CFA Zone

CHAPTER 1

The Context

Africa is a vast continent, and the CFA zone encompasses large parts of West and Central Africa. The continent's large size, its heterogeneity with more than 50 countries, and its unique history and tapestry make it a fascinating one for study. Africa is larger than China, India, and the United States combined, and the Sahara Desert is close to the size of the continental United States and represents one-quarter of the African landmass. Africa has been at the center of early civilization and has been enjoying economic growth before the pandemic. It is a heterogeneous continent, with a wide variety of countries, political systems, and development paths, as well as a diversity of landscapes. Besides the North African countries, which are more closely linked to the Middle East culturally, Sub-Saharan Africa consists of four main regions: West Africa, Central Africa, East Africa, and Southern Africa.

While Africa currently accounts for more than 1 billion people and close to 15% of the world population, it is less than 3% of the global GDP. Over the next two decades, its share of world population will increase. Africa can be the next development frontier, with a vast landmass, favorable demographics, rich resource endowment (oil, gold, diamonds, and other metals), and youthful population. After several decades during the postwar era of political crisis, poor economic performance, and sporadic conflict, by the 2000s, Africa may have turned a corner, guided by

A. Zafar, *The CFA Franc Zone*,
https://doi.org/10.1007/978-3-030-71006-4_1

rising commodity prices, a generation of new leaders, growing democratization, and greater sophistication in its macroeconomic management. Foreign investment in renewable energy, infrastructure, and finance has increased significantly, and there is a growing potential for public–private partnership (PPP) projects.

The two dominant economies in Sub-Saharan Africa are Nigeria and South Africa. Nigeria has emerged after decades of military rule and economic mismanagement with a democratic leadership, improved economic policies, and a greater pan-African vision. It has more than 200 million people and has been trying to diversify its oil-led economy but has been hit by the oil price volatility and Boko Haram terrorism. South Africa, which by some metrics is the most industrialized economy in Africa, has emerged from the shadows of apartheid to try to forge a path forward, but its success has been challenged by political crises, electricity shortages, growing debt, and rising crime. Over the next decade, these two economies will be important drivers of African recovery and growth.

Other regional powers have emerged and been among the faster growing global economies. Ethiopia, spurred by state-led public investment, a rising service sector, and a nascent manufacturing sector, has been one of the fast growers in Africa. Rwanda, which has recovered dramatically in the wake of one of the worst genocides in the twentieth century, is now an economy driven by service sector growth, business sector reform, and growing foreign direct investment. Mauritius, Botswana, and Ghana have also exhibited economic dynamism and have ridden on the back of the commodity boom and apt economic management. While in the past Africa was known for much corruption, the rise of countries with strong public administration, like Rwanda and Botswana, suggests a new forward path for the continent.

In the African continent, the CFA zone is a unique region. The CFA zone encompasses 14 low-income, mostly francophone countries in Central and West Africa, accounting for nearly a third of Sub-Saharan African states. Many of these countries have been left behind in terms of growth, development, and political evolution. Firstly, it has maintained a very tight link to its former colonial power France for more than 70 years. French influence reigns supreme—in language, in cuisine, in administration, in political system, and in the currency peg. Second, in recent years, it has a few of the faster growing economies in Sub-Saharan Africa, including Cote d'Ivoire, juxtaposed with many of the poorest ones. It is one of the parts of the world where poverty has not improved significantly despite decades of international aid flows. Fourth, the northern Sahelian part of the CFA zone has become afflicted by jihadist activity and terrorist violence in recent years.

As the development industry focuses more attention on the fragile states and on the countries that have failed to eradicate poverty, the CFA zone will be at the top of the list. It is a microcosm of many salient issues in international development, ranging from low human development to climate change, to conflict traps and to lack of economic diversification. Some of the CFA countries are countries where the government does not have full control of its territory (Mali and Central African Republic), where borders are porous (Burkina, Chad, Niger), and where the land-mass is too huge to administer. The fate of these countries depends on the politics of both France and the coastal countries who provide unique access to the sea.

Not only in a development sense, but in a macroeconomic sense, the CFA is fascinating. It is the oldest fixed exchange rate regime in the world. Its original acronym was CFA (*Colonies Francaises d'Afrique).* Dating from the end of the the Second World War, the CFA is a legacy of Charles de Gaulle and his vision for a tighter postwar Franco-African collaboration. There are two zones: the CFA *Communauté Financière d'Afrique* [Financial Community of Africa] in West Africa and *Coopération Financière en Afrique* [Financial Cooperation in Africa] in Central Africa).

The CFA predates the euro, which is of much more recent vintage. The CFA began as a currency union and now is trying to become a political union, while the euro began as a free trade area and political union, and then tried to become a monetary union as articulated in the 1992 Maastricht Treaty. The genesis of both arrangements has been one with a potentially good economic rationale—to create growth and development by leveraging the economies of scale. Like the EU, the CFA has multiple convergence criteria linked to inflation, debt, and interest rates to maintain a certain harmony. The EU has been a club that more countries have been joining, while the CFA has not attracted many new entrants since its origins.

The CFA zone is an important part of Sub-Saharan Africa in terms of size and influence. The two zones are around the same size in terms of output. With a total population of more than 150 million people and a combined gross domestic product (GDP) of more than $220 billion, the

CFA zone accounted for at least 15% of Sub-Saharan Africa's population and 15% of its GDP in 2020. None of the larger African economies—Kenya, Nigeria, South Africa—are in the zone. In this regard, one of the disadvantages of the CFA zone is the presence of many thinly populated countries with small domestic market size.

The two CFA subzones have several distinctive structural and economic features. The CFA franc is the common currency and the linchpin of the monetary architecture of the zone, which was fixed to the French franc before 1999 and has been fixed to the euro since 1999. Both CFA subzones peg their currency to the euro at the same parity. Around half of the economies in Sub-Saharan Africa are pegged currencies, either to the euro or the dollar, while the other half have an intermediate or floating regime. The larger economies, such as South Africa and Nigeria, tend to have managed floats, where the central banks intervene to smooth currency fluctuations.

There are many differences between the CFA zone and the rest of the developing world. First, these are old currency arrangements, having been preserved during all the ebbs and flows of the world economy for over 70 years. Second, the countries of the zone are highly heterogeneous, including poorer, landlocked, Sahelian economies and wealthier coastal countries. In the WAEMU, Côte d'Ivoire and Senegal are the dominant economies accounting for more than half the GDP, while the CEMAC is led by Cameroon and Gabon. From the oil wealth of Equatorial Guinea and Republic of Congo to the diamond wealth of the Central African Republic to the cotton base in Benin, Burkina, and Mali, the zone encompasses diverse geographies and economies. As in the EU, the zones are agglomerations of countries with significant differentials in GDP and poverty. The landlocked countries of the CFA zone have been vulnerable to terms of trade shocks, security threats, political instability, and difficult geography, and their fortunes are wrapped up with those of the coastal economies. In the last few years, there is greater political instability and a volatile security environment, especially in countries like Central African Republic and Mali.

Although there has been a strong recent push toward the creation of a single currency in the ECOWAS West African region and a common trading space, historically in the CFA zone, integration has not been viewed as a vehicle for greater integration with the global trading system. The subregions remain somewhat isolated from the global economy in a way that the Association of Southeast Asian Nations (ASEAN) and the Southern Cone Common Market are not. Intraregional trade in the UEMOA is still a bit above 10%, while within CEMAC, intraregional trade is even lower, currently at 5%. The countries trade mostly with Europe and Asia, rather than with each other, but there has been a growing shift to non-EU trade. In UEMOA, trade with France has fallen from more than half of total trade to a quarter in recent years. Oil is a dominant trade item in the CEMAC subzone; five of the six countries are oil producers. Cocoa, cotton, and iron ore are dominant in the WAEMU subzone. The recent environment for the two subregions has been shaped by price volatility, leading to fluctuations in output and revenue.

The CFA consists of two zones, which are different from one another—in wealth, in geography, and in politics. CEMAC represents a world of oil, of ecoforests, of ruling families, of dynastic politics, and of complex political economy. Besides having very low historical growth in per capita incomes, the zone is also characterized by a high dependence on oil and forest exports, volatility in economic growth, domination by two economies, very limited intraregional linkages, juxtaposition of richer coastal and poorer landlocked countries, and political instability within CEMAC and neighboring countries (Zafar and Kubota 2003). UEMOA is a world of contrasts, a land of cocoa and cotton, a land where the Sahara expansion south continues to shape the landscape. There are clear leaders and lagging countries in each of the two zones.

The Sahelian countries export raw materials and labor to Cote d'Ivoire, while the latter exports manufactured products to the hinterland, and the same happens to Cameroon in CEMAC. The inequality between the countries continues to be a problem. The zone has been shaped by history and migration. For the landlocked countries, migration has been part of the DNA. Pastoralists have migrated with their livestock searching for new pastures and water, while the youth have migrated both to the coastal countries, like Cote d'Ivoire, and abroad, to Europe and the United States. Many Sahelians live overseas now.

MAP: CFA ZONE

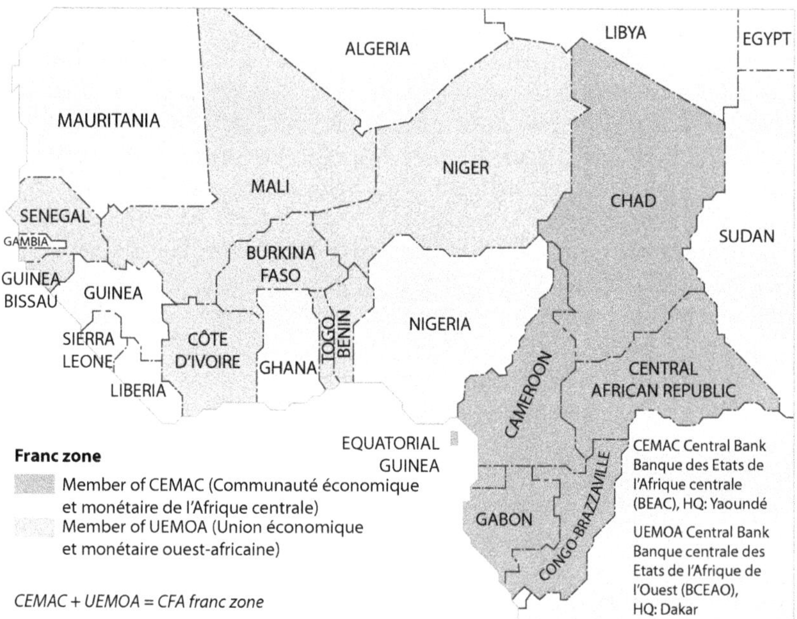

The CFA zone is the only region in the world whose exchange rate and institutional arrangements have persisted for so long with so little change amidst a world which has changed a big deal. Communism rose and fell, the euro was born less than twenty-five years ago, China moved from communism to a more capitalistic economy, Eastern Europe became independent from the Soviet Union, the subprime mortgage crisis happened, but the CFA zone has persisted with few institutional changes. It also survived the end of the fixed exchange regime of the Bretton Woods system in 1971. And it has survived the 9/11 terror attacks, the financial crisis, and the COVID-19 pandemic, although with modifications.

The French legacy remains strong and alive—from the baguettes in the cafes to the names of streets such as Avenue Charles de Gaulle, to the widespread use of the language to the cultural ties between the African elite and France. As can be seen by the composition of the French soccer team which won the World Cup, there are strong affiliations between France and its former colonies, with many of the players now French citizens. The political ties between the Francophone elite and France also remain strong. As was said long ago, the CFA zone gives France some vestiges of its lost empire and helps France have a strong geopolitical footprint. Many who tried to dissent from the political equilibrium, like Thomas Sankara of Burkina Faso and Sylvanus Olympio of Togo, were pushed aside and were assassinated. There have been dark chapters in the history of the CFA but the potential of the region has always been there.

Whatever happens in the CFA zone can have an impact beyond the CFA zone—in terms of migration, of terrorism, and of famine. It is an area of potential in terms of resource endowment, human capabilities, and aspiring entrepreneurs and social activists. The CFA zone can benefit from the support of the international community to become a prosperous zone, but it will also require its own governments to accelerate the development and reform path. In words that can be partly relevant to the CFA zone, academic Collier (2007) has argued in his study of the "bottom billion" of the world's population:

> Let me be clear: we cannot rescue them. The societies of the bottom billion can only be rescued from within. In every society of the bottom billion there are people working for change, but usually they are defeated by the powerful internal forces stacked against them. We should be helping the heroes. So far, our efforts have been paltry: through inertia, ignorance, and incompetence, we have stood by and watched them lose.

However, in the case of the CFA zone, outsiders, particularly France, and the aid community have continued to play an important role, affecting the evolution and nature of reform. The CFA zone has not been on the radar screen on many Anglo-American policymakers and travelers, but is only associated with crisis, as was seen in the Sahel recently. Travel and plane connections are difficult, and for those without knowledge of the French language, it is not easy to navigate the culture. English-speaking investors have been reluctant to invest in Francophone Africa due to a combination of language, security, and bureaucracy.

CFA economies tend to be poorer than many emerging market economies, as measured by per capita income, and the CEMAC economies are richer than UEMOA economies on a per capita income basis, mostly due to oil abundance (Table 1.1). They are also countries with lower inflation than others, but they have lower growth. One does not see in the CFA zone the likes of Ethiopia or Rwanda. Compared to East Asian countries, neither the CFA zone nor other African economies have performed well. Competitiveness rankings from the World Economic

Table 1.1 CFA zone in Africa: data and comparisons 2019

	GNI	*Real GDP*	*Inflation*	*Fiscal balance*	*Current account balance*	*Govt debt*	*Competitiveness*
	Per capita/Atlas ($)	*(%)*	*(%)*	*(% GDP)*	*(% GDP)*	*(% GDP)*	*Ranking/141*
CFA ZONE		4.6	0.2	−1.5	−4.2	47.6	
UEMOA		6.0	−0.6	−2.4	−5.0	45.0	
Benin	1250	6.9	−0.9	−0.5	−4.3	41.2	125
Burkina	790	5.7	−3.2	−3.5	−4.8	42.7	130
Cote d'Ivoire	2290	6.5	0.8	−2.3	−2.7	37.9	118
Mali	880	5.1	−2.9	−1.7	−4.2	40.5	129
Niger	560	5.9	−2.5	−3.6	−12.6	41.7	NA
Senegal	1450	5.3	1.0	−3.8	−7.7	64.1	114
Togo	690	5.3	0.7	2.1	−4.3	70.9	NA
CEMAC		2.0	1.8	0.0	−2.8	51.8	
Cameroon	1500	3.9	2.5	−3.3	−4.4	42.7	123
CAR	520	3.0	2.7	1.4	−4.9	47.2	NA
Chad	700	3.0	−1.0	−0.2	−4.9	44.3	141
Congo, Rep of	1750	−0.6	2.2	5.8	3.5	83.7	NA
Equatorial Guinea	6460	−6.1	1.2	1.8	−5.9	41.1	NA
Gabon	7210	3.8	2.0	2.1	−0.3	62.4	119
Other African							
Ethiopia	850	9.0	15.8	−2.5	−5.3	57.6	126
Ghana	2220	6.5	7.2	−7.3	−2.7	62.8	111
Kenya	1817	5.4	5.2	−7.7	−5.8	62.1	95
Nigeria	2030	2.2	11.4	−4.8	−3.8	29.1	116
Rwanda	820	9.4	2.4	−5.2	−9.2	51.4	100
South Africa	6040	0.2	4.1	−6.3	−3.0	62.2	60
Other Asian							
Bangladesh	1940	8.2	5.5	−5.3	−1.7	35.9	105
Indonesia	4050	5.2	3.1	−1.8	−2.9	30.2	50
Malaysia	11,200	4.5	0.7	−3.4	3.5	57.1	27
Philippines	3850	6.0	4.5	−2.7	−1.6	38.9	64
Thailand	7260	2.4	0.7	−0.2	5.4	43.0	40

Source IMF, World Bank (GNI per capita), World Economic Forum
Note The fiscal and current account balances include grants

Forum place the CFA countries below even African comparators like South Africa and Kenya.

References

Collier, Paul. 2007. *The Bottom Billion: Why the Poorest Countries Are Failing and What Can Be Done About It*. Oxford: Oxford University Press.

Zafar, Ali, and Keiko Kubota. 2003. *The CEMAC: Regional Integration in Central Africa: Key Issues*. The World Bank Working Papers-Africa Region Working Papers 52, Washington, DC.

CHAPTER 2

The Institutional Arrangements That Govern the Zone

The CFA zone has several interesting features—including a particular set of exchange rate arrangements and its own currency pegged to the euro. Printed in a town called Chamalières in France by the Banque de France since 1945, the currency is used as legal tender in each of the two subzones. As part of the common zone, countries do not pursue an independent monetary policy, but instead use a collective monetary policy to support the fixed exchange peg. Monetary policy for the countries is managed by two central banks, the *Banque des États de l'Afrique Centrale* (Bank of the Central African States, BEAC) and the *Banque des États de l'Afrique de l'Ouest* (Central Bank of the West African States, BCEAO), with the overriding goal of maintaining price stability and low inflation. This arrangement is unique in the developing world, where monetary policy is more typically managed by national authorities.

As part of the CFA setup, there are several key elements.

- Firstly, the anchor of the system is a **fixed rate of exchange** with the euro set at 1 euro = 656 CFA francs. In macroeconomic terms, it is a hard peg that can be only altered with a devaluation or revaluation. According to the conventions of the CFA, France has had the ultimate say in parity adjustment.
- Second, there is a centralization and **pooling of reserves in an Operations Account with the French Treasury.** Where they are

A. Zafar, *The CFA Franc Zone*,
https://doi.org/10.1007/978-3-030-71006-4_2

required to pool 50% of reserves in an overdraft facility, representing 50% of the net foreign assets of the two regional central banks.

- Third, the French Treasury acts as a provider of a **convertibility guarantee.** Under the agreement, the French Government agrees to buy CFA and sell euros at a fixed exchange rate in unlimited amounts, and the French Treasury also pledges support for balance of payments imbalances. Although the BCEAO and BEAC have an overdraft facility with the French Treasury, the drawdowns on such facilities are subject to the consent of the French Treasury and based on strictly commercial terms.
- A final feature of the system is the **free capital transfer** between the two zones and France, leading to a situation of minimal exchange rate risk. There is no friction in currency movements within each zone. Profit repatriation of foreign companies is done without major issues.

The Operations Accounts have played an important role in the architecture of the CFA and are mostly the deposits of CFA African export receipts. They are unique in international monetary circles and imply an unconditional support to convert the money. It is a de facto overdraft facility of the French Treasury that absorbs unlimited CFA exchange rates so there is never any depressed demand for the CFA. Immediately following independence, this figure stood at 100% (and from 1973 to 2005, at 65%). It was reduced to 50% following the surpluses in CEMAC in the 2000s, leading to the French desire for fewer reserves. As CEMAC reserves accumulated in the wake of the oil boom in the early 2000s, there was less need for such a large share, although there has never been a precise rationale for the percent of reserves in the Operations Account. Until recently, France was given a minority of seats on the governing board of each of the two regional central banks.

The management of the Operations Account has been a subject of debate. It is important to centralize reserves to defend the fixed exchange rate. Reserves at 3 months of imports are a standard reserve adequacy metric, but there are several perspectives for optimal reserve management.

The conventional IMF view is that the Operations Account is required to guarantee the convertibility of the currency. From the French Treasury perspective, the Operations Account is necessary for the maintenance of the system. A recent report from September 2020 commissioned by the French Senate and conducted by Nathalie Goulet and Victorin Lurel argues that France does not gain financially from the centralization of reserves.[1] France pays an annual interest rate with a ceiling of 0.75% to the region's two central banks. Rather, France has paid 40.6 million euros in 2018 and 40.4 million euros in 2019, as the remuneration for the BCEAO reserves managed by the French Treasury. From the African civil society perspective, the Operations Account represents a use and control of African resources without a clear accounting.

In reality, it is challenging to understand the Operations Account as there has not been a formal audit. On the one hand, the combined reserves represent a small portion of French public debt. The guarantee constitutes a contingent liability of the French Treasury in case of a drawdown of outstanding balances of the Operations Account (Hadjimichael and Galy 1997). However, it is unclear if some of the funds are invested in French government debt instruments, as is common for many central banks.

One important point that has been lost in the debate is the exact nature and degree of the French guarantee. For one thing, at a practical level, it is hard to change CFA francs either outside the zone or in other parts of the world, including France. The legal tender does not have a recognized market value or acceptability. Moreover, it has rarely been tested. First, there are certain fiscal rules and conventions in the zone that prevent the buildup of deficits in the accounts. The two central banks, BEAC and BCEAO, each must maintain foreign exchange coverage of at least 20% of liabilities, and the institutional rules restrict governments from borrowing domestically above 20% of the tax revenues of the previous year. These are meant to prevent the monetization of fiscal deficits, where central banks are used by governments for their own fiscal needs.[2]

Second, for much of the recent history, both the BCEAO and the BEAC Operations Account have been in surplus, with only a few years

[1] https://www.seneplus.com/economie/le-senat-francais-valide-une-reforme-cosmetique-du-fcfa.

[2] The rules of the Franc zone are designed to ensure that there is a ceiling on global credit growth that matches the GDP growth in the individual countries. The main policy target of the BEAC and BCEAO is to maximize the role of net foreign assets in the banking system. By design, the CFA arrangement limits two financial flows: private sector borrowing from the central government and statutory advances to governments. These must be contained to prevent a situation where the reserves are not sufficient to maintain the convertibility of the currency and where excess fiscal spending can lead to a decline in the country's net foreign asset position.

where there was a deficit. The BCEAO's Operations Account was in deficit from 1980 to 1984 and in 1988–1989, while drawings on the Operations Account in BEAC were generally in more surplus, except during the difficult 1993–1994 period. During the 2000s and 2010s, the accounts were most in surplus, except for challenges in CEMAC in 2015. Third, in a point that is frequently misunderstood, the pooling of reserves guarantees a surplus. One countries surplus will compensate for another country's deficit. So frequently, it is the surplus countries in the zone financing the non-surplus countries. For example, according to the IMF, in 2019, the net foreign assets in the BEAC Operations Account, representing half of total net foreign assets, were in surplus in Cameroon (CFA 80 billion) and the Republic of Congo (CFA 156 billion), while the accounts for Gabon (CFA 17 billion) and Equatorial Guinea (47 billion) were in deficit.

Finally, the changing finances in France, who faces fiscal challenges in the context of the EU convergence criteria, and the growing financial clout of the IMF post-2010 mean that it is the IMF, with French support, that is the lender of last resort for CFA countries when facing protracted balance of payments problems. While France pumped billions into the CFA economies in the 1990s, it is the IMF that has been bailed out by the CEMAC economies in recent years, especially after the oil price shocks in the mid-2010s. It is frequently the IMF and World Bank who provide the necessary financing support to support the budget.

In the CFA system, monetary policy ceases to be a powerful tool of macroeconomic management and the central banks do not pursue active interest rate policy as a key goal to safeguard the currency.[3] As policy instruments, the central banks of the CFA zones use ceilings on government credit, reserve ratios, and quantitative targets on central bank refinancing of commercial banks. The system survives because there is an implicit commitment by French authorities to support the currency. The technical features of the system combine with other elements of the Franco-African political relationship and also involve aid coordination.

[3] One important nuance to recognize is that while the CFA franc is the same parity to the euro, the two CFA Francs are not directly convertible into each other. Once when I tried to convert Cameroonian CFA into West Africa CFA with an authorized dealer in Dakar, he looked with surprise at the Cameroonian note. When I reminded him that the currency was the same name and same worth, he was even more surprised and looked at the CEMAC currency in a dismissive way. In practice, the CFA francs are issued by two distinct central banks.

The system revolves around a coordination framework involving consultations between French and African states, including biannual meetings of the Ministers of Finance and Governors of the central banks of the Franc Zone countries. The policy objectives for both CEMAC and UEMOAare usually decided by an Annual Conference of Heads of State and focus on regional integration, competitiveness, and macroeconomic policy convergence.

The institutional structure has been developed over the last two decades, and there are an array of institutions, including a Court of Justice, a UEMOA Commission in Bamako and a CEMAC Secretariat in Bangui, and a business council. Regional legislation has been developed under the "*l'harmonisation en Afrique du droit des affaires*" (OHADA). OHADA is a system of corporate law which provides the legal framework and texts for the two zones. The architecture of the two zones is modeled on the European Union and has evolved over time.

France has been the anchor of the system in some ways, and gives a degree of credibility, but it has also impacted the countries' sovereignty. Although France's formal powers under its monetary cooperation agreements with CEMAC and UEMOA are limited, it has been the underwriter of the Zone's exchange rate and plays an informal policy leadership role as the de facto enforcer of rules. Under the agreements, any change in the parity can be done after consultations between regional authorities and the French government. Van de Walle (1991) argues that the arrangements of the Franc zone take sovereignty of monetary matters away from member states and once the decision has been made to remain in the zone, this makes the exchange rate exogenous to policy. He also notes that the conservative rules in theory put a limit on deficit spending taking away one development tool.

However, the French role has decreased in recent years, as France does not get involved in the regional trade organizations or the conferences with heads of state. French aid, which was very important in the 1980s, has dwindled by the 2000s, as France has reoriented itself to domestic and global priorities. Other actors and players are becoming more involved in the CFA zone, including China and Morocco. Multilateral institutions, such as the IMF, World Bank, and African Development Bank, have become more important players.

Regional Surveillance and Convergence Criterion

Membership in the subregional groupings provides a framework for shared economic policy. The membership in the CEMAC and the WAEMU has created a zonal framework for macroeconomic surveillance and an institutional forum for policy dialogue through adherence to a set of subregionally determined convergence criteria. These are a set of fiscal and structural targets to which the countries adhere to contain monetary and fiscal expansion. Modeled on the EU's growth and stability pact, the convergence criteria for the CFA countries focus on budget balances, debt levels, and inflation rates with a goal of ensuring sustainability of national fiscal policies and public debt sustainability. The idea of the convergence policies was that the fiscal system should be balanced as unsustainable spending in some part of the zone, as was seen in Southern Europe with the euro, will undermine the credibility of the zones. The rationale was to prevent the zones from fiscal indiscipline.

The latest surveillance framework, adopted in 2015, centers around a 3% of GDP central government overall fiscal deficit ceiling, nominal debt at 70% of GDP for the region as while, and a 3% target for a country's annual average inflation. The CEMAC criteria are similar but include an additional one on preventing an accumulation of arrears. In practical terms, there has been an uneven success with regard to meeting the convergence criteria. Both zones are better at managing deficits and arrears compared to the 1990s, when deficits reached more than 5 percent of GDP. In UEMOA, all countries have recently been compliant with inflation and debt targets; however, in 2017, five countries were non-compliant with the fiscal deficit target, and in 2019, 2 were non-compliant. The terms of trade shocks faced by many countries have made it difficult for policymakers to comply. From the perspective of the Bank of France, Cabrillac and Rocher (2013) find that while macroeconomic convergence programs in CEMAC have led to a convergence of debt levels, fiscal deficits have tended to diverge. Moreover, in the early years, the CFA countries relied on statutory advances, and in some cases indirect financing of budget deficits via domestic commercial banks to bypass some of the fiscal rules of the zone. In theory, countries that deviate from the "convergence criteria" have to develop a corrective program, but it is in practice, hard to implement. After rules were put into place to reduce central banks financing the government deficits, the countries turned to the bond markets and there was a large increase in the issuance of government bonds and local currency debt.

Uniqueness of CFA

From a global perspective, the CFA regime remains an anomaly. The system is designed to insulate the economies from excess volatility by providing a strong nominal anchor, but there are several difficulties. First, the general tendency has been to move from fixed to more floating systems. Second, the deposits of 50% of reserves in a foreign country have been unique to the CFA arrangement, as has been the loss of sovereignty. Third, as opposed to many central bankers, the CFA monetary authorities have not demonstrated a strong concern about avoiding currency overvaluation. Finally, the CFA zone defies the emerging consensus among macroeconomists of the ability of well-designed managed float regimes to intervene to smooth excessive fluctuations of a currency in response to trade shocks.

Not all economies in the world are floating exchange rates. But hard pegs to expensive currencies are the aberration, not the norm. Years of macroeconomic research have demonstrated the ability of exchange rates to respond to real shocks. Kenneth Rogoff, former IMF Chief Economist, has provided an interesting description of fixed exchange rate.

> Perhaps economic historians will look back on today's patchwork global exchange rate arrangements as a latter-day Tower of Babel. But what other system is there? With freely flowing capital, a fixed exchange rate has the life expectancy of a Hollywood marriage. (Rogoff 2002)

There are several countries in the Middle East and East Asia that are still pegged to the dollar. Lebanon has kept a dollar peg for more than two decades as an anchor for economic stability, but that is currently under threat given the recent economic crises affecting that country. Lebanon's currency peg, an anchor of financial and social stability for more than two decades, is struggling and attempts to stabilize the exchange rate in the wake of the 2020 political and economic crises as well as the aftermath of the explosion at the port are adding to the chaos.

Saudi Arabia, the world's largest oil producer, has kept a peg to the US dollar for more than three decades. Partly due to the fact that oil is priced in dollars and partly due to the clout of the US economy, the Saudi authorities have seen the dollar as an anchor for monetary stability. But Saudi Arabia is sitting on an asset that the whole world craves. China, once pegged to the dollar, abandoned the dollar peg in the mid-2000s, and developed a managed float system, partly in response to global pressure accusing it of currency manipulation. Hong Kong, pegged to the US dollar in 1983, has based its decision on the need to protect its status as a financial hub and as a US dollar trading area.

Then there is the case of the Eastern Caribbean countries. Nine of the 14 independent Caribbean Community (CARICOM) countries are pegged to the dollar for many years: Antigua and Barbuda, Bahamas, Belize, Barbados, Dominica, Grenada, St Kitts-Nevis, St Lucia, and St Vincent and the Grenadines. By statute, the Eastern Caribbean Central Bank (ECCB) is mandated to maintain foreign exchange reserves at not less than 60% of demand liabilities, with member countries surrendering and pooling their reserves to the ECCB. There is no convertibility guarantee with the US Treasury, and the reserves are maintained in the Caribbean. While in the past these economies used to export sugar and bananas, tourism has become the key foreign exchange earner. Since the main source of revenue is tourism linked to the US dollar, the peg helps these economies with a stable foreign exchange inflow. In southern Africa, the Rand Monetary Area, made of South Africa, Lesotho, and Swaziland, the latter two peg their currencies to the South African but keep independence in changing the parities and do not coordinate monetary policy.

These arrangements are not academic arrangements but affect the life of an economy, the competitiveness of its exports, and the well-being of its citizens, given that many of these economies are open commodity-exporting economies that trade with the world and not autarchic economies. It is the exchange rate the governs their relationship with the outside world. From a macroeconomic standpoint, the exchange rate remains the principal instrument for adjustment. Foreign trade usually means that the costs of production are in one currency and the revenues from exports are in another currency. Exchange rates respond to economic shocks by fluctuating, affecting the incentives to export and to import. It is no accident that many countries' currencies are linked to the price of their commodity export—Canadian dollar and oil, Australian dollar and iron ore, and Russian ruble and oil.

References

Cabrillac, Bruno, and Emmanuel Rocher. 2013. Les Perspectives des Unions Monétaires Africaines. *Revue d'économie financière* 110 (2): 99.

Hadjimichael, Michael T., and Michel Galy. 1997. The CFA Franc Zone and the EMU. *IMF Working Papers* 97 (156): 1.

Rogoff, Kenneth. 2002. Managing the World Economy, Economic Counsellor and Director of the Research Department, International Monetary Fund, The Economist, London.

Van de Walle, Nicholas. 1991. The Decline of the Franc Zone: Monetary Politics in Francophone Africa. *African Affairs* 90 (360) (March): 383–405.

CHAPTER 3

History of the CFA Zone

Origins

The sixteenth century marks some of the beginnings of the wave of European colonization of the Americas and of Africa. Around the time that the Mayflower was arriving in Massachusetts in 1620, the French were starting to build trading outputs in West Africa, especially Senegal. By the 1800s, this process had accelerated, leading to a "Scramble for Africa" toward the end of the nineteenth century. While there was a booming slave trade, France abolished slavery in the colonies in 1848. Capitalizing on the decline of the Ottoman Empire, France expanded its West African empire and started settling these areas and expanding in geographical reach. Military administrators were increasingly accompanied by civilians. Over time, the French administrative system evolved, and the colonies developed a formal structure. The colonial experience created flourishing commercial and cultural interactions. By the end of World War II, there were new developments in the French colonies.

The CFA zone has a very colorful and long history. The initial phase was the creation of the CFA. It was based on a currency that had been created during the prewar era because it was too difficult to transport cash from France to its colonies. It was officially created on December 26, 1945 by General Charles de Gaulle in order to strengthen French and African commercial and political times in the aftermath of World War II.

A. Zafar, *The CFA Franc Zone*,
https://doi.org/10.1007/978-3-030-71006-4_3

De Gaulle was the French statesman who tried to cement France's postwar imprint and create a sphere of influence by solidifying ties between France and its African colonies. Probably the most towering French political figure of the twentieth century, de Gaulle was many things. It is no accident that Paris's airport is named after him. The former French army officer, the statesmen and leader of Free French Forces against the Nazis, the founder of the Fifth Republic, de Gaulle was the mastermind of the French modern state and of continuation of its leadership role in Africa. In spite of decolonization, de Gaulle wanted to maintain a strong French footprint in Africa. The idea was to build political and economic institutions that can support these links.

France was not unique as the UK also had the sterling zone and the Commonwealth, but the French connections were deeper and more pervasive. There was a debate at the beginning on the nature of the post-colonial state and if the CFA zone was to remain as two federations or as multiple independent states. De Gaulle's purpose was also for France to continue to have a global footprint. Humiliated by the war and worried about the ascent of American power, de Gaulle struggled to preserve the French global role. Unfortunately, the absence of discussion and debate with local leaders meant that there was never any real consultation on setting up the CFA system.

The right-hand man of De Gaulle, and the main architect of France-afrique was a man called Jacques Foccart. By all accounts, he was a charming but secretive man. As adviser to three French presidents on African affairs, and as a political fixer, Foccart played a central role in the development of France's relations with the ex-colonies. Most importantly, he created the network of arrangements and connections that allowed the flows of finance, intelligence, and ideas. He was a master strategist. From the France-afrique, there was continued French influence in the politics, the administration, and the economies of the countries. Foccart was connected to many of the postcolonial rulers in the CFA and had a close understanding of the African political and social landscape. As opposed to the rupture many countries had with their ex-colonies, Foccart's work allowed the umbilical cord between France and its ex-colonies to not be severed. When he died of Parkinson's in 1997, he also took with him to his grave many experiences and secret knowledge.

On the African side, the French relied on Felix Houphouet-Boigny, the former tribal chief and union leader, who led Cote d'Ivoire after independence in 1960, serving as its first President from 1960 to 1993. He was a planner and the architect of the Ivorian economic boom in the early years and managed to maintain good relations with the international community. Under Boigny, Cote d'Ivoire became a strong agricultural nation, with a vibrant coffee and cocoa industry. From his perspective, a strong relationship with France was in the best long-term interests of Cote d'Ivoire. The CFA architecture cemented the deal, and Boigny was one of the more prominent supporters and fought hard against opponents of the Government's Francophone policy. He had celebrated fights with Kwame Nkrumah, the visionary leader of Ghana and first President who advocated a more nationalist road with a stronger rupture in ties with the West. Their celebrated wager in the 1950s on which country would become more prosperous—Ghana or Cote d'Ivoire, is the story of legend but has continued to reverberate to this day.

Then you have the story of Thomas Sankara, the President of Burkina Faso from 1983 to 1987, and a man diametrically opposed from most of the African leaders in the CFA. He was a sort of West African Che Guevara. While not known widely in the Anglophone role, Sankara was a revolutionary and pan-Africanist leader who felt that the best path for his country was a rupture with France. His politics was anti-imperial, and he believed in the reduction of what he termed "odious debt." As opposed to Houphouet-Boigny, Sankara felt that the ties with France, the CFA, and the international world had to be severed. His vision was for a home-grown African development. Domestically, he focused on land reform, a nationwide literacy campaign and promoting public health by vaccinating more than 2.5 million children against meningitis, yellow fever, and measles. Feminism was also a central part of his political ideology. On October 15, 1987, Thomas Sankara was killed along with twelve other officials. However, his name is still widely known among the youth of the CFA countries. His tomb on the outskirts of Ouagadougou has been a visiting site for many pan-Africanists and humanitarians.

Early Years

During the 1950s and 1960s, the system was being set up and developed. In 1958, General de Gaulle modified the CFA franc into the "Franc of the French Community of Africa" (FCFA), for both West and Central Africa. The early decades of the CFA were relatively better for the economies compared to those of other African countries. Growth and inflation rates were better in the CFA zone than other African countries (although with large differentials between countries), and the institutional apparatus was developed with French support. Under the leadership of Félix Houphouet-Boigny in Cote d'Ivoire and others, the CFA zone attracted some prestige due to the stability that was offered and the consistent rules of the games. The two monetary unions operate under cooperation agreements signed between 1959 and 1962, which articulated the principles governing the monetary architecture of the Franc Zone.

During its early years, the CFA arrangement was perceived by some as a good marriage between the French leadership and Francophone African elites. Some of the CFA leaders had served in the French parliament at one point in time. As opposed to the British colonial experience, the French experience was based on a greater degree of interaction between the Africans and the former colonial power. France received a stable environment for its investments, and African elites enjoyed good purchasing power. Some have argued that the zones made sense for most Francophone leaders:

> As a group, the founding father generation of leaders – the so-called collaborator generation in the creation of the French connection – was not composed of stupid men. These leaders understood that genuine independence...would entail economic costs none were willing to bear ... much better to have juridical independence with monetary and economic links to France. In most cases that simply meant continuing the existing commercial and trading links, accepting French advisors, and technical assistants to operate behind the scenes and integrating finances and money into the new franc zone system and institutions. If it also meant French military assistance in putting down local rebellions..that was a fine job. (William Le Vine as quoted in Kavanagh 2006)

Continuing this analysis, Kavanagh (2006) argues that the political economy of the system had produced a group of African winners—the African elite—and some individual French companies benefited from France's relations with the ex-colonies, but not the French economy as a whole.

Over time, there was some growing dissent against the CFA, both in the political community and African intellectual world. In Mali, Modibo Keita's Parliament refused to sign in May 1962 the treaty establishing the West African Monetary Union (WAMU), the predecessor to the West African Economic and Monetary Union (UEMOA), in 1994. The story told is that President Keita had the Malian franc made in Czechoslovakia.

He was undermined and eventually overthrown by a military coup in 1968, and Mali eventually returned to the CFA franc. Another skeptic was Nigerian President Hamani Diori, who commissioned the Samir Amin report to study the CFA matter. Samir Amin, who has articulated the "dependency" thesis lamented the lack of independence of the currency and the pooling of reserves in France and proposed to have separate national currencies. Academic Sylla (2020) has questioned the parity and the arrangement. He argues that the new currency came with a fixed parity—1 CFA franc equal to 1.7 metropolitan francs, which was further revised to 1 CFA franc to 2 metropolitan francs, which he contrasts with the British colonies in Africa had an exchange rate value lower than the British pound. Presenting a historical perspective on the CFA system he argues[1]:

> French economy needed access to sources of raw materials that it could buy in its own currency, at below world-market prices....first, France could pay its imports from franc zone countries in its own currency.... French companies operating in the zone moreover benefit from large — and stable — outlets for trade...French companies also have the guaranteed freedom to repatriate their revenue and capitals without any foreign exchange risk, thanks to the free-transfer policy and the fact that France decides the zone's exchange and monetary policy...

By 1970, there the beginning of institutional reforms to start to modernize the existing institutions. The African governments increased their negotiation power with France, and obtained greater control of their fiscal policy and slightly more autonomy of the monetary accounts. In 1972, during an official visit to Paris, Togolese leader Eyadema challenged French leader President George Pompidou on reform of the CFA. There was a reduction in French presence on the boards of directors of the BCEAO and BEAC and the transfer of the headquarters of BEAC to Yaounde Cameroon in 1977 and BCEAO to Dakar in 1978. Over the years, the system was gaining institutional strength, but the fundamental parity was never questioned.

[1] https://www.jacobinmag.com/2020/01/franc-zone-french-neocolonialism-africa#:~:text=Indeed%2C%20from%20its%20creation%2C%20the,face%20up%20to%20international%20competition.

As in any monetary club, there was some exit of members. Guinea left in 1960, Mali left in 1962 but returned in the mid-1980s, and Madagascar and Mauritania left in 1973. Some faced more costly exits than others. Two new members were Equatorial Guinea in 1985 and Guinea-Bissau in 1997. Countries like Morocco, Tunisia, Algeria, and Vietnam were part of similar French-style arrangements, although they all went their separate ways. Some of the exits from the CFA were from countries that wanted to pursue a more independent economic and foreign policy.

The Crisis in the 1980s

Beginning in the mid-1980s and leading up to the 1994 devaluation, the zone suffered from stagnant growth but benefitted from low inflation. A global commodity price collapse hurt the CFA leading to an overvalued currency. There was a significant decline in cocoa, cotton, coffee, and oil prices. (Some suspect that this particular fall in oil prices in the Soviet Union also played a part in the collapse of communism.) Terms of trade shocks led to deteriorating external and fiscal balances and led to external borrowing at first to protect the now unsustainably high levels of spending. Internal adjustment efforts, which is a way to adjust the economy without touching the exchange rate, to depreciate the inflation levels failed. Essentially, governments tried to deflate the domestic prices and achieve the required depreciation in the real exchange rate using a combination of deflationary macroeconomic policies, internal structural reforms, and "second best" trade policies.

French bilateral aid and generous credit from the central banks were deployed to sustain the economies. The IMF and World Bank warned of the excessive size of civil services in these countries and the bloated fiscal budgets. Countries tried what became known as an internal adjustment strategy by subsidizing exports and increasing import tariff rates. These failed to work for administrative and governance reasons. Defending an unsustainable exchange rate became a costly proposition. The economies were in a major depression with per capita GDP falling by 3.9% annually between 1985 and 1993. Regional GDP also declined by more than 30% over this eight-year period. The economies contracted leading to revenue falls, while their expenditures remained largely unchanged because political constraints made it difficult to reduce the wage bill, the single largest component of the expenditures.

For the first time in history, the Operations Account had a deficit as the reserves of both zones were plunging. Some scholars have argued that during the period the Franc Zone was costing France a tremendous amount of money; after 1987, French support of the balance of payments deficits surpassed a billion dollars a year (Kavanagh 2006). By the early 1990s, the system was in crisis and required some corrective action. Policy adjustments of the national authorities had failed to reach both internal and external balance. As opposed to the wave of liberalization that had taken place in the late 1980s and early 1990s, with the support of the World Bank and the IMF, many of the larger economies in the region, especially Nigeria and Ghana were undertaking significant liberalization both in terms of exchange rate management and in terms of fiscal policy, while CFA economies were trying to adjust to trade shocks through internal adjustment policies.

The Devaluation of 1994

In order to address the growing overvaluation of the currency in the face of global commodity shocks of the late 1980s and early 1990s and with the support of France, the IMF, and the World Bank, in January 1994 there was a devaluation of the CFA franc in 1994 of 100% in local currency terms to correct the overvaluation. Estimates of the overvaluation had ranged from 20 to 50% depending on the nature of the models that were used. This devaluation was the result of a prolonged deterioration in the terms of trade of member countries and a nominal appreciation of the French franc against the US dollar, all of which resulted in an overvalued exchange rate among CFA member countries. The goods produced in the CFA zone were priced out of the world market when the CFA franc exchange rate was artificially high in the 1980s.

Because of the loss in competitiveness, the CFA economies grew little during the 1980s and early 1990s and suffered major investment and export reductions. To remedy the situation, there was a joint historic decision to devalue the CFA franc, thus boosting export competitiveness and addressing fiscal considerations. The devaluation was accompanied by a package of fiscal, monetary, and wage policies designed to support the new parity. Initially, there was some resistance to devaluation from France, who had tried hard to bail out these economies during the difficult 1986–1994 period. French aid had been used to try to help sustain the currency but over time, it became too costly to do so. In 1993, motivated by the crisis in the CFA countries and supported by French Prime Minister Edouard Balladur, France adopted the Abidjan Doctrine, which conditioned its financial support on the adoption of the IMF program. This set in place an even stronger proximity between France and the IMF on the CFA franc.

Over time, with the support of the World Bank and IMF, and the leadership of Prime Minister Balladur, who recognized the financial strain on the French Treasury of the CFA zone economic crisis, the devaluation happened. The prominent President of Cote d'Ivoire and the founding father Houphouet-Boigny was opposed to the devaluation until his untimely death. The consensus is that the devaluation was eventually decided in Paris, although some African leaders agreed on this measure. Per the informal rules of the CFA, it was France that decided on the parity of the currency.

The post-devaluation effect was generally positive on the macroeconomic side. It had a positive effect on agriculture and farming but negative effects on the urban middle class who was importing more expensive food and had lower purchasing power. There was an improvement in growth as well as the fiscal and current account balances, but there were differences across countries. The devaluation helped in reducing the twin deficits. However, the rise in prices of food and services caused concern, leading to aid packages to stabilize prices and plug the fiscal holes in the budget.

Between 1994 and 2001, total output in the CFA zone expanded at an annual rate of more than 4%, and per capita income of CEMAC as a whole grew at an annual rate of more than 1%, rebounding from the 1986–1993 depression during which it fell by more than 3% annually. French foreign aid has continued to provide support to these economies coupled with the support from the World Bank and IMF.

In 1994, CEMAC was created to deepen the regional integration process to support the reforms that had been done in the aftermath of the devaluation (Zafar and Kubota 2003). On March 16, 1994, shortly after the devaluation, the member countries of BEAC signed a treaty to create an umbrella organization, the Communauté économique et monétaire de l'Afrique Centrale (CEMAC) over existing Union douanière et économique de l'Afrique Centrale (UDEAC) and BEAC. The treaty was formally ratified by the countries in 1999. The reforms aimed at converting UDEAC into a more outward-oriented, rational, functioning customs union included the introduction of a new common external tariff with four categories (a four-rate escalated structure: 5% for essential goods; 10% for raw materials and capital goods; 20% for intermediate goods; and 30% for consumer goods), as well as reductions in quantitative restrictions. The mindset was to complement fiscal reforms with trade reforms in order to jumpstart growth.

One of the interesting post-devaluation changes was the push toward regional integration and the setting up of a system of macroeconomic convergence, which was modeled on the European Union. Both UEMOA and CEMAC tried to create stronger regional integration and market integration in labor, agricultural, and manufactured goods market. There was a good-faith effort to create a set of regional institutions to help remove competitiveness barriers between the countries of the zone. The idea was also to create some centralized system of monitoring that ensured that countries had fiscal and monetary discipline. In parallel, the two regions committed to accelerate their progress toward regional integration by dismantling tariffs and pledging to improve transit corridors. Financial sector reforms were enacted to improve financial integration and banking supervision.

By 1999, the euro was introduced, and the CFA peg to the French franc was replaced with a peg to the euro. The other institutions and arrangements were left intact. After the 2000s, macroeconomic management has improved, and reserves continued to get stronger, providing buffers to shocks. Macroeconomic reforms were accompanied by measures to make the economies more vibrant through policies such as privatization, financial sector reforms, and trade liberalization, with mixed results. Some of the major issues with government arrears and public enterprise borrowing, that were more prominent in the 1980s, diminished twenty years later in the wake of many reforms.

The 2000s

In the 2000s, there was a commodity boom, more so in CEMAC than in UEMOA. Oil price, which was less than $30 a barrel in 2000, reached $100 a barrel a decade later, as there was increasing demand from Asia, particularly China. From a buyer's market, oil became a seller's market, and CEMAC became quite wealthy in total GDP. Macroeconomic management in the 2000s had improved relative to the 1980s, and there was a concerted effort to make sure fiscal policy was well-managed during this time. The oil boom declined in the aftermath of the financial crisis but increased again by the mid-2010s.

With the advent of the euro and the consolidation of the institutions in CEMAC and UEMOA, there was a push for further regional integration in both zones. By 2000 officially, there was supposed to be free movement of goods, services, capital, and labor, but as has been the case, there was a marked gap between official declarations and on-the-ground implementation. The countries also became greater recipients of multilateral aid, Chinese aid, and FDI inflows.

Both the CEMAC and WAEMU subregions were affected by the trade shocks in the mid-2010s in the aftermath of the global financial crisis, the recession in developed countries, and the economic slowdown in China. First, as oil proceeds fell by more than 30%, there has been a strong deterioration in the current account balance of 6% of GDP and the fiscal balance of 9% of GDP, especially in the oil economies—Gabon, Republic of Congo, Chad, and Equatorial Guinea. CEMAC growth slowed to 1.9% in 2016 compared to 4.9% in 2014 in the wake of reduced public investment and lower oil production. The spillover effects of Nigeria's slowdown in the wake of the oil price fall have been difficult for Benin, which has seen a significant crisis in its reexport business.

Second, there has been a major impact on reserves as they have dwindled to less than 4 months of imports by 2018, prompting concerns about capital flight not only in CEMAC but also in UEMOA. Third, given the internal challenges that countries like Senegal, Cameroon, and Cote d'Ivoire were going through, it is difficult for them to contribute to regional reserves accumulation through fiscal consolidation. In recent years, UEMOA's performance has been better than CEMAC's, reversing a previous trend. During the 2010s, the increase in the bilateral exchange rate between the euro and the dollar led to greater exchange rate appreciation and a loss in CFA zone competitiveness.

The New Shocks in the Mid-2010s

By the late 2010s, the CFA zone was facing new challenges and crises, as oil price still had not recovered and was averaging closer to $50 a barrel than the $100 that CEMAC policymakers were envisioning, and the Sahel was facing difficulties with commodity prices and extremist violence. Terms of trade shocks and conflict were leading to stresses on both the Eastern front of the CFA zone and the Western front. There was a clear weakening of macroeconomic fundamentals and significant widening of both the current account and fiscal deficits as well as a decline in reserve coverage.

In December 2016, the Heads of State met in Yaounde and while rejecting any devaluation of the currency in the interests of what they perceived as macroeconomic stability, tried to restore the conditions for macroeconomic stability and growth through concerted efforts. They asked IMF support to help finance the balance of payments deficit and agreed on the importance of having IMF programs in each of the CEMAC countries. The general attempt was to drive to preserve the peg and plug the deficits through aid and stabilization programs. A series of IMF programs were designed for most of the CEMAC countries.

By 2020, there was a new menace which appeared in the form of the COVID-19 pandemic, the defining crisis of modern times and the greatest shock to the world economy since the Great Depression of the late 1920s and early 1930s and the global financial crisis in 2009. Originating in Asia, COVID-19 has had a ripple effect and impacted millions across all the major continents. Leading to deep lockdowns as countries try to stem the tide of the pandemic, it has had severe shocks on economic output, trade, and food security throughout the world economy. In March 2020, the Economic Commission for Africa (ECA) warned that the unfolding crisis could dent Africa's already stagnant growth with oil-exporting nations losing up to US$ $65 billion in revenues as crude oil prices continue to tumble, and Africa losing half of its GDP with growth falling from 3.2% to about 2% due to a number of reasons which include the breakdown of export trade and disruption of global supply chains. Other analysts have pointed to the growing poverty impact and risk of widespread hunger in the face of job loss.

References

Kavanagh, Michael. 2006. *The 1994 Devaluation of the CFA Franc and the Changing Role of France in African Development, International Affairs Council*. Working Paper Number 06–04, New Haven, CT.

Sylla, Ndongo Samba. 2020. *The Franc Zone, A Tool of French Neocolonialism in Africa*. https://www.jacobinmag.com/2020/01/franc-zone-french-neocolonialism-africa.

Zafar, Ali, and Keiko Kubota. 2003. *The CEMAC: Regional Integration in Central Africa: Key Issues*. The World Bank Working Papers-Africa Region Working Papers 52, Washington, ssDC.

CHAPTER 4

The Macron and Ouattara Reform of the CFA

On December 21, 2019, in an epic speech in Abidjan, Macron and Ouattara announced the end of the CFA. Four decisions were announced to the international community.

- First, the CFA franc would cease to officially exist and shed its colonial baggage by being renamed the "eco" in 2020.
- Second, to increase African sovereignty, French officials were no longer to be represented in the regional governing bodies or central banks, the BEAC and the BCEAO.
- Third, there was to be a delinking between the regional reserves and the Operations Accounts in the French Treasury. BCEAO would move its reserves away from the French Treasury.
- Finally, the peg to the euro was to be maintained.

President Ouattara stressed the importance of moving forward but at the same time keeping a degree of stability amidst the changes. To the audience, this was a significant change as it represented an end to one of the most long-lasting exchange rate regimes in the world. However, France was supposedly going to provide a guarantee and a credit line assuming the reserves continued to be pooled. The details of the new French arrangement have not been publicly discussed.

A. Zafar, *The CFA Franc Zone*,
https://doi.org/10.1007/978-3-030-71006-4_4

For the first time in its more than 70-year history, the CFA regime was facing an important change. For the status quo forces, the reforms were too radical, and for the radicals, the reforms were not enough. However, the significance of the reforms cannot be understated.

The system of the CFA was challenged from the top of the French and African political establishments. The first shots of the revolution had been fired by the technocratic leaders. This was the first substantive reform since Charles de Gaulle established the institutional framework for the CFA monetary system more than 70 years ago. It was a historic moment, the beginning of the unraveling of the umbilical cord that had bound France and the CFA zone.

The IMF Chief Kristalina Georgieva welcomed the reforms and supported the contribution to the modernization of long-standing arrangements between the West African Economic and Monetary Union and France. Many Africans were surprised by the move because it was unexpected. Other commentators supported the move but felt that it was not enough.

However, in January 2020, the Anglophone countries in ECOWAS (which included Nigeria, Ghana, Gambia, Liberia, Sierra Leone, and the Francophone Guinea Conakry), issued a statement condemning the WAEMU's decision to unilaterally rename the West African CFA franc as "Eco" as it was meant to be the name for the West African ECOWAS currency. Subsequently, the Nigerian President asked for a postponement in the launch of the single ECOWAS currency but will be based on the countries meeting the convergence criteria.[1] Already in 2019, the ECOWAS had expressed interest in a flexible exchange rate regime with a monetary policy framework based on inflation targeting, which put it in conflict with the euro peg of the CFA zone.

There is also a significant change in Central Africa. On November 22, 2019, there was an Extraordinary Summit of Heads of State and Government in Yaounde, Cameroon. During this summit, the six CEMAC unanimously agreed to reflect on the CFA arrangement and reform its currency to have a stable and strong legal tender capable of giving the

[1]The four criteria for ECOWAS common currency integration are: (i) to maintain the budget deficit at a level below or equal to 3% of nominal GDP, (ii) to maintain an annual average inflation rate below 10%, (iii) to ensure that the budget deficit/central bank ratio is below 10% of the previous year's tax revenues, and (iv) to hold a 3-month or more gross reserves in months of imports.

economies the boost for better development and population's livelihood. Under the direction of BEAC, there will be further exploration of this.

Due to these changes, there is now an even greater debate on the CFA zone. Together with the political class, many African artists and intellectuals are calling for a debate on the future of the monetary union in the CFA zone in the aftermath of the announcement by Macron and Ouattara. This has spawned a continent-wide debate on the future of the zone and the additional reforms that may be needed. Macron and Ouattara, for both domestic and external reasons, decided to act together. Part of the motivation was to stem the tide of growing anti-French sentiment, which had been growing in the continent.

The relationship between the Anglophone and the Francophone African countries is also now a subject of a growing debate as there is an inconsistency with the flexible Nigerian naira and the CFA/eco which is pegged to the euro. From the Nigerian perspective, the using of the eco, which was meant to be the currency of the ECOWAS, for the new CFA regime, meant that there was a lack of coordinated effort and communication in ECOWAS. The incompatibility of the Nigeria naira with the new currency means that there will be a delay in the ECOWAS common currency.

Nigeria has had a managed float exchange rate regime in recent years to respond to oil shocks.[2] In May 2016, the Central Bank of Nigeria (CBN) announced the reintroduction of a flexible exchange rate to prevent the decline in foreign exchange reserves that has been the result of the CBN's policy of maintaining the naira-US dollar peg. As Phyllis Papadavid from Overseas Development Institute (ODI) and others have argued, the operationalization of the new naira regime has been challenging as there is a continued shortage of dollars in the official and parallel currency markets despite inflows into local currency bonds. In April 2020, the IMF announced it approved Nigeria's request for emergency financial assistance of $3.4 billion under its Rapid Financing Instrument (RFI). As part of the discussions with the IMF, the Nigerians have been working on a unified flexible exchange rate regime.

The implications of this are that there is an inconsistency between the Nigerian and other Anglophone positions on the currency and the

[2] In practice, Nigeria operates a system of multiple exchange rates to control demand for dollars. While the official rate has been about 307 naira per dollar for government agencies and fuel importers, a cheaper rate is used for exporter and importers.

Francophone one and a barrier to an ECOWAS single currency zone. Moreover, the fact is that Nigeria is an oil exporter and the UEMOA countries' oil importers may further complicate the situation. This divergence can prevent the development of the Africa Continental Free Trade Area, a free trade area which was signed in Kigali in 2018 by 44 of the 55 African Union member states, and is the largest in the world in terms of number of participating countries. A speedy launch of the Eco is now stoking divisions among the 15 members of the Economic Community of West African States (ECOWAS). The five anglophone countries of ECOWAS want to adopt the new currency following a slower timetable and as a new currency for the whole region, not just as a replacement for the CFA franc.

Former Togolese Minister Kako Nubukpo, and current adviser to UEMOA on the exchange rate reform, has foreseen four scenarios on the future of the relationship between the Anglophone and the Francophone countries in ECOWAS.

> **Option 1: The Eco as simple avatar of the CFA franc.** This plan, which seems to have been inspired by Ouattara's announcement in Abidjan on 21 December 2019, is based on meeting nominal convergence criteria and highly favors a fixed exchange rate with the euro. It assumes that the UEMOA will gradually expand to include ECOWAS economies.
>
> **Option 2: An Eco based on real convergence: GDP per inhabitant.** ECOWAS economies would have to converge toward the three top-performing countries, i.e., Cabo Verde, Nigeria and Ghana. The Eco would have a flexible exchange rate regime governed by inflation targeting.
>
> **Option 3: The Eco-naira.** On 20 April 2000 in Accra, Ghana, six West African countries (Gambia, Ghana, Guinea, Liberia, Nigeria and Sierra Leone) announced that they intended to create a second monetary zone in West Africa which would use the Eco as its currency, alongside the CFA franc of UEMOA… In April 2002, WAMZ was established and each country made a commitment to maintain its domestic exchange rate within a fixed range of 15% against the dollar.

Option 4: The Eco, a common, but not single, currency. This plan would be a less onerous agreement compared to a single currency agreement.[3,4]

COVID-19 AND CFA

Unfortunately, due to the COVID-19 pandemic, the CFA reforms have been put on hold. Uncertainties regarding timing and implementation have led to a slippage in the calendar for CFA reform. Due to the sharp deterioration in regional macroeconomic indicators and the policy measures to combat the pandemic, the reform has been put on the back burner. The project started by Presidents Macron and President Ouattara to replace the CFA franc with the "Eco," has been officially delayed. Moreover, there appears to be strong behind-the-scenes diplomacy led by Ghana's President Nana Akufo-Addo to bridge the rift between the UEMOA countries and the remaining Anglophone ECOWAS countries, who have resented the Macron–Ouattara use of the ECO, which was meant to be the ECOWAS currency. There have been several recent developments in the last months of 2020 and early 2021.

- There has been no further communication by France and the UEMOA on a timeline for the rollout of the reform. The UEMOA Commission is currently working on a plan to be disseminated at the Conference of Heads of State in April 2021. The focus is to prepare a transition plan to the ECO and to prepare a longer term plan to integrate with a West African common currency. The idea that is being floated is to start implementing the new UEMOA ECO between 2023 and 2025.
- On December 10, 2020, after much consultation, the French Senate has signed revised monetary cooperation agreements with the UEMOA countries. The exact agreement is not publicly available, and it is not clear what the French Government is guaranteeing. Anecdotal evidence and media reports suggest that the French have

[3] The idea, a first step toward an integration process between countries, was first suggested in 1960 by Senegalese economist Daniel Cabou, who would later become the first secretary general of the Central Bank of West African States (BCEAO), as well as Samir Amin, one of the leading African development experts.

[4] https://www.sunnewsonline.com/eco-and-cfa-franc-four-weddings-and-a-funeral/.

agreed to a credit line and some form of guarantee in return for a pooling of reserves, regardless of whether they are at the French Treasury or the Bank of International Settlements. France would have a representative to monitor and verify the reserves. These agreements will now need to be adopted by the UEMOA's parliaments in 2021.

- The UEMOA Commission has issued a semi-annual report on the implementation of multilateral surveillance in which it has expressed concern about the adverse impact of the COVID-19 pandemic on the West African region's economies[5] The UEMOA Commission has forecast the GDP growth rate at 0.9% for 2020 compared to 5.8% in 2019, the budget deficit at 5.5% in 2020 compared to 2.4% in 2019, the inflation rate at 2.2% in 2020 compared to –0.7% in 2019, and a debt ratio at 49.3% in 2020 compared to 44.1% in 2019. In light of this, the Commission has urged member states to adopt a new convergence pact guaranteeing macroeconomic stability in the medium term. The precise terms of the new UEMOA convergence pact remain unclear.
- On January 23, 2021, there was a virtual ordinary session of the Assembly of Heads of State and Government, during which the ECOWAS regional bloc decided to suspend the convergence criteria for the year 2021 due to the degradation of African economies hard hit by the COVID-19 pandemic.[6] According to media reports and the official communique, the Conference instructed the ECOWAS Commission, in collaboration with the West African Monetary Agency (IMAO), the UEMOA Commission, and the Central Banks of the Community, to submit a draft of a new convergence and macroeconomic stability pact on January 1, 2022.

[5] Is West Africa's CFA reform a collateral victim of COVID-19? (theafricareport.com).

[6] ECOWAS suspends Eco convergence agreement - Journal du Cameroun.

CHAPTER 5

The Problem with the CFA Zone

The CFA zone remains important and interesting for several reasons as it is at the heart of development challenges—poverty traps, climate change, terrorism, and food security, among others. A rich CFA zone is Europe's interest as it can stem the flow of migration to Europe. As the international community's attention will shift away from health in a post-COVID-19 world and development will shift back to the battle against poverty and fragility, the CFA zone will only acquire more prominence.

Unfortunately, the current reforms are not sufficient to address the development challenges amplified by the pandemic.

- First, they focus on maintaining the overvalued fixed parity
- Second, they are silent on the issue of merging UEMOA with countries like Ghana that have asked for a flexible parity
- Third, they propose a longer term merger with Nigeria without clarity on the issues of linking an oil exporter to an oil importer in a currency union.

The adoption of either the euro peg by Nigeria or adoption of the naira by the UEMOA countries is technically complex. The analysis will show several key problems with the CFA zone:

A. Zafar, *The CFA Franc Zone*,
https://doi.org/10.1007/978-3-030-71006-4_5

- In terms of development success, the CFA has **underperformed** compared to the expectations in the postwar era and has been falling behind, especially in terms of growth and poverty. However, compared to the 1990s, the CFA zone has improved several aspects of its economic and political governance.
- The peg to the strong euro and the inability to adjust to trade shocks has led to the maintenance of an **overvalued currency** with adverse effects on competitiveness.
- There has been some policy credibility and a degree of macroeconomic stability with low inflation, but that has become a **costly and outdated policy**.
- It has not allowed sufficient national **sovereignty** in decision-making.
- The Sahelian twin challenge of **famine and conflict** remain major concerns, while the CEMAC oil economies are facing **governance challenges** and oil price declines.
- The landlocked countries are not **converging in incomes** with the coastal countries. There is no mechanism of **fiscal transfers** to the poorer economies from the richer ones, as in the EU, nor no mechanisms to deal with asymmetric shocks.
- **The CFA is not an optimal currency area**: no free flow of capital, limited labor mobility, limited fiscal transfers, and somewhat idiosyncratic shocks faced by individual countries (although there is some degree of synchronicity).

First, the economies of the CFA zone are falling behind the better performers in Africa including the Anglophone ones. The CFA countries have not had high per capita income growth compared to many of the better performing African groupings, such as COMESA and ECOWAS (Fig. 5.1). The CFA countries and the two zones lag in both growth per capita and in doing business. In a ranking of the ten richest economies in Africa—Nigeria, South Africa, Egypt, Algeria, Morocco, Kenya, Angola, Ethiopia, Ghana, and Tanzania, there is no country from the CFA. The CFA economies also tend to perform worse on the World Bank's Doing Business Indicators, with Republic of Congo, Chad, and CAR ranked towards the bottom of the list (Fig. 5.2).

Second, the excessive focus on very low inflation, significantly lower than in non-CFA zone, has contributed to lower growth in the CFA zone. Pegging to the euro essentially means tying monetary policy to the

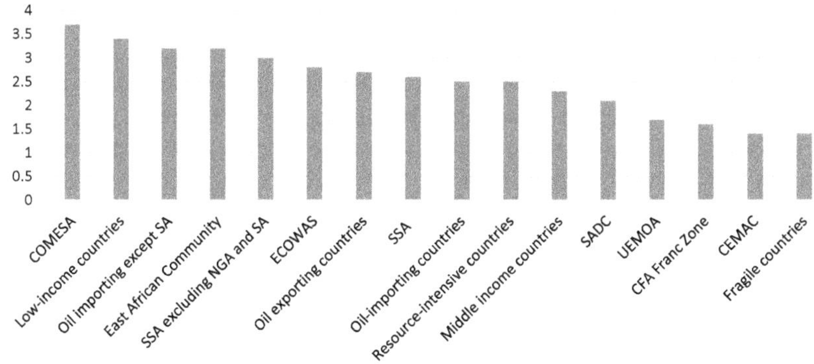

Fig. 5.1 Average Annual Per Capita Growth by Cluster 2004–2017 (%) (*Source* IMF, author calculations)

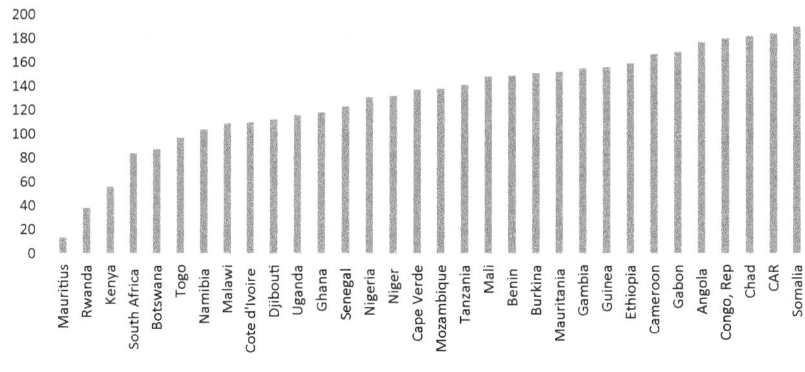

Fig 5.2 Ranking in the Doing Business Indicators 2020 (*Source* World Bank)

monetary policy of the ECB in Frankfurt and keeping the same interest rate policy, which is at a different economic cycle. There is a view among academic economists that there is a trade-off between inflation and unemployment and that there are growth consequences. Ed Phelps and Milton Friedman who argued that the Phillips curve becomes vertical in the long run accepted the trade-offs in the short run.

Third, in the last five years, the CFA euro has tended to be significantly overvalued, especially in CEMAC due to the oil price fall, and this has hindered structural transformation and impeded competitiveness.

Oil, which was close to $100 in 2014 has fallen to $40 by July 2020 but has been rebounding in 2021. There has been a major impact on the oil market due to the twin shock of rising US shale production coupled with declining Chinese demand as China rebalances its economy. The extent of overvaluation is significant, but the magnitude is sensitive to the methodologies used. By using a methodology to account for trade shocks, by December 2020, the Central African CFA is overvalued by more than 30%, and the West African CFA by close to 20%

Fourth, fiscal policy has tended to be procyclical, and countries do not adjust to shocks well. Either debt accumulates, as was seen in UEMOA and CEMAC in recent years, or public investment is cut during shocks to adjust to shocks, as was seen in CEMAC in the mid-2010s. Since the countries cannot use the exchange rate to adjust to shocks, they either borrow or they use costly internal adjustments, which cut development expenditure.

Fifth, the high dependence on imports contributes to weak productive structures in the countries. The region manufactures very little. Many of the bigger enterprises are foreign-owned. The CFA countries produce very little that is non-commodity. Chronically in current account deficits, the excessive reliance on foreign products is an unfortunate feature of their economies. Almost everything is imported, from processed agriculture to consumer products to health masks to capital machinery. Even mango and salt are exported in crude form to Europe, processed as mango pulp and iodized salt, and re-exported back to the CFA zone.

Sixth, the region has been dealing with rising debt dynamics which have worsened due to the pandemic, and can impede future recovery. In the aftermath of COVID-19, there are great concerns about a new global debt crisis. World Bank President David Malpass has spoken of the overwhelming impact of budget deficits and debt payments on many countries. The debt servicing costs in Africa have reached more than $50 billion forcing many governments to make a choice between paying debt service and financing investment in health and schools. There are several CFA countries at a rising rate of debt distress.

However, this is not to say that there has not been any progress in the CFA zone, as there has been progress both in CEMAC in the first decade since 2000 and UEMOA in the second decade. Inflation has been contained. Since the 2000s, macroeconomic management has improved, including fiscal management. Tax mobilization, especially in countries like Senegal, has been good, with a more competent fiscal administration.

Public investment in infrastructure in the two leading UEMOA countries has been a major driver of growth, and Eurobond issuance has been a success, although there are increasing risks now due to COVID-19. A few of the countries have been able to access international capital markets. In 2015 Cameroon issued its maiden Eurobond at $750 million, while in 2018, Senegal's bonds were oversubscribed, as the country received more than $10 billion of potential orders for a $2.2 billion Eurobond. Discovery of oil in Senegal has also helped the economy.

CHAPTER 6

Reforming and Modernizing the Zone with Currency Flexibility

In the CFA zones in West and Central Africa, the COVID-19 shocks are amplifying existing competitiveness challenges, reducing growth prospects, and worsening poverty and welfare. The CFA zone has fewer policy tools at its disposal to cope with shocks. In a world of climate change, increased migration, food insecurity, and deep poverty, the CFA zone will benefit from a policy regime that is well-suited to address multiple shocks.

The announcement in December 2019 that the West African currency CFA would be replaced by an independent currency to be called Eco has been hailed as a major event in Africa.

- What prompted this decision? Who were behind this action?
- What advantages and disadvantages does the new currency arrangement bring to the poor West African countries? What further reforms are necessary for growth and poverty reduction?
- How will the COVID-19 pandemic affect the timeline and the will for CFA reform?
- What are the policy options for oil-rich CEMAC in a world of volatile oil prices?
- What can the CFA zone learn from the experience of countries like China, Bangladesh, Russia, Turkey, and others who have succeeded in moving up the development ladder?

A. Zafar, *The CFA Franc Zone*,
https://doi.org/10.1007/978-3-030-71006-4_6

- How will other countries use macroeconomic policy and exchange rate policy to manage the shocks linked to the pandemic and enhance competitiveness?
- How will the complex political economy between France, the African governments, and the IMF be shifted?

This book will thoroughly examine these and other issues.

The book will argue that the further reforms are necessary to reduce vulnerability to shocks, address multiple development challenges, and build economic resilience against future crises. The exchange rate arrangement and peg to the euro will require further modernization and flexibility. Some of the problems of the CFA zone are uniquely linked to the currency, while others are linked to broader structural factors specific to political economy dynamics in Africa.

It is time to modernize the arrangements and replace an outdated system and adapt the exchange rate to the changing realities of the world economy. The eco is a step in the right direction, but it is neither sufficient nor helpful to stronger growth and poverty alleviation unless it remains flexible and is decoupled from the euro. In a volatile post-COVID-19 world, the countries should have the fiscal and monetary policy arsenal to deal with these shocks. The existing CFA arrangement served a purpose but in the world of the twenty-first century, it is outdated.

Addressing deep poverty and managing post-COVID recovery in the short and medium term will require a full arsenal of weapons—exchange rate flexibility, more targeted fiscal policy, and countercyclical monetary policy—that are necessary in the CFA zone. Moreover, the subregions need a set of incentives that sees the return of private and foreign investment. The provision of liquidity to firms, the building of social safety nets, the increase in public investment in infrastructure and health, and the development of more diversified exports will all necessitate a refined exchange rate setup. Aid is needed but cannot be a panacea for a long-term structural challenge. The CFA zone can learn from the history of exchange rate arrangements in the developing world, including from Bangladesh, China, and Mauritius, which shows that the power of a managed but flexible exchange rate to foster growth and development.

CHAPTER 7

The Roadmap for a Better Future

The book argues for several important exchange rate reforms that can help improve the CFA zone development performance, notably the movement to a more flexible parity delinked from the euro. This is a new perspective in the literature and in policy circles. This book will argue that there are several possible alternatives. It will try to fill the gap in the literature and provide an integrated approach for both zones.

1. For UEMOA, the **fixed exchange rate should transition to a basket peg (a mix of currencies reflecting international trade weights) in the medium-term and a more market-determined managed float regime in the long term once there is a more explicit fiscal union and consensus among countries.** Reflecting the growing trade with Asia and the declining trade with the euro zone, one formula can be a tripartite peg to the euro, the dollar, and the Chinese renmimbi. The optimal basket peg can be determined with econometric models. It can be managed by the BCEAO using well-tested principles of monetary management with the support of international expertise. After the COVID-19 recovery is starting, there can be a detailed analysis period and an orderly transition. In the long run, the peg can be designed around a band, and there are many international examples, especially from

A. Zafar, *The CFA Franc Zone*,
https://doi.org/10.1007/978-3-030-71006-4_7

Asia. The size of the band will depend on the potential market reaction. The currency will likely depreciate initially in UEMOA.

2. For CEMAC, the **current peg arrangement is challenging in the medium-term** in the face of volatile oil prices, declining production, low reserves, and widening fiscal and current account deficits. CEMAC should move to **a new currency with a basket peg linked to a tripartite formula** based on euro, dollars, and the price of oil. CEMAC can learn from the rich experience of Nigeria, Russia, and Kuwait in terms of management of oil shocks. A **transition period** of several years to the new arrangement will be necessary. The **new currency** will most likely be **at lower parity and cheaper** than the current CFA franc.
3. The two CFA zones should have **separate currencies with different parities** as one is oil importer and the other is oil exporter. There is **no need to link two currencies** in any way. The parities should be more **market-determined** than they are at present based on the supply and demand of foreign exchange. A foreign exchange trading platform and market can be developed.
4. There should be **a greater modernization of BCEAO and BEAC**, the conservative regional central banks, in line with **global best practices**. The banks can evolve from a system uniquely focused on foreign exchange reserve accumulation to approaches used by Asian central banks. **The shift in the pooled reserves**, intended to diversify risk, from the Operations Account in the French Treasury to the Bank of International Settlements and elsewhere (including repatriation to Yaounde and Dakar), as envisaged in UEMOA now, is a promising step. Reserves can be managed for both macroprudential purposes and development purposes including sovereign wealth funds. New guidelines for fintech regulatory framework, credit bureau coverage, regional payments interoperability, and offshore finance can be adopted.
5. **The architecture of the CFA zone** should help support **a modernized regional convergence pact and greater harmony between the convergence criteria of ECOWAS and those of UEMOA.** This pact can include a higher upper bound on inflation, a fiscal convergence criterion that factors in asymmetric shocks faced by countries, and debt targets that factor in the impact of the COVID-19 pandemic. In UEMOA, the current 6 percent regional fiscal deficit will require time to reduce. For CEMAC, focus on

non-oil balances will be key. Central bank reserves above the 3 to 4 month import thresholds can be allocated for regional emergencies. The Sahelian countries may need to have fiscal deficits above 3 percent to address the triple shocks of post-pandemic recovery, climate change, and security costs. A system of fiscal transfers or insurance mechanisms as well as compensation to support the fiscal positions of revenue-constrained poor Sahelian landlocked countries' path to convergence should be envisaged. Given the multiple violations of convergence criterion by many countries, especially on the fiscal front, there should be a creative design of new criteria post-pandemic that make sure to incorporate the negative effects of trade shocks.[1]

6. **The French convertibility guarantee** will have to be clarified and revisited. There should be an **evolution** to a system where there is a **euro or dollar swap line at the two central banks to the European Central Bank or the Federal Reserve Board**. This is especially true for CEMAC, which is a region in need of significant macroeconomic reform. In UEMOA, the nature of the French guarantee remains unclear, especially the link to a fixed parity and reserve pooling.
7. **The adoption of either the euro peg by Nigeria or adoption of the naira by the UEMOA countries is technically challenging.** In UEMOA, greater exchange rate flexibility can help reduce trade frictions and support the West African vision for a common currency and a **pan-West African free trade zone**. Integration between the Francophone and Anglophone members of ECOWAS can be facilitated with a flexible arrangement. The CFA countries should focus on integration with countries like Ghana and Liberia at the first stage. Since Nigeria is an oil exporter, the link between UEMOA and Nigeria will have to be carefully thought given macroeconomic challenges of putting oil importers and oil exporters in the same arrangement.
8. In CEMAC, given the primacy of oil, **a new currency** will be able to support adjustment in a post-COVID world and provide **more fiscal space** that can be used **for targeted transfers and**

[1] Zafar (2005) shows the typical fiscal challenge for a Sahelian country like Niger, which suffers trade shocks as well as the fiscal impact of trade liberalization, without benefiting from any compensation.

social safety nets. Post-pandemic, CEMAC should return to fiscal sustainability once the recovery happens.

9. **Supportive structural policies** are necessary to complement sound exchange rate management including regulatory simplification, reform of agricultural taxation, trade liberalization, financial sector modernization, and more targeted industrial policy.
10. It is important to improve **communication and dialogue** with the public on the CFA and consult with Parliaments, academics, civil society groups, and nongovernmental organizations (NGOs) of the relevant states in West Africa and Central Africa. One can use the momentum from the Black Lives movement to internationalize the issue. The idea that Africans are incapable of managing their own currency should be relegated to the dustbin of colonial history. It is also important to have regular **South–South forum on the CFA**, with officials and bankers from emerging markets to share best practices with CFA zone officials.

Reference

Zafar, Ali. 2005. Revenue and the Fiscal Impact of Trade Liberalization: The Case of Niger. World Bank Policy Research Working Paper No. 3500. World Bank, Washington, DC.

PART II

CFA Zone Development Puzzles

Despite decades of policy reform, and support from the international financial institutions, the CFA zone faces several development challenges. Many of the CFA countries embarked on significant policy reform but have been unable to overcome these challenges.

CHAPTER 8

Poverty Traps in the Sahel

The key challenge of the CFA zone is the high poverty rate. Despite many years of political independence, significant economic aid, and reforms over the years, the average poverty rate for CFA countries stands at about 40%. Impacted by trade shocks, difficult geography, and climate change, many of the countries have not had significant success in reducing poverty, with a few exceptions. Although in the postwar years, Africa was supposed to take off and Asia was not imagined to be successful, the realities changed after several decades of economic development. China, which once had a poverty rate of more than 60% in 1981, now has become one of the most powerful economies in the world.

According to a recent World Bank study, of the world's 28 poorest countries, 27 are in Sub-Saharan Africa all with a poverty rate above 30%. Poverty in Africa has fallen substantially—from 54% in 1990 to 41% in 2015, while the number of poor has increased, from 278 million in 1990 to 413 million in 2015. Projections show that extreme poverty is showing few signs of improvement in Sub-Saharan Africa and may keep countries from ending extreme poverty by 2030. This recalcitrant poverty tends to be concentrated in rural landlocked economies.

A review of poverty trends in the CFA region indicate:

A. Zafar, *The CFA Franc Zone*,
https://doi.org/10.1007/978-3-030-71006-4_8

- The significant average of poverty across the CFA region is quite high. Using a headcount index based on $1.90 a day, the average is more than 40% across the CFA.
- There are similar poverty patterns in CEMAC and UEMOA, despite the divergence in geographies, economic structure, and commodity export.
- The CFA economies have not had success in poverty reduction. The most successful poverty reducers in SSA have been Ethiopia, Ghana, Uganda, and Botswana. Even Cameroon, Cote d'Ivoire, and Senegal have high poverty rates.
- Economies with strong natural resources in the CFA, Equatorial Guinea, Central African Republic, and Chad are the ones with the highest poverty rates (as measured by national poverty lines).
- Initial conditions seem to be an important factor explaining poverty trends across countries.
- Between 1985 and 1992, poverty rate in Cote d'Ivoire doubled from 30 to 60% partly suggesting the negative effects of an overvalued currency.

Over the years, the CFA zone has not performed well in terms of per capita income growth, although there have been differences between the Sahelian economies, the oil-rich CEMAC economies, and the richer coastal countries. In a review of the growth performance of all African economies, Arbache and Page (2008) find no evidence of income convergence and very little evidence of significant income mobility across countries in the continent. Low and volatile growth in Africa has been associated with a remarkably stable structure of incomes, and initial income in 1975 tends to equal average income for the entire period 1975–2005.

In per capita terms as well as GDP growth, the CFA countries have lagged their non-CFA African counterparts. Figure 8.1 shows the poverty rates in Africa, and Fig. 8.2 shows the growth rate of annual average GDP per capita for the last two decades for CFA countries and their comparators. Only Burkina Faso and Chad feature in the top 15 growth performers, significantly lagging the best African performers—Ethiopia, Rwanda, Mozambique, Ghana, and Tanzania. The latter include some countries that have a good trajectory in poverty reduction. However, there are some African countries, such as Democratic Republic of Congo

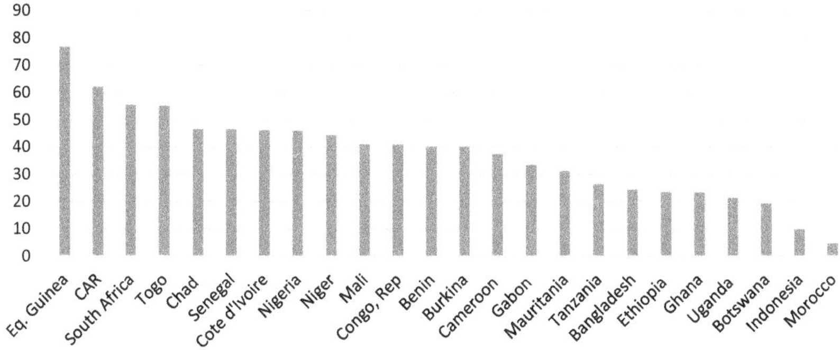

Fig. 8.1 Poverty Rate (National Poverty Line %) (*Source* World Bank dataset; latest year available)

and Liberia that have a worse per capita income growth record than many CFA countries.

Then there are the Sahelian economies. Spanning close to 6000 km from the Atlantic Ocean to the Red Sea, the Sahel is the belt south of the Sahara that is a mixture of grassland and savanna. The Sahel is a high-risk zone. Five CFA countries—Mali, Burkina, Niger, Chad, and Central African Republic are Sahelian. These countries have been frequently afflicted by more than one of the four development traps that Collier (2007) elaborated—"The Conflict Trap," "The Natural Resource Trap," "Landlocked with Bad Neighbors," or "Bad Governance in a Small Country." Most importantly, the economies may be locked in a poverty trap. While there is a debate on the nature of these traps, there is a growing consensus that poverty trap means that an economy is caught in a low-level equilibrium and underdevelopment.

The Sahelian economies have an inadequate manufacturing base, subsistence farming, and primary product dependence. While the economies have a degree of macroeconomic stability, that is somewhat artificial. The lack of per capita income growth coupled with weak governance has exacerbated tensions. Even if the economies are not tightly integrated with the world economy in terms of trade and financial flows, any world event, such as the 2008 financial crisis or the 2020 pandemic, has impacted them. These countries also rank among the world's lowest on the Human Capital Index, which measures the contribution of health and education to the productivity of the next generation of workers.

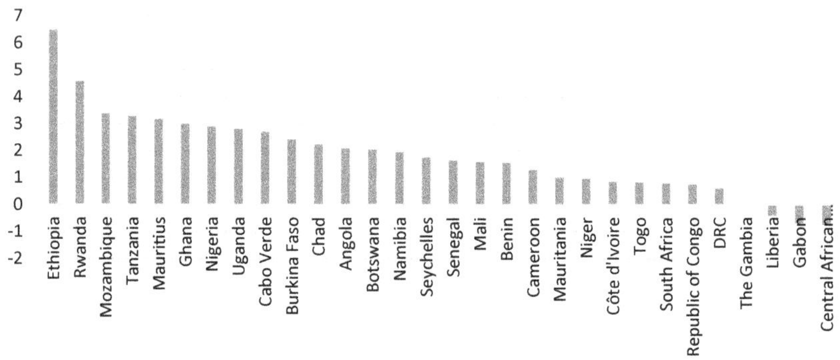

Fig. 8.2 Average Annual GDP per Capita 2000–2019 (%) (*Source* IMF, author calculations

They tend to be very large countries with very low populations of less than ten million people, while some of their individual land size is as big as Western Europe. It is difficult to get any type of agglomeration economics happening there due to the lack of density of markets that one sees in Asia. In terms of agriculture, the Sahelian countries are largely subsistence agriculture with millet and sorghum as staples and cotton and groundnuts as cash exports. There is also a livestock sector and a fisheries sector that has been threatened by overfishing and climate change. They are all fragile economies vulnerable to trade shocks. But each has a precious metal, Burkina and Mali have gold, Niger has uranium, Chad has oil, and the Central African Republic has livestock. Converting these into windfalls has still been a challenge for these countries.

There is evidence that these Sahelian countries are in a poverty trap. The combination of poor land, adverse climate, and low density translates into negative development outcomes. Sachs et al. (2004) find that tropical Africa, including some of the better governed parts, is stuck in a poverty trap and too poor to achieve robust, high levels of growth. The extreme poverty leads to a low national savings rate leading to poor economic growth.

Over the years, there has been more data and refinement of analysis on household vulnerabilities. Using an innovative empirical methodology classifying household as chronically poor, non-resilient and resilient, Alfani et al. (2015) finds that Niger, Burkina, and Northern Nigeria have high percentages of chronically poor: respectively, 48, 34, and 27%, while for Senegal, the percentage of chronically poor is only 4%. In terms of the non-resilient, they account for about 70% of the households in Senegal, while in the other countries, it ranges between 38 and 34%. Resilient households account for about 33% in all countries except Niger, where the share is around 18%. Marginal increase in malnutrition for children ages 1–3 years from exposure to an extreme shock in the West African Sahel notes that while around 20% of the children in the sample are stunted or underweight, more than 30% of the children in the sample are highly vulnerable to either form of malnutrition.

The Sahelian countries are landlocked and face very high transport costs to get to the ports, one of the most expensive transit corridors in the world. Being near to the sea and to international shipping is important for the export growth of many of these countries. Being Switzerland—with its web of transit connections to the outside world via France, Germany, and Italy—is different from being Burkina Faso or Niger.

Over the years, they have faced droughts and food insecurity. According to the Food and Agriculture Organization of the United Nations (FAO) and the United Nations World Food Program (WFP), in early 2020, more than 3.3 million people required immediate assistance in the Central Sahel, and close to 4.8 million people in the Central Sahel were at risk of food insecurity during the lean season summer season.

One historical example of the challenging situation in the Sahel was the food crisis of 2011. The impact had been felt strongest in countries with strong underlying vulnerabilities, especially Mauritania, Mali, Gambia, Niger, and Burkina Faso. Cereal production across the Sahel in September 2011 was 25% lower than in 2010, leading to a deficit of 2.5 million tons, and contributing to a significant decline in GDP among the vulnerable countries. There were also price increases in regional markets in Burkina, Niger, and Mali of close to 50%. Food inflation led to CPI inflation increases of more than 1% in the affected countries. The Sahelian countries have relied on a depletion of grain reserves and dependence on costly food imports leading to fiscal pressures on the budget. In Burkina Faso, an ambitious food security plan involving the purchase of grains from surplus areas and the sale/distribution to deficit parts of the country as well as the tapping of food reserves cost CFA 65 billion ($130 million). In Cote d'Ivoire, increases in the price of flour in the wake of the crisis caused public discontent, where there are demands for the government to raise the bread subsidy. Restrictions on export of grains imposed by countries such as Mali and Burkina Faso also exacerbated problems in vulnerable areas.

The Sahelian countries have faced challenges from Islamist extremist groups, linked to the post-Libyan war, which have unleashed violence in the area, leading to a volatile security situation and humanitarian crisis. Burkina Faso and Mali, which used to be a bastion of stability, have dangerous security situations with several major terrorist attacks and security incidents in Bamako and Ouagadougou in recent years. Estimates of the number of internally displaced people in Burkina Faso have reached more than 500,000 by end of 2019. The situation in the Central African Republic has been difficult because sectarian conflicts between Christian and Muslim groups are exacerbating conflicts between sedentary populations and pastoralists. (Even Cameroon, which is non-Sahelian is facing increased conflicts between the Anglophone and Francophone populations for territory.)

References

Alfani, Federica, Andrew Dabalen, Peter Fisker, and Vasco Molini. 2015. Can We Measure Resilience? A Proposed Method and Evidence from Countries in the Sahel. World Bank Policy Research Working Paper 7170.

Arbache, Jorge Saba and John Page. 2008. Hunting for Leopards: Long Run Country Income Dynamics in Africa. Policy Research Working Paper Series 4715. The World Bank.

Collier, Paul. 2007. *The Bottom Billion: Why the Poorest Countries Are Failing and What Can Be Done About It*. Oxford: Oxford University Press.

Sachs, Jeffrey, John W. McArthur, Guido Schmidt-Traub, Margaret Kruk, Chandrika Bahadur, Michael Faye, and Gordon McCord. 2004. Ending Africa's Poverty Trap. *Brookings Papers on Economic Activity* 2004 (1): 117–240.

CHAPTER 9

Governance Challenges in the CFA Zone

One challenge for CFA countries has been centered around governance. The CFA countries, particularly CEMAC, have faced challenges around natural resource management, decentralization, and transparent public financial management. As defined by the World Bank, the African Development Bank, and other multilateral organizations, governance relates to the methods and mechanisms through which power is exercised while managing a country's economic development. From the African Development Bank's (2000) perspective, good governance can be built on three foundations: effective states, mobilized civil societies, and an efficient private sector. Good governance centers around accountability, transparency, combating corruption, and citizen participation. The idea of governance also centers around state accountability to its population, especially related to the predictability of resource management. From an economic angle, this also includes debt management, transparent natural resource management, and mobilization of domestic revenues.

In terms of governance, the CFA zone lags behind the global trends. According to a variety of indicators and metrics, the governance in the CFA zone, especially CEMAC, is not optimal. Institutional strength, accountability, and business environment lag in the CFA zone. In terms of government effectiveness and in terms of corruption, CEMAC and UEMOA are both lagging subregions compared to international norms. In CEMAC, the situation is impacted by the political economy of oil

A. Zafar, *The CFA Franc Zone*,
https://doi.org/10.1007/978-3-030-71006-4_9

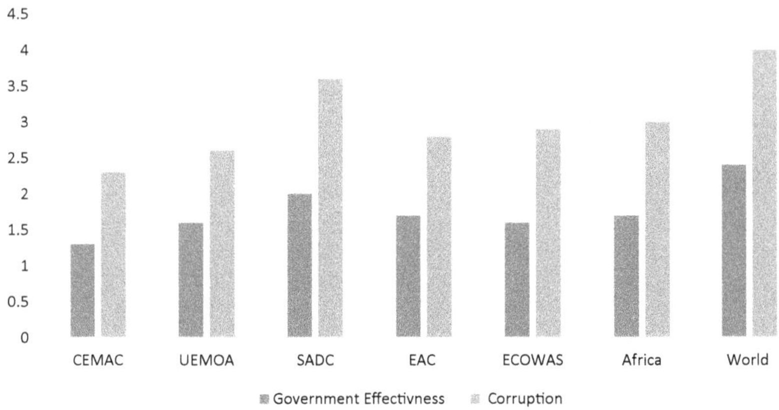

Fig. 9.1 Governance Indicators in CEMAC and UEMOA (*Note* Higher numbers indicate better governance. *Source* Akum and Donnerfeld [2015], World Bank database)

revenue management. Akum and Donnerfeld (2015) note that CEMAC states should address the issue of state capture and poor governance by regimes (Fig. 9.1).

Conceptual Framework

Political economist Brian Levy (2014) has introduced an interesting typology to help explain the variations in governance around the world. He focuses on three concepts: "political settlements" where settlements can lead to consolidated power in the hands of a dominant party or political leader or can be organized around a truce in which rival forces agree on peaceful rules for political competition; "institutions"—depending on whether the rules of the game are personalized or impersonal and codified in formal written law; and "rents"—based on distinctions between rules versus discretion.

According to this framework, CEMAC would be #4: rule-by-law dominant, where institutions are more impersonal, but political control remains monopolized. In CEMAC, family and patronage politics is strong with powerful and sometimes dynastic families in power, but there has been some formal development of institutions. When public institutions are weak (personalized), the politics are maintained by clientelism. By contrast, UEMOA has a #5 Rule-of-law competitive, where the political and economic rules have become more impersonal but not perfect Westminster democracies. In a competitive trajectory, political and social stability is based on agreement about peaceful rules of competition among elite groups, generally via elections (Fig. 9.2).

The difference between CEMAC and UEMOA lies in the freedom of the political space and the opening of centers of power to new social forces. CEMAC has seen a combination of dynastic politics with authoritarian management, while UEMOA has seen more political pluralism, greater mobilization by civil society, and a more mature discourse. In UEMOA, the incumbents must face stronger political opposition and rely on demonstrated success and legacies. The civil society and the press are also stronger in West Africa and have been a counterbalance to political power. In Senegal, during the 2012 elections it was the civil society which promoted genuine democracy and help spearhead a successful political transition. There are more than 300 nongovernmental organizations in Senegal, and this has provided an important glue to ensure social peace. In Burkina, it was civil society that helped usher in a new era of democracy from authoritarian rule. By contrast, in Gabon and Equatorial Guinea, civil society have little political clout or presence and face action if they get involved in social or political processes. There is an inherent contestability of political space in UEMOA, while in CEMAC, similar to oil economies

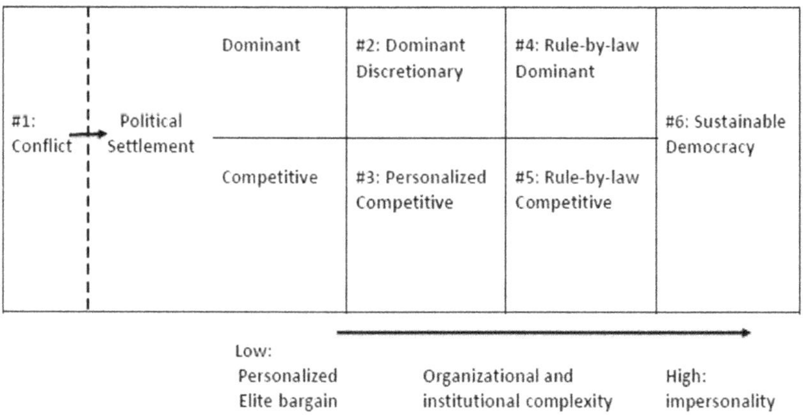

Fig. 9.2 Political Economy (*Source* Levy [2014])

in the Gulf and in Central Asia, there is a tendency for authoritarian impulses and the political economy of rentier states. Except for Gabon, all five CEMAC countries have faced civic and political unrest in the last twenty years, and strong challenges for internal stability.

Political Economy of Oil in CEMAC

The CEMAC area has a very different landscape from the Sahel. The two regions are poles apart in mindset and resource abundance. The political economy in these countries has defined the management of these revenues. CEMAC is home to many natural resources and minerals including oil, what some commentators have called the Devil's Gold. Part of the problem with oil is that the extraction costs of oil have been low relative to the windfalls. But countries that have it tend to depend too much on it leading to an unhealthy addiction. The oil-rich economies, especially Gabon, Republic of Congo, and Equatorial Guinea, have fallen victim to the "boom and bust" cycles associated with fluctuations in the global oil market. Except for oil-importing Central African Republic, the CEMAC region is vulnerable to oil price shifts affecting both fiscal and current account deficits. A very rough calculation indicates that a dollar decline in oil price can shave off close to 0.1% of GDP growth for CEMAC.

Most of the CEMAC countries suffer from the resource curse and "Dutch Disease." Drawing on the experience of the Netherlands, this resource curse refers to failures of resource-rich economies to translate natural resource wealth into sustainable economic development. The resource wealth has sometimes led to increased corruption, volatile growth, and conflict. In a survey of the literature, Ross (2014) finds that one type of mineral wealth, petroleum, has at least three harmful effects: it tends to make authoritarian regimes more durable, to increase certain types of corruption, and to help trigger violent conflict in low- and middle-income countries.

Economies with abundant natural resources have tended to grow less rapidly than natural-resource-scarce economies (Sachs and Warner 1995). In these countries, the increase in oil rent has helped develop the sector and the non-tradable sectors linked to the oil economy. However, due to the increase in factors costs, manufacturing and agricultural sectors have tended to stagnate. Years after oil was discovered, Gabon, Republic of Congo, and Equatorial Guinea have become food importers and have no vibrant agro-processing and industrial capability outside oil. There has been a difficult quest for diversification as non-oil growth has averaged 2% in CEMAC since 2015. Another tragedy is that human development indicators remain the same as in countries where there is no oil and consistently rank in the lowest out of 189 countries in the Human Development Index. Since oil in CEMAC is not expected to last more than a few decades, this lack of development presents a cause for concern.

Oil movements in the last decade have been unpredictable and like a roller coaster. Oil used to be dominated by international companies but by the 1970s, the Organization of Petroleum Exporting Countries, which was created at the Baghdad Conference in September 1960, by Iran, Iraq, Kuwait, Saudi Arabia, and Venezuela and which expanded membership after that, revolutionized the oil market. As a cartel that can unify its members amid the common objective of stabilizing petroleum prices, OPEC played a role in the 1970s by restricting output to lead to higher prices. Over the years, due to OPEC's deft maneuvering and increasing demand from emerging markets such as China and India, the oil price had a steady ascent, with occasional downturns. From the late 1990s, where it was $10 a barrel to the mid-2010s where it reached $100 a barrel, oil has had a volatile history.

However, by the 2000s, the world witnessed the spectacular emergence of US shale, which has been a game changer in the oil market and led to the United States becoming a large energy producer, exporting close to 3 million barrels a day in 2019. Supported by advanced technologies and horizontal fracking and benefiting from America's generous oil endowment in areas such as North Dakota, Texas, and Pennsylvania, the US shale production has surged leading to an abundance of oil and gas. It gave the United States the energy independence it had been seeking for years and affected the world geopolitical calculus. In 2019, the United States was the world's largest oil-producing country in 2019 with more than 12 million barrels per day.

The rise in shale—coupled with decreased demand in Asia, inability of OPEC to have a united front, and the rise of renewable energy (like wind and solar) led to oil falling from its $100 dollar a barrel in 2014 to less than $40 a barrel in 2016. Measures by the Saudis and the Russians led to production cuts and a price increase. Although it is not a formal member of OPEC, Russia collaborates with OPEC in areas of mutual interest. Since both Russia and Saudi Arabia are dependent on fiscal revenue from oil, there has been a convergence of interests.

After increasing in recent years, the COVID-19 pandemic has once again led to volatility in oil prices, which at some point have gone below \$10 a barrel. However, by February 2021 there has been a bit of a rebound in the oil market leading to oil prices above \$50. In particular, US shale, which is quite leveraged, had a very bad year in 2020, and many industry analysts are speculating that the industry will only recover in 2022. Despite the rise of US shale, OPEC (mostly Saudi Arabia) still controls about 75% of the world's total crude oil reserves. The future of oil is uncertain, especially in a world of renewables, such as hydro, solar, and wind, and the \$100 that CEMAC economies benefited from in the heyday seem like a thing of the past. As a result, CEMAC has been on a roller-coaster path, its macroeconomic stability jeopardized by the commodity swings (Fig. 9.3).

Oil results in a unique political economy. Oil economies become defined as rentier states, where governments depend on oil rents and income streams to finance the core activities of the state. The distribution of the rents is then done according to the political economy considerations of the government. Oil windfalls are used to finance high government spending, especially wages and salaries. Usually, in these countries, there is little investment in human or social capital. Capital flight prevails.

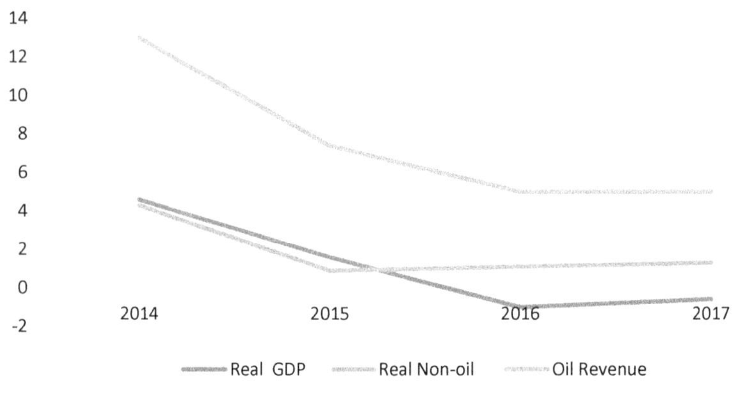

Fig. 9.3 CEMAC: Growth and Revenue: 2014–2017 (*Source* IMF)

The relationships between the national government and the oil companies are frequently not transparent.[1] The press coverage of the depletion of millions of dollars in the reserves of Sonangol, Angola's state-owned oil company, is testament to the difficulty in managing oil windfalls well. Empirical evidence suggests that there is significant capital flight out from CEMAC and large deposits by CEMAC resident in foreign countries, perhaps estimates at more than $5 billion, which are beyond what is allowed by CEMAC's foreign exchange regulation. The ability of individuals and companies to bypass the national legislation and provide incorrect customs declarations, coupled with the weak oversight of the tax authorities, reveals the extent of the governance challenges.

In a World Bank study, Devarajan and Singh (2012) find that poor performance stems from a fundamental feature of mineral extraction, that goes through the government but that does not have the oversight from the citizenry. The authors present the case for government failure and are in favor of a direct transfer of resources to the citizens who can also be taxed and argue that their proposal would prevent the CEMAC political elites from squandering the natural resource wealth.

Public Financial Management and Lack of Fiscal Decentralization

Public financial management in the CFA zone has had mixed record, in spite of multiple reforms. Over the years there have been improvements in budget preparation, budget reporting, and reductions in arrears due to better management. However, gaps persist in implementation. In their attempts to harmonize and improve public finance systems, the WAEMU Commission in 2009 and the CEMAC one in 2011 adopted a number of new Directives to strengthen the new legislative framework for public finance management in the CFA zone. While these Directives are strong from a public finance perspective, they have been delayed in being transposed to national legislation and implementation lags persist.

[1] Oil contracts in CEMAC tend to be either Production-Sharing Agreements (PSAs), whereby a CEMAC government makes an deal with a foreign company to provide technical services for exploration and development in return for a share of production or a tax concession regime, where a government transfers the title to the oil and resources to the oil company and imposes tax and royalties.

A research note by the International Budget Partnership (2014), using the results from the 2012 Open Budget Survey, finds the performance of most of the CFA countries surveyed to be particularly poor: the average score of 14 is three times lower than the world average score (43) and two times lower than Sub-Saharan Africa's average score (31). Citizens have no opportunity to participate in the budget debate, making them unable to express their expectations but also to assess their government policies and actions. Of all the countries surveyed, only Mali seems to perform relatively well in the subregion, and can be a benchmark for other WAEMU and CEMAC countries.

One problem with the Francophone countries is the excessive centralization. The existing system in CEMAC and UEMOA, which gives greater power to Ministry of Finance officials, and less autonomy to line ministries, prevents a smooth execution of expenditures and results in a long process. While de facto the system has controls, in practice, the controls are more procedural than on the verification of the quality of expenditure.

Francophone countries lag behind Anglophone ones in the extent of fiscal decentralization. Since the 1980s, based on a mindset of bringing resources closer to populations, decentralization has been transforming governance structures and development possibilities in Africa. The leaders in the process—Ghana, Ethiopia, and Uganda—have succeeded in transferring power and resources to subnational governments and local communities. Unfortunately, Francophone CFA countries have lagged. More than 80% of revenues in Niger are spent in Niamey, and similar patterns are throughout the Sahel and CFA zone. Even in cases where local governments have been entrusted with ambitious mandates, fiscal decentralization has proceeded much more slowly.

A recent study finds that countries like Mali, Burkina, and Niger have been involved in decades-long decentralization efforts with channeling of resources to strengthen local governments, but decentralization has not been a panacea. It has brought national challenges to the local level: poor institutional capacity, elite capture, and political conflict (Clingendael 2020).

A parallel problem is the lack of good data and accounting standards reflecting a lag in the convergence between Francophone practices and best practice norms.

Samia Msadek from the World Bank has noted:

> In many parts of Francophone Africa, accounting practices have a lot of room to improve. In particular, financial reporting and auditing need reforms... Policy-makers do not always have accurate information about the money available to provide vital and quality public services, such as school-teachers or the construction of health clinics or roads. They also don't always know how such funds are used...Governments with poor accounting practices are unable to make fully informed decisions about the allocation and use of scarce resources... This also means that citizens, in turn, do not have a way of knowing how their tax money is being used.[2]

A final problem is the persistence of graft and inefficiency due to opaque public expenditure management. Prominent examples for CEMAC cited by Devarajan and Singh include the following:

- The costs of construction classrooms in Chad are the most expensive in Africa and four times the next most expensive country.
- Cameroon spends $50 per capita on health, but it has the epidemiological profile as countries who spend $10 per capita.
- Road maintenance costs in Cameroon are twice the average for Sub-Saharan African countries.
- Republic of Congo electrical utility suffers from 47% transmission losses compared to 27% for the rest of Africa.
- Capital flight from CEMAC is more than $140 billion between 1975 and 2015 (Ndikumana and Boyce 2018).

References

African Development Bank. 2000. African Development Bank, Bank Group Policy on Good Governance Abidjan.

Akum, Fonteh, and Zachary Donnerfeld. 2015. Gathering storm clouds: Political and economic uncertainty in Central Africa. Institute of Security Studies.

Clingendael. 2020. Decentralisation and Inclusive Governance in Fragile Settings: Lessons for the Sahel, Netherlands Institute for International Relations. CRU Policy Brief.

[2] A conference to improve public finance management in Francophone Africa A conference to improve public finance management in Francophone Africa | World Bank Blogs.

Devarajan, Shantayanan, and Raju Singh. 2012. Government Failure and Poverty Reduction in the CEMAC. In *Oil Wealth in Central Africa*, ed. Bernardin Akitoby and Sharmini Coorey. Washington, DC: IMF.

International Budget Partnership. 2014. Are New PFM Reforms in the WAEMU and the CEMAC Working? Lessons from the Open Budget Survey, by Babacar Sarr, IBF Research Note.

Levy, Brian. 2014. *Working with the Grain: Integrating Governance and Growth in Development Strategies*. Oxford University Press.

Ndikumana, Leonce, and James K. Boyce. 2018. Capital Flight: Updated Methodology and New Estimates. Political Economy Research Institute (PERI) University of Massachusetts at Amherst.

Ross, Michael. 2014. What Have We Learned about the Resource Curse? University of California, Los Angeles (UCLA)—Department of Political Science.

Sachs, Jeffrey, and Andrew M. Warner. 1995. Natural Resource Abundance and Economic Growth. NBER Working Papers 5398, National Bureau of Economic Research, Inc.

CHAPTER 10

The Underperforming Private Sector

The three leading countries—Cote d'Ivoire, Cameroon, and Senegal have been unable to develop a strong manufacturing sector and increase the processing of agricultural commodities. There are several dynamics, including the lack of mid-sized firms, the partial retreat of the state, the politically connected oligopolies, and the trifecta of high energy costs, difficult financing, and high transport costs.

Cote d'Ivoire, by some definitions the locomotive of the UEMOA, has had an average real GDP growth rate of close to 7% since the end of the civil war in 2011 fueled by agriculture, investment, services, and an improved business climate. It has become one of the better performers in the region. Unique among the CFA zone, it attracts much migration from the Sahelian economies. Together with Ghana, it is the top exporter of cocoa and raw cashews, and has a diversified agro-processing sector of some scale. Recently, it has even ventured into chocolate production, trying to bring in value added in some of its exports.

One area where Cote d'Ivoire has had a divergence with other CFA countries is that large public and private investment in infrastructure and power projects (bridges, economic zones, roads, power plants, hydroelectric dams). Cote d'Ivoire has had a major change in agriculture production, which has grown by 50% from 15.8 million tons in 2011 to 23.7 million tons in 2017—almost 30% points faster than in Africa and 20% points faster than in West Africa (IFC 2020). Cote d'Ivoire has

A. Zafar, *The CFA Franc Zone*,
https://doi.org/10.1007/978-3-030-71006-4_10

emerged as a regional leader for the CFA zone, but it still has poverty levels that average more than 40%.

Cameroon, the leader of CEMAC together with Gabon, was post-independence one of the powerful economies in Africa, but its momentum has stalled despite oil reserves, a coastal location, and favorable agricultural conditions. It remains a well-endowed primary commodity economy, but it has considerable potential to be a manufacturing exporter. If Cameroon is to become an upper middle-income country by 2035, Cameroon's real GDP will have to grow by roughly 8% (or 5.7% per capita) between 2015 and 2035, which in turn will require the investment share of GDP to increase from about 20% in 2015 to 30% in 2035 (World Bank 2017).

The Senegalese economy is the other leading economy in UEMOA after the Ivory Coast. It has considerable potential, but it has not been able to diversify away from phosphates, fish, and groundnuts. Since 2014 the government has been implementing the Emerging Senegal Plan (PSE), trying to become an emerging country by 2035. However, it has not yet been able to capitalize on its administrative elite and coastal location to develop manufacturing, agro-processing, and mining. Senegal still faces some of the same per capita income that it did since independence many years back.

Senegal is also interesting because its geography and history make it an ideal country to have a manufacturing hub exporting garments to Europe. Several studies in the early 2000s demonstrate that the country has key advantages in the textile industry: a decline in labor costs because of a 1994 devaluation; good access to European and US markets because of proximity, trade agreements, or preferential treatment; and highly skilled informal sector producers including weavers in Casamance and experienced tailors.

In a recent study, Golub and Mbaye (2020) find that Senegal has considerable export potential but major challenges. Once upon a time, it had a well-developed formal industry inherited from the colonial era and a tradition of skilled informal tailors, but the industry collapsed due to overly protection and highly ineffective industrial base, as well as smuggling and trade liberalization of the 1980s. Currently, it is unable to attract investment and outsourcing from global retail chains looking for new manufacturing hubs due to a deficient investment climate and high unit labor costs. Both for Senegal and other countries, anecdotal evidence suggests that wage costs in Francophone Africa tend to be high, a legacy of the higher civil servant salaries in the past.

Cameroon, Ivory Coast, and Senegal face limited poverty reduction. Growth-poverty elasticities have remained low in all three countries. Every percentage point of growth led to 0.2% points of poverty reduction in Côte d'Ivoire (vs 2.5 ppt in lower middle-income countries and 1.6 ppt in Sub-Saharan Africa).

In most of the CFA countries, manufacturing as a percent of GDP has stagnated for the last few decades, mostly below 15% of GDP. Almost all the manufacturing in the CFA zone is conducted by small firms, sold domestically, and focused on internal demand and local markets, even among the three leading countries—Cote d'Ivoire, Senegal, and Cameroon. Despite this favorable coastal location, relative abundance of natural resources, and valuable inputs for light manufacturing industries serving local, regional, and global markets, the manufacturing exports have not been able to take off. The resources include wood products for the furniture industry, cotton for the textile and garment industry, and ample agricultural land, adequate rainfall, and favorable meteorology that supply a clear comparative advantage in agro-processing and agribusiness. In Gabon, the oil sector is an enclave with not enough backward linkages to the rest of the economy. Despite favorable agricultural endowments, wood processing and agro-industry have failed to establish themselves, only reaching 10% of non-oil GDP. In sum, the CFA leading countries have been unable to take advantage of unique coastal locations.

Some features of these economies are:

- The economies are bifurcated between large, formal, well-established firms (more than 500 in Cote d'Ivoire) and many microenterprises, and there is the absence of strong mid-size firms.
- The formal sector is small accounting for less than 5% of economic units in the CFA zone, and SMEs making up the rest of the units.
- The large firms specialize in agro-industry (horticulture, fish, etc.), food processing, chemicals, metals, wood, cement, plastics, and basic machinery. There is the absence of garments and textiles, furniture, and more technologically sophisticated products. These firms are competitive only in regional markets and not globally.
- Private investment in CFA zone as a percent of GDP remains low. In Cote d'Ivoire, private sector investment increased from 10.3% of

GDP in 2015 to more than 12% in 2018. In East Asia, private investment is close to 30% of GDP, and in Bangladesh, it is more than 22%.

- Cote d'Ivoire has a formal industrial sector that includes very few firms that are labor-intensive and consists mostly of subsidiaries of multinationals (primarily European-owned), involved largely in the commodity sector (cocoa, oil and gas, cashew, rubber). It is also a major cocoa producer, accounting for about 40% of the global market, but the transformation and processing have been limited. The top five export items—cocoa, horticulture, petroleum products, gold, and rubber—constitute 75% of exports. In private investment and FDI inflows, it is lower than its peers (IFC 2020). Agro-business accounts for approximately 30% of the manufacturing sector (predominantly cocoa products, oilseeds, dairy products).
- Close to 80% of the working-age population operates in the private sector informal sector, which tends to have low productivity and be poorly regulated.
- In most of the CFA countries, there is a government presence in agro-processing and manufacturing sectors (cotton, fertilizer, etc.), but the state has exited many industries. It still influences the prices of many staples, including rice, edible oils, sugar, fertilizer, bread, and agricultural products.
- Sectors such as the transport and telecom sectors are dominated by politically connected oligopolies and state enterprises. There is a lack of competition in many industries and connected firms do well, while new firms have high barriers of entry. Mbaye et al. (2015) find that formal firms in Senegal in import-competing industries such as sugar, vegetable oil, and wheat flour benefit from protected rents, either in the form of high import taxes, monopoly rights to import key inputs, or privileged access to government contracts.
- CFA manufacturing is further hindered by the trifecta of high energy costs, difficult financing, and high transport costs, especially container transport. A 40 ft container from Abidjan to Long

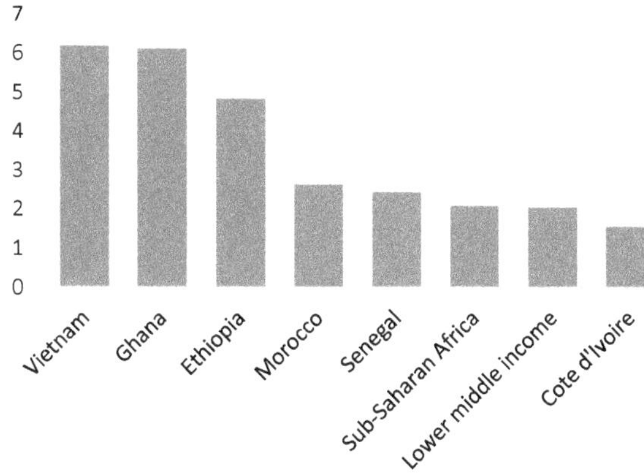

Fig. 10.1 FDI inflows, 2015–2017 average (% of GDP) (*Source* IFC CPSD Cote d'Ivoire 2020)

Beach costs $4,000 to transport compared to $2,000 from Dhaka or Shanghai to Long Beach.

- Integration into global value VCs remains low. The CFA zone lags behind both other regions and subregions of the world in integrating into GVCs. The export of intermediate goods is very low.
- CFA firms tend to be smaller than firms in other regions with lower labor productivity.
- Foreign investment is not high, and the CFA zone has not been successful at gathering the attention of the international private sector. CFA countries have a less successful record of FDI mobilization compared to aspirational peers. Two of the FDI leaders in the CFA zone have levels of FDI at 2% of GDP, much less than the 5% of Ethiopia, Ghana, and Vietnam (Fig. 10.1). There is also lower private investment in Cote d'Ivoire and Senegal than Ethiopia (Fig. 10.2).

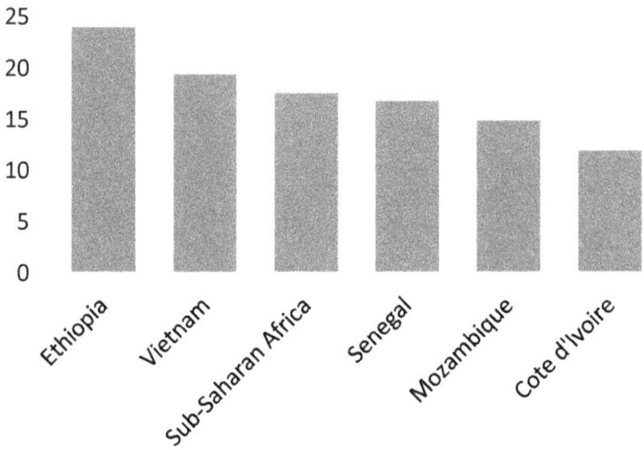

Fig. 10.2 Private investment, 2015–2017 average (% of GDP) (*Source* IFC CPSD Cote d'Ivoire 2020)

References

Golub, Stephen, and Ahmadou Aly Mbaye. 2020. *Removing Impediments to Export-Led Growth in Senegal: Groundnuts, Fishing, Textiles, Fruits, and Vegetables*. Washington, DC: Brookings. https://www.brookings.edu/blog/africa-in-focus/2020/09/01/removing-impediments-to-export-led-growth-in-senegal-groundnuts-fishing-textiles-fruits-and-vegetables/.

International Finance Corporation. 2020. Creating Markets in Cote d'Ivoire: Mobilizing the Private Sector in Support of Economic Transformation in Côte d'Ivoire. Washington, DC.

Mbaye, A.A., S.S. Golub, and Phil English. 2015. Policies, Prices, and Poverty: The Sugar, Vegetable Oil, and Flour Industries in Senegal. World Bank Policy Research Working Paper 7286. Washington, DC.

World Bank. 2017. *Cameroon Country Economic Memorandum: Markets, Government, and Growth*. Washington, DC: World Bank.

CHAPTER 11

Lack of Dynamic Agriculture and the Limited Structural Transformation

The CFA economies do not have a very dynamic agriculture. CFA farm yields are among the lowest in the world. Farmers pay three times the price and use one third of the fertilizer compared to other emerging economies. Despite progress in certain crops, such as coffee, cocoa, and cotton, West Africa continues to import large supplies of rice and faces challenges with nontraditional agricultural exports. Many countries, such as Cameroon and Senegal, imported more than half a billion dollars of cereal imports in 2020.

Food production is low due to more smallholder farmers, lower productivity, and poor infrastructure for crop processing and transportation, as well as a deficiency in agriculture and extension services. The soils also tend to be of poorer quality and deprived of nutrients. The absence of domestic input manufacture and strong agricultural research makes the situation more challenging. The experience of China, Vietnam, and Bangladesh, who benefited from government policy support and private investments, suggests that better agricultural productivity can catalyze strong development success.

Ethiopia has had very strong agricultural GDP growth in the last decade averaging more than 8%, while Kenya has become a large horticulture producer. Its exports increased from $70 million in 1991 to close to $1.5 billion in early 2020 before the COVID pandemic. In the last decade, Rwanda has increased crop production through supportive

A. Zafar, *The CFA Franc Zone*,
https://doi.org/10.1007/978-3-030-71006-4_11

macroeconomic policies and public investment in agriculture. As opposed to the CFA economies, the Eastern African nations are all committed to maintaining exchange rate flexibility as the key tool for external adjustment and for promoting domestic production. As a result, the exchange rates of Kenya and Rwanda have been kept on a managed float to adjust to market forces within the equilibrium range. In 2019, Ethiopia also committed to a fully floating currency.

The African Development Bank finds that the African continent can also double its market share to select processed commodities and that Africa's agribusiness sector can reach one trillion dollars by 2030, describing it as the next oil sector. There is considerable potential for expanded regional trade to foster the substitution of locally processed starchy staples for imported rice during times of high grain prices. There is considerable scope for investment in agriculture and value-addition in African agriculture, in crops such as wheat, cereals, vegetable oils, poultry, and vegetable.

A recent FAO study on African agriculture finds a disturbing picture regarding African agriculture. In 1980, Africa had an almost balanced agricultural trade with both agricultural exports and imports at about USD 14 billion, but by 2007 its agricultural imports exceeded agricultural exports by about USD $22 billion (FAO 2012). The study notes a striking increase in food imports since the mid-1970s for basic foodstuffs such as dairy products, edible oils and fats, meat and meat products, sugar, and especially cereals. The food trade deficit, which started in the mid-1970s, has been accelerating until recent years. By 2020, during the COVID pandemic, it is estimated that Africa imports roughly 80% of its food. The situation is particularly challenging in West and Central Africa. The CEMAC economies are even more dependent on food imports than the UEMOA economies.

Another problem for CFA agriculture is problems competing with non-CFA agriculture as well as European agriculture due to the overvalued currency, which makes African farmers less competitive. A secondary challenge is the competition from European agriculture, despite the large amounts of fertile land. EU farmers benefit from subsidies and agricultural support programs under the Common Agricultural Policy (CAP) and are able to sell at prices which do not cover production costs.

In terms of structural transformation, the process of moving resources from less-productive to higher productive activities, most successful countries have gone through a process where they have moved from being agrarian economies to moving to manufacturing and then to services. City-states, like the Vatican and Singapore, never were big agricultural producers, while countries like India have moved directly from agriculture to services. Growth can also be realized by raising productivity within sectors, such as capital deepening, by adopting new technologies, or by improving the quality of services.

One phenomenon in the CFA countries has been the rise of urbanization fueled by rural migrants who have left stagnating agriculture to seek opportunities in the city. Unfortunately, the urbanization process has been chaotic and disorderly with rural migrants moving to overcrowded cities and joining the ranks of the informal sector and low productivity service sector, as opposed to countries like China, Bangladesh, and Indonesia, where the rural poor joined productive jobs in manufacturing. The CFA capital cities—Bamako, Niamey, Ouagadougou, Bangui, and Yaounde—have all become booming cities that have far more population than was originally planned. In a study of West African urbanization, World Bank (2018a) finds that urban areas account for roughly half of the national GDP in both Mali and Niger but represent only 1% of their landmass; Bamako represents 34%, while Niamey represents 27%. Until 2030, Mali and Niger will welcome at least 400,000 and 190,000 people, respectively. The cities will need to develop the infrastructure and services to absorb the inflows of people.

The contrast with Asia is clear. In Asia, it was productive agriculture in the latter that allowed the strong food surpluses that allowed the city dwellers to be well-fed and not depend on expensive food imports. In Indonesia, the high productivity of rice in the 1960s and 1970s allowed the movement of factory workers to Jakarta to work. In the CFA zone, the emigration from the cities was spurred by droughts and agricultural hardships and not by a productivity revolution.

By moving economic activities from low-productive sectors to high-productive sectors (the between-sector effects), the CEMAC and WAEMU countries can achieve long-lasting economic growth. These economies were overwhelmingly rural in the 1960s and 1970s. Over time, migrants left the cities to travel to the growing urban centers, including

Abidjan, Yaounde, Bamako, and Ouagadougou. The shift out of agriculture does not seem to have been accompanied by improvements in rural labor productivity. McMillan and Rodrik (2011) note:

> Labor productivity growth in an economy can be achieved in one of two ways. First, productivity can grow within economic sectors through capital accumulation, technological change, or reduction of misallocation across plants. Second, labor can move across sectors, from low-productivity sectors to high-productivity sectors, increasing overall labor productivity in the economy… a high rate of productivity growth within an industry can have quite ambiguous implications for overall economic performance if the industry's share of employment shrinks rather than expands. If the displaced labor ends up in activities with lower productivity, economy-wide growth will suffer and may even turn negative.

In many of the WAEMU countries, the service sectors account for over 50% of economic activity, while agriculture and industry represent around 30% and less than 20%. In some countries, modest deindustrialization has been experienced, with the share of manufacturing in output falling from 15 to 10% in the WAEMU.

In an analysis of African countries along with others, McMillan et al. (2014) note the reallocation of factors has been observed in the opposite direction, meaning that the labor factor moved to below-average productivity, indicating reverse structural transformation. Africa and Latin America are the only two regions in the world where this occurs. Many of the poorer agricultural laborers in Africa moved to the sprawling urban informal sector, and many of them have been trapped in low productivity jobs. This is different from the experience in Asia, where workers moved to the growing manufacturing sector. McMillan et al. (2017) find that structural change played a small role in the recent growth performance of the middle-income countries of Brazil and Botswana, although it did play a key role in launching them into middle-income status, and that structural change contributed significantly to growth in Vietnam and Ghana over the past two decades, although in different ways.

Dinh (2017) analyzes this pattern in Senegal to measure the contribution of employment reallocation to productivity growth. Using this methodology and data from 1999 to 2010 in the Penn World Table database, which consists of consistent data for a group of developed

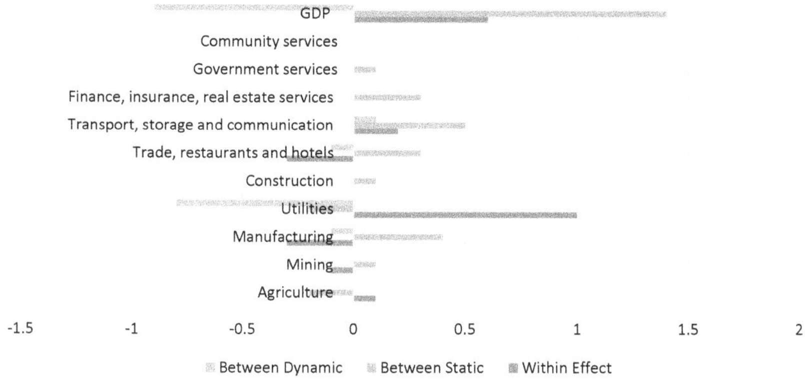

Fig. 11.1 Sectoral contribution to productivity growth, by Type of Effect, Senegal (*Source* Dinh 2017)

and developing countries on employment, value adding, and productivity up to 2014, he finds evidence of reverse structural transformation.[1] Figure 11.1 presents the results of the analysis and Fig. 11.2 shows how Senegal's performance in structural transformation compared with the performance of other countries in Africa and with countries in Asia. According to the analysis, transport and finance exhibit greater productivity than manufacturing, but they do not absorb many workers, and their rising productivity means that fewer and fewer workers will be employed as the economy grows. In fact, over the period, the three sectors that absorb the most workers are still agriculture, trade and hotels, and manufacturing.

The analysis shows the impact on Senegal and other African countries of shifting resources to conform to the resource structure in developed countries, while maintaining the same level of sectoral productivity in the African countries. In other words, even if productivity within sectors

[1] The method is to estimate a decomposition equation using the weighted sum of productivity growth within individual sectors. The weights are the employment share of each sector at the beginning of the time period. This is the within component of productivity growth, which comes into play if there is capital deepening in the sectors or the application of new technologies (high-variety yields, better inputs, and so on), assuming no change in the sectoral distribution of employment. The second term captures the productivity effect of labor reallocations across sectors.

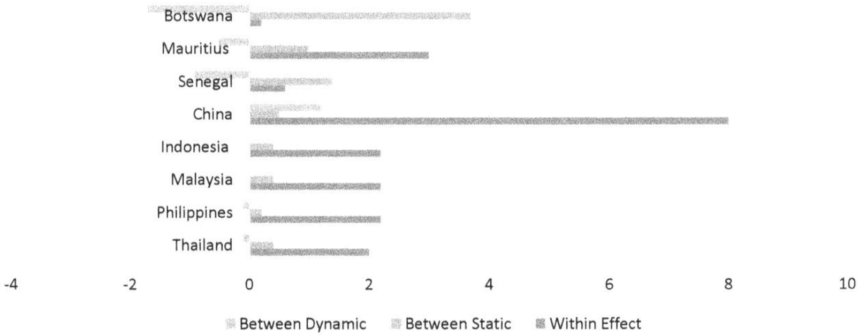

Fig. 11.2 Decomposition of productivity growth, various countries, 2000–2010 (*Source* Dinh 2017)

does not improve, Senegal can gain tremendously by creating opportunities outside agriculture to which resources may be moved. While all African countries in the sample seem to gain from such a shift in resources, Senegal gains the most: over ten times the average productivity.

References

Dinh, Hinh. 2017. Industrialization, and Globalization. OCP Policy Center, Morocco.

FAO. 2012. Why Has Africa Become a Net Food Importer? Explaining African Agricultural and Food Trade Deficits. In *FAO Trade and Markets Division*, ed. Manitra A. Rakotoarisoa, Massimo Iafrate, and Marianna Paschali. Rome.

McMillan, Margaret S., and Dani Rodrik. 2011. Globalization, Structural Change, and Productivity Growth. NBER Working Paper 17143, National Bureau of Economic Research, Cambridge, MA.

McMillan, Margaret S., Dani Rodrik, and Íñigo Verduzco-Gallo. 2014. Globalization, Structural Change, and Productivity Growth, with an Update on Africa. *World Development* 63 (C): 11–32.

McMillan, Margaret S., Dani Rodrik, and Claudia Sepulveda. 2017. Structural Change, Fundamentals and Growth: A Framework and Case Studies. NBER Working Paper No. 23378, May.

World Bank. 2018a. The Challenges of Urbanization in West Africa. AFCW3 Economic Update, Washington, DC, Spring.

CHAPTER 12

Climate Change and Migration

Climate change has been one of the challenging crises of our times. As global temperatures increase, climate change is affecting resource scarcity, leading to migration, exacerbating conflict, and reducing water and food availability. Climate change can also have a profound impact on socioeconomic dynamics in the countries and have adverse political implications. By definition, climate change includes changes both in emissions of greenhouse gases and in changing weather patterns. The pace of climate change has accelerated in the last few years galvanizing growing international attention. There has been an increasing number of weather-related events, whether hurricanes, forest fires, and storms. A wide spectrum of economic activity risks being affected by climate change, including agriculture, forestry, and fisheries. Some estimates suggest that by 2050 cumulative damages from climate change may reach $8 trillion affecting 3% of gross world product.

Global warming may also be exacerbating global income equality. First, many poor countries are closer to the tropics and in regions where global warming is having a greater impact. Second, because of limited fiscal space, their coping and adaptation mechanisms are somewhat limited. Third, due to the parabolic relationship between temperature and economic growth, warming is increasing growth in cool countries and decreasing growth in warm countries (Diffenbaugh and Burke 2019). According to their analysis, per capita gross domestic product (GDP)

A. Zafar, *The CFA Franc Zone*,
https://doi.org/10.1007/978-3-030-71006-4_12

has been reduced 17–31% at the poorest four deciles of the population-weighted country-level per capita GDP distribution, yielding a ratio between the top and bottom deciles that is 25% larger than in a world without global warming. Smaller poorer countries will disproportionately face the impact though they are not the prime originators of global emissions and have relatively a lower carbon footprint.

According to NASA, the Earth's average global surface temperature in 2019 was the second warmest recorded year. At the same time, there has been the emergence of El Nino, which is itself a complex weather pattern that results when ocean temperatures in the Pacific Ocean near the equator vary from the norm and where accumulation of warm water in the west Pacific adds heat to air. There has also been a decrease in the ice mass, with a decrease in the mass of the Greenland and Antarctic ice sheets, as well as a rising sea level, which is rising faster than it did in the last century. In California in 2020, there has been a very large wildfire, leading to temperature records and increased smog and air quality in many northern California cities.

Global Findings

According to the 2013 special UN Intergovernmental Panel on Climate Change (IPCC), the world's foremost institutional authority on the subject, finds overwhelming evidence of climate change. The Fifth Assessment Report finds that climate change is a real threat to the globe (IPCC 2013). Estimating cumulative CO_2 emissions since premodern times and providing a CO_2 budget for future emissions to limit warming to less than 2 °C, the panel has argued that the global community should seriously try to reduce the emissions. Many organizations and institutions have been redirecting their aid to factor in the emerging climate crisis.

Among the IPCC findings:

- From 1880 to 2012, the average global temperature increased by 0.85 °C.
- Oceans have warmed, the amounts of snow and ice have diminished, and the sea level has risen.
- From 1901 to 2010, the global average sea level rose by 19 cm as oceans expanded due to warming and ice melted; average sea level rise is predicted to be 24–30 cm by 2065 and 40–63 cm by 2100 relative to the reference period of 1986–2005.

- Most aspects of climate change will persist for many centuries, even if emissions are stopped.
- Limiting warming to 1.5 °C is possible within the laws of chemistry and physics, but doing so would require unprecedented changes in land, energy, industry, buildings, transport, and cities.

Africa and Climate Change

One continent where climate change has had an impact is Sub-Saharan Africa, which has seen greater weather extremes in the last thirty years. The Intergovernmental Panel on Climate Change finds that Africa is among the most vulnerable continents to climate change influenced by factors such as weak adaptive capacity, high dependence on ecosystem goods for livelihoods, and less developed agricultural production systems. In a general sense, the key impacts of these record greenhouse gas emissions will be higher temperatures, drought, changing rainfall patterns and increased climate variability.

For many reasons, including geography and low adaptive capacity, Africa is highly vulnerable to the impacts of climate change (Engelbrecht et al. 2015). According to one model, which is the first model developed by African researchers tailored to African realities, African annual average near-surface temperatures over the last five decades reveals drastic increases, particularly over parts of the subtropics and central tropical Africa where temperatures have been rising at more than twice the global rate of temperature increase. The model indicates that African annual-averaged temperatures may plausibly rise at about 1.5 times the global rate of temperature increase in the subtropics, and at a somewhat lower rate in the tropics.

West Africa has emerged as one of the world's next hotspots, and the Sahel, where many of the CFA countries is located, is particularly vulnerable. It is one of the world's regions that can see temperature increases of between 2 and 5 °C by 2050. West and Central Africa will see particularly large increases in the number of hot days at both 1.5 and 2 °C. Some climate change models find that temperature increases in Sub-Saharan Africa will be higher than the global mean. There will be a very pronounced impact on crops leading to crop failures and general damage to agricultural productivity. The impact on food security will be very damaging, leading to even greater imports of food. Agricultural losses caused by climate change in western and central Africa are expected to range from 2 to 4% GDP, and losses of 0.4% to 1.3% of GDP are predicted for northern and southern Africa (Mendelsohn et al. 2000). Some models are also predicting the lengthening of drought periods in much of Africa (WBGU 2007). The effects are supposed to be significant on the livestock and cropping sectors, which already suffer from a limited ability to control water and limited adaptation from farmers.

According to Brookings, global temperatures rising as much as 3 °C by 2100 would have a disproportionate impact on Africa with aggregate GDP potentially dropping by as much as 8.6% after that year. Many are in agro-ecological belts most vulnerable to climate change. Already there is evidence of early departure of herds and growing fights between migrating pastoralists who frequently conflict with local farmers for scarce water. Exhibit A of the climate change dynamic is the situation with Lake Chad. Once a major lake in Central Africa, with over 30 million people relying on its freshwater, over the last few decades, it has reduced in size, although there is a debate on the actual reduction due to climate change. The impact on livestock rearing, fishing, and irrigation has been immense. The Sahelian climate change situation has not been escalated at the level of the United Nations Security Council, which has increasingly recognized the role of climate change in exacerbating conflict.

However, there are still differences among different climate change models of the impact of the change on precipitation and rainfall patterns, but the consensus is that these will not stay the same. In relation to the CFA zone, the current modeling projections show that there will be longer dry spells in the Western Sahel region, while Central Africa may have a decrease in wet spells. However, given the lack of a consistent time series, it is also hard to fully understand the impact from the general climate change to the particular local models.

The growing violence in Mali and Burkina, the depletion of Lake Chad, the threat to cotton production, and the possible increase in famine are all linked to climate change. The conflict between pastoralists searching for grazing land and water supply for livestock with more sedentary farmers can spiral out of control and lead to violence. The combined effect of all these issues could dampen the economic future of the Sahel and push many more people into poverty, reversing some of the positive development impacts of recent years.

In another study, the negative effects of climate change on the Sahel are further highlighted. Dell et al. (2012) analyze historical fluctuations in temperature within countries to identify its effects on aggregate economic outcomes and find three primary results. First, higher temperatures substantially reduce economic growth in poor countries. Second, higher temperatures may reduce growth rates, not just the level of output. Third, higher temperatures have wide-ranging effects, reducing agricultural output, industrial output, and political stability.

In response to these changes, all the CFA countries have signed the 2015 Paris Agreement dedicated to reducing climate change. The CFA countries will have to get used to the increased financial support from developed countries to develop a coherent action plan for monitoring climate change impact on their economies and have a revamped regional food security framework.

A recent World Bank study (2018b) finds that by 2050 the worsening impacts of climate change in three densely populated regions of the world could see more than 140 million people move within their countries' borders. Focusing on three regions—Sub-Saharan Africa, South Asia, and Latin America—the report argues that unless urgent action is taken, these three regions could be dealing with a combined total of over 140 million internal climate migrants by 2050. These people will be forced to migrate from one part of Africa to another, pushed out by droughts, failing crops, rising sea levels, and storm surges. The largest climate-related migration pressures will likely result from diminishing agricultural opportunities. Internal climate migration will increase in all parts of Sub-Saharan Africa including the CFA due to lower water availability and crop productivity alongside rising sea level and storm surges. The study finds that by 2050, the projected total number of potential internal climate migrants could be as high as 85.7 million or four percent of the region's total population under the pessimistic reference scenario, which is more than in South Asia and Latin America. With reform and action, the worst scenarios can be avoided.

References

Dell, Melissa, Benjamin Jones, and Benjamin Olken. 2012. Temperature Shocks and Economic Growth: Evidence from the Last Half Century. *American Economic Journal: Macroeconomics* 4 (3): 66–95.

Diffenbaugh, Noah, and Marshall Burke. 2019. Global Warming Has Increased Global Economic Inequality. *Proceedings of the National Academy of Sciences*, ed. Ottmar Edenhofer. Potsdam, Germany: Potsdam Institute for Climate

Impact Research, and accepted by Editorial Board Member Hans J. Schellnhuber March 22, 2019.

Engelbrecht, F., J. Adegoke, M.-J. Bopape, M. Naidoo, R. Garland, M. Thatcher, J. McGregor, J. Katzfey, M. Werner, and C. Ichoku. 2015. Projections of Rapidly Rising Surface Temperatures Over Africa Under Low Mitigation. *Environmental Research Letters* 10 (8): 085004. https://www.csir.co.za/nre/coupled_land_water_and_marine_ecosystems/pdfs/CCAM_African_temps.pdf.

Intergovernmental Panel on Climate Change. 2013. Fifth Assessment Report, United Nations.

Mendelsohn, R., A. Dinar, and A. Dalfelt. 2000. *Climate Change Impacts on African Agriculture*. Preliminary analysis prepared for the World Bank. Washington, DC: World Bank.

WBGU (German Advisory Council on Global Change). 2007. *Climate Change as a Security Risk*. London: Earthscan.

World Bank. 2018b. Groundswell: Preparing for Internal Climate Migration.

PART III

The Taboo Around the CFA Zone

For many years, among many policy circles, the CFA was considered a taboo topic. It was perceived as a sensitive topic, even within the development community. Except for a limited debate during the 1990s, the broader academic and policy community on the whole has not been engaged on the CFA. Only among a very specialized community of academics and policymakers was there a debate on the working on the CFA zone. The persistence of the taboo for so long is a fascinating story. There are a wide range of factors—individual, cultural, economic, political, and institutional—that prevented this discussion. The taboo has many origins and explanations.

CHAPTER 13

The Tragedy of Lower Quality Economic Analysis for Poorer Countries

The CFA zone has suffered the lack of quality scholarship. The circle of professionals interested in the CFA zone has been narrow, beyond a small circle of Francophone scholars. There was a flourishing of scholarship around the World Bank and the IMF due to the innovative work of macroeconomists such as Shanta Devarajan and Lawrence Hinkle, work at the IMF under the guidance of Benedict Clement, analysis by former Togolese minister and academic Kako Nubukpo, work in France under the Cerdi Institute, associated with Patrick and Sylvaine Guillaumont and pioneering academic work with David Stasavage, Eliot Berg, and few other scholars. Boughton (1991) and Devarajan and Rodrik (1991) provide some of the dueling perspectives on the debate.

Moreover, as Professor William Easterly has noted, the poorer the country, the lower the quality of economic analysis done for it. Young and promising academics worldwide were more interested in working on the EU, China, international trade, and finance than on the CFA economies. Top-notch academics graduating from elite universities were interested in topics that were more prestigious. Spending years working in conflict-ridden countries was not perceived as a career move, save with some international peacekeeping or relief organization. Most journals and books did not accord prominence to the CFA zone. In many of the leading academic and policy journals, the discussions on the CFA zone are not very visible.

A. Zafar, *The CFA Franc Zone*,
https://doi.org/10.1007/978-3-030-71006-4_13

In the international development circuit, visits to Bangui, Bamako, or Brazzaville were not considered interesting or enticing. Among international organizations, until recent years, careers were not made in these places but in the donor capitals and hobnobbing with more powerful players. While the tide is slowly turning, it has always been a challenge for the best global experts to visit CFA countries in Africa. None of the top global economists, perhaps with the exception of Dani Rodrik, has written about the CFA. Emerging economies such as India, China, South Korea, Mexico, and Brazil were considered far more interesting.

Even in cases where outsiders arrived in the CFA zone, there was frequently a lack of interest in the cultures, the nuances, and the history of the zone. A sort of developmental tourism emerged where visiting development experts moved between ministries, airports, and hotels. There was easy in and out movement without a deeper understanding. Reports were written by experienced economists with hardly a visit to the countries or an engagement with the manufacturers and agriculturalists of the countries. Overreliance on development indicators produced without engaging in adequate consultation with local authorities and entrepreneurs led to analytical weaknesses. Knowledge produced in a Northern research center was valued more than a report in the South, regardless of quality. Some CFA studies were prepared by supposed academic experts without ever having visited any of the CFA countries.

As veteran economist Celestin Monga (2020) has argued about many of the experts in Africa, and applicable to the CFA zone:

> Many of the development experts who set the policy agenda across Africa are recent university graduates with very little professional experience in any field, and none about life and policies in developing countries. Yet, they do not lack supreme confidence in their diagnostics of the problems or in the pertinence of their prescriptions. Not surprisingly, their policy advice, provided on the basis of a fuzzy understanding of country context, is often of poor quality, irrelevant, and harmful. The myth of dominant "donor" knowledge and the power of money (channeled through loans and grants to cash-strapped governments constantly facing crises) can seal the fate of nations.[1]

[1] https://www.brookings.edu/blog/future-development/2020/07/15/discrimination-and-prejudice-in-development/.

A related problem around the CFA is the paucity of data. When I asked academics and friends why they were not working on CFA issues in Africa, they said they did not know the countries, and the quality of data was too weak to be able to prepare publications for academic journals. While there are some good macro numbers, there has been a challenge to get good and regular household survey data since they are done every few years. One prominent factoid that has been talked about is that despite comprising 12.5% of the world's population, Africa still accounts for less than 1% of global research output.

The Sahel became more interesting when there were discussions on international terrorism. The only interest seems to be from journalists, anthropologists, and civil society, who were passionate and committed but perhaps lacked the empiricism and analytical experience to assess the common currency dynamics. Lately this tide is starting to turn as the Sahel is getting more interest from the development partners, and fragile states are moving to the higher ranks of the development agenda.

Also, the CFA arrangement has been considered technical as it had to do with exchange rates and monetary economics, and there was a broad unfamiliarity in the workings of the system. The discussions about overvaluation, misalignment, and optimal currencies turned out to be esoteric. Most of the existing analysis on the CFA zone was in French. Much of the literature was not translated and known. Most people, even among global development professionals, could not name many of the countries of the zone.

References

Boughton, M. 1991. The CFA Franc Zone: Currency Union and Monetary Standard. IMF Working Paper (WP/91/133), Washington, DC.

Devarajan, Shantayanan, and Dani Rodrik. 1991. Do the Benefits of Fixed Exchange Rates Outweigh Their Costs? The Franc Zone in Africa. NBER Working Papers 3727, National Bureau of Economic Research, Inc.

CHAPTER 14

Geopolitics, France, and African Elites: The Political Economy

The architects of the system view the fixed exchange rate arrangement and institutional setup to provide stability. The nominal anchor to a stable currency protects countries from inflation. And it is thought to be mutually beneficial for the African economies and France. The idea is that African countries benefited from French aid and anchorage to a stable currency, while France benefited from its aid, trade, and investments in Africa. The unlimited convertibility regime and the smooth rules on capital transfers provided security for foreign investments, and it was easy for French and other European companies to repatriate capital back to France. Exchange rate risk is minimized under the arrangement, and there is some discipline on fiscal and monetary policy of member nations.

The international system perceived the zone as a *fait accomplit*, and there was never a strong interest in challenging the existing regime. In a volatile world of the 1960s and 1970s, the CFA zone was perceived as a beacon of stability, especially in an environment where macroeconomic mismanagement and high-inflation among other African countries was common. However, Konnert (1998) argues that the free convertibility and fixed parity guaranteed by the French Treasury serve a narrow political elite in Africa, and this has been done at the expense of both the African poor and the French taxpayer.

A. Zafar, *The CFA Franc Zone*,
https://doi.org/10.1007/978-3-030-71006-4_14

There has been a complex political economy that was difficult to break, and there were monetary and political benefits from the existing arrangement. There has been a thick web of commercial interests, networks, and relationships between France and West and Central African elites, mixed with close political, economic, military, and cultural links. Much of this was not even known among the broader public in France or Africa. The world of the 1950s and 1960s and 1970s was different from the world of the 2000s and 2010s.

In those early postwar days, secret deals were more prevalent, and there were financial flows between French Africa and France that eluded the scrutiny. There are stories of agreements containing secret clauses, giving France a monopoly on the rights to exploit natural resources, especially oil, timber, and uranium, in the CFA countries. Popular knowledge or accountability was less common. The lack of social media did not allow visibility on many fronts. The strong currency benefited the urban elite who benefited from cheaper imports and penalized the tradable sectors, who had less political and lobbying power. The trading relationships were based on history and connections. CFA countries were able to export raw materials to France at prices secretly negotiated and import European machinery and capital goods. Many of the CFA countries had large endowments of oil, uranium, phosphate, cocoa, coffee, rubber, and cotton, all useful for European economies.

Many French and overseas companies benefited from the stability of the system and from a privileged access to rents and markets. Companies such as Orange (telecom), Bollore (transport), Thales (Arms), and Total (petroleum) had captive and successful markets in Sub-Saharan markets. Some powerful French firms have lobbied together with importer associations to keep the exchange rate as it, while African exporters have not had the clout or power to lobby. Importers in Francophone Africa frequently operated as powerful cartels, and it was hard to challenge their position. There are also Lebanese and Indian diaspora entrepreneurs who provide needed services but sometimes collude on pricing to make it hard for new African firms to enter the market. There has historically been the lack of an effective competition policy. ECOWAS, which comprises both Francophone and Anglophone countries, adopted a Regional Competition Rules in 2008 and a regulatory body, but it has taken more than a decade to launch the agenda to protect consumers in the region from market-distorting pricing.

This system started to slowly evolve by the late 1990s, in the face of French integration into the EU, more public awareness, fiscal considerations, and economic and security challenges in Africa. However, there had been a stability and inertia in the system, and none of the key players—France, the EU, the IMF, and the African governments—had a strong desire to challenge the status quo. The only major change was an adjustment of the parity in 1994, but it is only in 2019, that there was another significant change.

Many of the elements of the status quo—the French Treasury and some of the Ministries of Finance in Africa—had an interest in maintaining a stable system compared to what they perceived to be chaos which may emerge in the aftermath. The French Treasury demonstrated a willingness and secrecy to manage large pools of West and Central African reserves. France remained Africa's largest trading partner and was responsible for from one-fourth to one-third of European Union exports to the African continent.

But the political economy ran a bit deeper. There were two sides to the equation and two parties to the agreement. It was not unilaterally imposed by France, and exit was an option, although one with consequences. There has been a convergence of interests. One of the more perceptive commentators on the CFA, Stasavage (2003) has viewed the CFA arrangement with a wider political economy lens and made the important point that French support for political and macroeconomic stability was matched by African support:

> For participating African governments, continued membership in the CFA zone has been inextricably linked to...fear of losing privileged aid and security arrangements has raised the cost of exits for a number of governments that would have otherwise sought to establish their own currencies...It is not difficult to show that countries in the CFA zone have enjoyed important benefits from their relationship with France in areas other than monetary cooperation....

References

Stasavage, David. 2003. When Do States Abandon Monetary Discretion, Lessons from the Evolution of the CFA Franc Zone. In *Monetary Orders: Ambiguous Economics, Ubiquitous Politics*, ed. David Kirshner. Ithaca, NY: Cornell University Press.

Konnert, Dirk. 1998. The Euro, a Blessing for Africa? Consequences of the Peg of the African Franc CFA to the Euro, Munich. MPRA_paper_5777.pdf.

CHAPTER 15

The Triumph of Politics Over Economics

The CFA is an exhibit A of the triumph of politics over economics. Political factors continued to weigh despite the growing international economic evidence of the risk and consequences of overvalued currencies. The defenders of the system exaggerated the benefits, while the critics of the system could not propose concrete workable alternatives. The CFA survived because of the legacy effect and the belief that the zone needed a strong nominal anchor.

First, political and bureaucratic careers were not made challenging the CFA but in supporting it. The defenders of the system were focused on the stability dimension and not enough on the development angle. Until Macron and Ouattara began the reform, it was never in anyone's interest to "rock the boat." Ignoring the East and South Asian experiences with competitive exchange rates, many experts did not imagine a modernization of the exchange rate arrangements. There has been a deficiency of courage on the CFA and not enough attention to find a solution that was compatible with African development goals.

Even the IMF, which is technically sophisticated, has chosen to focus on short-term macro-stabilization compared to longer-term growth. By ignoring its own advice to other countries on the importance of market-based exchange rates, the IMF has not proposed CFA exchange rate reform in its macroeconomic reports. By the mid-2010s, the IMF was on the front lines defending difficult programs in the CEMAC region that

A. Zafar, *The CFA Franc Zone*,
https://doi.org/10.1007/978-3-030-71006-4_15

did not fully address debt sustainability challenges. Anecdotal evidence suggests that there was growing resistance to some of the Fund bailout programs for CEMAC countries, even at the level of the IMF Board. The Republic of Congo program took many years to be approved by the IMF Board because it was difficult to have a consensus around the macroeconomic framework.

The World Bank, which is the global development agency, took a more prominent position on the CFA exchange rate in the 1990s, increasingly took a back seat to the IMF on macroeconomic considerations in the 2000s and 2010s, and no longer played a visible role in the global debate. Over the years, it shifted focus to digital finance, gender and social protection, and climate economics. However, it should try to get a seat at the table on the macro dialogue given the impact of the exchange rate on development and poverty outcomes.[1]

Second, there has been an asymmetry of power between the defenders of the system and the critics. Some heads of state, including in Mali, who challenged the system, faced political risks and even personal death. Even among prominent and educated Africans, there was a fear of discussing a topic, which was so important to the development path of their countries.[2] For years, France and the African elite controlled the parity and had strong influence on the discourse around the CFA, and it was hard to get alternative perspectives.

Third, a problem in the CFA world has been the division between "insiders" and "outsiders." Those who learn about the mechanics and details of the CFA become captured by the organizations or bureaucracies and tend to support the status quo. Outsiders are not frequently aware of the exact details to make a compelling case. Those challenging the CFA

[1] The World Bank and IMF agreed to a Concordat in 1989 which stipulated that IMF would focus on the sustainable macroeconomic framework and the World Bank would focus on sharing developmental policy. The core focus of IMF would be on macroeconomic policies including fiscal policy and revenue mobilization, wage policy, monetary policy, and exchange rates. The Concordat says that in case of differences of opinion, the institution without the primary responsibility for the issue at hand is expected to "yield to the judgment of the other institution."

[2] The story of Kako Nubukpo is interesting. Currently, Dean of the Faculty of Economics at the University of Lomé, Togo, he has divergent views on the CFA. He has moved from former Togolese Minister of Prospective and Evaluation of Public Policy of Togo to the Director of the International Organization of the "Francophonie," to being an academic to returning as advisor to UEMOA Commission on the move to the eco.

have been far from the decision-making. In a story that can be relevant to the CFA discussion, during a celebrated discussion on the euro, US Treasury Secretary Larry Summers spoke to Yannis Varoufakis, the ex-Greek Finance Minister and academic who had voiced some skepticism of the Euro arrangement and was intent on reforming the system:

> 'There are two kinds of politicians,' he said: 'insiders and outsiders. The outsiders prioritize their freedom to speak their version of the truth. The price of their freedom is that they are ignored by the insiders, who make the important decisions. The insiders, for their part, follow a sacrosanct rule: never turn against other insiders and never talk to outsiders about what insiders say or do. Their reward? Access to inside information and a chance, though no guarantee, of influencing powerful people and outcomes."[3]

Fourth, there is also an intellectual gap in the debate on the CFA that has to do with the academy's specialization. Microeconomists are trained to count the poor and to analyze household survey data, while macroeconomics analyze more explicit macro variables such as trade shocks and balance of payments disequilibria. Microeconomists tend to look at individual consumers and firms and study economic welfare, consumption patterns, and poverty dynamics, while macroeconomists are more concerned with national income, aggregate output, and the price level. There have been some attempts by the intellectual research community to remedy these shortcomings. There are general equilibrium models, which suffer from data gaps, and randomized control trials (RCT's), which are interesting but often not generalizable. On top of that, models were not designed to deal with low-income countries or were not conceptualized to address data limitations in these poorer economies, many of which had poverty and household surveys every five years. Agenor (2005) argues that much research on poverty has been distorted by an excessive focus on micro and measurement issues, and it has focused insufficiently on transmission channels of macro shocks to the poor.

Some of the more promising work has revolved around models such as the Integrated Macroeconomic Model for Poverty Analysis (IMMPA), which is a dynamic quantitative macroeconomic framework for analyzing the impact of policy and exogenous shocks on income distribution and

[3] https://www.armstrongeconomics.com/uncategorized/insider-v-outsider/.

poverty, mainly in low-income countries. One example of an area where economics trumped politics was the analytical work in the 1990s and 2000s that helped guide some of the thinking behind the 1994 CFA devaluation. There was a new class of simplified computable general equilibrium models (CGE) models that were prepared to find ways to guide policymakers with accompanying strong empirics.[4] This kind of analytical work was very useful in the context of the 1994 devaluation and allowed policymakers to understand the ways commodity shocks were hurting individual welfare.

Reference

Agenor, Pierre-Richard. 2005. The Macroeconomics of Poverty Reduction. *Manchester School* 73 (4): 369–434.

[4] As opposed to existing macroeconomic models of the 1960s and 1990s, including the IMF Financial Programming model, the 1–2–3 model developed by Shanta Devarajan, Robinson, and Jeffrey Lewis at the World Bank does not treat economic growth and relative prices as exogenous. Instead, it seeks to link the CGE model with household survey data to measure the effects of macro policy changes on household poverty. The models are simple in that they are not very data-intensive (especially important given the African context), but they use existing data to try to understand the effect of macro shocks on individuals.

CHAPTER 16

How Britain Was Different: The Story of the Sterling Zone

The contrast between the CFA franc zone and Britain's sterling zone is interesting. The pound is the world's oldest currency and has a medieval vintage. Britain, the world's top imperial power in 1900, had a very strong pound, which was fixed to gold. However, as time went on and Britain's economy became eclipsed by the United States, the pound's role declined.

After World War II, although Britain emerged as a victor, the war had left its economy decimated. However, sterling was made up of 80% of global foreign exchange reserves, and half the world's trade was denominated in sterling, although there had been a growing competition from the dollar in the interwar years. Britain, like France, wanted to maintain a link with the former colonies. At Atlee started to quickly dismantle the British Empire by the late 1940s, beginning with India, and 1950s, there was a general British retreat from the ex-colonies. Winston Churchill and others had wanted to keep the empire longer, but under Clement Atlee, the British Labor Party realized the economic and political costs of keeping the empire were very large. As a result, in a span of few years, Britain shifted its position and left many of its colonies in the wake of postwar sociopolitical global changes.

In order to keep links with the former colonies, by the London Declaration of 1949, the British created a Commonwealth of Nations which provided an institutional and cooperation framework with the various member states, most of which were British colonies or former

A. Zafar, *The CFA Franc Zone*,
https://doi.org/10.1007/978-3-030-71006-4_16

British colonies. A new sterling area was created, including many of the Commonwealth countries and former British colonies in the Middle East (including Egypt, Jordan, and Kuwait). This zone consolidated many of the existing currency arrangements. Many of the former colonies stayed in the sterling area and continued to peg their currencies to the pound under a broader Bretton Woods framework of fixed exchange rates to the US dollar. Under the Bretton Woods agreement, the dollar was pegged to gold, since the United States held most of the world's gold reserves, and other European countries had a fixed exchange rate to the dollar. But more important than that was the issue of war debts. Historian Catherine Schenk has argued that:

> Britain's war debts defined the early years of the sterling area. These debts were popularly known as the "sterling balances" and were owed primarily to colonies in South Asia, which were due for independence, including India, Pakistan, and Ceylon… At the end of the war, these debts amounted to four times British foreign exchange reserves so they could not immediately be redeemed in dollars or other currency. Instead, the creditors were forced to continue to hold their assets in sterling or to spend them on imports from the UK or other sterling area countries who would accept sterling. Britain engaged in a long and complex set of negotiations with its primary creditors (especially India) in the late 1940s and early 1950s.[1]

Like the French, the British were motivated by a combination of political and economic interests, though the British interest in keeping the culture was less prominent. From the British perspective, the former colonies could peg their currencies against the pound in order to have free trade with Britain and freer access to the British capital. Similar to the French Treasury arrangements in the CFA franc, the Bank of England in London guided coordination of monetary policy in the currency area, while countries had reserves as sterling balances in London, and the countries were able to access the capital markets in London.

However, there were a few key differences with the CFA arrangement. First, the sterling area was never a formal monetary union with precise rules and regulations but was rather an area where exchange rates were linked. There were certain regulations and exchange controls on

[1] https://link.springer.com/referenceworkentry/10.1007/978-981-10-0622-7_29-1.

capital transactions within the zone that persisted for some time. Countries could change their parities to the British pound without a decision from London, although there were clearly conversations between UK Treasury officials and central bank officials from the respective countries. Even when the pound devalued, countries like Pakistan, Australia, and Hong Kong, did not adjust their parities symmetrically.

Second, the British did not replicate the structure of the regional central banks, the BCEAO and the BEAC, in the Commonwealth countries. Third, countries had distinct national currencies, including in the Indian subcontinent, rather than one uniform currency. Fourth, the British never offered the convertibility guarantee that the French gave and never wanted to ask as the guarantor for external liquidity to support balance of payments problems. Even in cases of the East African schilling, when British support was needed in the 1970s and 1980s, the British were not interested in guaranteeing convertibility. Finally, there was never the express desire of the former British colonies, including India, to maintain a very tight relationship, as was the case with the Francophone political elite.

The case of the Indian rupee is interesting. During the independence in 1947, the rupee was pegged to the pound sterling. It continued to be the currency in parts of East Africa and the Persian Gulf. However, by 1975, it delinked from the pound sterling and moved to a basket peg. It is interesting that by 1971, many of the sterling countries had ended their pegs to the pound. Among West African countries, Nigeria ended its sterling parity in 1962 and Ghana ended it in 1965. After the Indian reforms of 1991, India moved to a managed float system to handle its economic reality, and many of the ex-British colonies moved toward managed float regimes in the 1980s and 1990s.

The sterling zone did not survive more than thirty years. With the decline of the Bretton Woods system in 1971, the system began to unravel, and the pound was floated in 1972. As Britain declined in global significance, the pound lost its glamor and stature as a reserve currency, and there was less interest among all the members in monetary cooperation. With less than 5% of the world's reserves currently denominated in pounds, the pound's decline was matched by the dollar's ascent. The combination of the difficult negotiations of Britain to enter the European Economic Community in the early 1970s, the changing trade relationships as many commonwealth countries were trading with Asia, and the general unraveling of the post-Bretton woods system led to the end of the sterling zone. According to the IMF, the only areas in the world that fix their currency to the British pound are the Falkland Islands, Gibraltar, Guernsey, Isle of Man, Jersey, and St. Helena, none of which is formally independent.

CHAPTER 17

Myopic Macroeconomic Considerations and Inflation Focus

A key argument of the proponents of the CFA zone is that the zones promote macroeconomic stability, low inflation, and import policy credibility. There is some truth to this view in the early decades of the CFA but one which has diminished relevance in today's world. First, the severity of the current COVID crisis is testing the resilience of highly indebted countries. A robust policy response is needed, including flexible currencies which can soften the blow on the domestic economy in the short-run and discourage the buildup of substantial balance sheet mismatches and ward of large exchange rate misalignments in the longer term (Kose et al. 2020). Second, inflation is less a problem than in the past. Among emerging market and developing economies, inflation fell from 17.3 percent in 1974 to 3.5 percent in 2017 (Ha et al. 2019). Third, the CFA zone has its particular institutional peculiarities that make it non-adaptable to the pandemic shock. Devarajan (1992) has argued that the very rules that have kept inflation low in CFA countries have served to exacerbate the effects of these external shocks on their domestic economies.

From this perspective, the years of low inflation were perceived as a big advantage of the zone compared to the neighbors, who frequently had to deal with double-digit inflation. In the early years, the CFA zone was not facing strong shocks, or the types of economic mismanagement seen in

A. Zafar, *The CFA Franc Zone*,
https://doi.org/10.1007/978-3-030-71006-4_17

some of the other countries on the continent. Many countries, particularly Anglophone ones, suffered currency crises and large black-market premiums, as well as excessive fiscal capture of the central bank and monetization of deficits. The CFA was a safe universe as it put the brake on poor macroeconomic management and runaway inflation. A currency that floats excessively, that does not have a clear policy objective, that leads to a big black-market premium, and where there is not institutional oversight illustrates the challenges of a freely floating or mismanaged exchange rate.

However, this view ignores a growing body of academic and historical evidence, especially from Asia.

First, the excessive focus on inflation and insistence on low inflation thresholds of 2 or 3% ignores the policy tradeoffs. There has been a willingness to sacrifice growth to keep inflation so low. Tapsoba and Bicaba (2014) find the growth costs of UEMOA membership to outweigh by far the price stability benefit. Second, there has been a growing sophistication of macroeconomic management in Africa, especially in terms of policies and capacities (Kasekende 2011). Many developing countries are independently managing their exchange rates. Third, there exist alternatives to the CFA, and there are multiple transition regimes and currency arrangements that can help support growth. Finally, the perception that the CFA zone lacks the institutional capacity to manage a floating exchange rate rests on outdated ideas and ignores the technocratic competence in BCEAO and growing knowledge in BEAC.

Moreover, over the years, there have been increasing criticisms of the fixed currency unions for failing to deliver on growth and stability. In a discussion that can be linked to the CFA, Nobel Prize winner Joseph Stiglitz (2016) has recently expressed concern about the euro zone (which the CFA has tried to model):

> But for a single currency to work over a region with enormous economic and political diversity is not easy. A single currency entails a fixed exchange rate among the countries, and a single interest rate… there needs to be an array of institutions that can help those nations for which the policies are not well suited. Europe failed to create these institutions….worse still, the structure of the eurozone built in certain ideas about what was required for economic success – for instance, that the central bank should focus on inflation, as opposed to the mandate of the Federal Reserve in the US, which incorporates unemployment, growth and stability. It was not simply that the eurozone was not structured to accommodate Europe's economic

> diversity; it was that the structure of the eurozone, its rules and regulations, were not designed to promote growth, employment and stability.[1]

Of course, the exchange rate is not the only reason for the CFA zone falling behind, but it is the most important one. Structural issues, such as transport costs, lack of financial intermediation, security issues, and regulatory environment, are also quite important. Some of the problems faced by CFA countries are similar to those faced by Kenyans and Nigerians and Zambians, but some are truly unique to the zone. Structural policies also matter but they tend to be linked to macro management. From the macroeconomic research, the exchange rate is the most important relative price and it tends to dwarf other factors.

Nevertheless, there are some academic defenses of the existing system. Two of the more prominent academic advocates, Guillaumont and Guillaumont (2017) find a more adaptable system than is frequently perceived. They have argued that while the basic principles of the exchange rate system have been maintained, the Franc Zone has shown its capacity to adapt to new situations: African governance of central banks, establishment of Economic Unions, control of capital transactions, replacement of the French franc by the euro, independence of the central banks. In their view, the Franc Zone can appear as a genuine and effective cooperation regime.

References

Devarajan, Shanta. (1992). Preserving the Union: Lessons of History, Theory and Thirty Years of Experience, speech delivered at 30th Anniversary of UEMOA in Dakar, Senegal.

Guilllaumont, P., and S. Guillaumont Jeanneney. (2017). La Zone franc en perspective, Revue. Fin du franc CFA en Afrique de l'Ouest, quel avenir pour l'éco? FERDI.

Ha, Jongrim, M. Ayhan Kose, and Franziska L. Ohnsorge. (2019). Understanding Inflation in Emerging and Developing Economies, World Bank Policy Research Series 8761, Washington, DC.

Kasekende, Louis. (2011, January 26). The Evolving Nature of Macroeconomic Management in Sub-Saharan Africa and Its Implications for IMF Programs

[1] https://www.theguardian.com/business/2016/aug/10/joseph-stiglitz-the-problem-with-europe-is-the-euro.

Speech by Dr Louis Kasekende, Deputy Governor of the Bank of Uganda, Kampala.

Kose, M. Ayhan, Franziska Ohnsorge, Peter Nagle, and Naotaka Sugawara. (2020, June). *Caught by a Cresting Debt Wave, Finance and Development* 57 (2). Washington, DC.

Stiglitz, Joseph. (2016). The Problem with Europe is the Euro. Interview with the Guardian. https://www.theguardian.com/business/2016/aug/10/joseph-stiglitz-the-problem-with-europe-is-the-euro.

Tabsoba, Rene, and Zorobabel Bicaba. (2014). Low Inflation Luxury. Economic Lindau Nobel Laureate Meetings.

CHAPTER 18

Exits from the CFA-Style Arrangements: Experience of Mauritania, Morocco, and Vietnam

There has been a perception that there are no good alternatives to the CFA. However, most countries who left the CFA zone or similar arrangements have performed better. The defenders of the CFA have rightly pointed to some of the countries in Sub-Saharan Africa that have not managed exchange rate well, such as Nigeria in the 1980s and 1990s, or Guinea.[1] However, these are exceptions, rather than the norm.

Mauritania exited the CFA in 1973 and replaced the CFA with the ouguiya. At the time of its exit, the prediction was that Mauritania would be forced to reenter the CFA. The country pursued a relatively tight managed float regime, which allowed it to have stable growth while keeping inflation low. The country has depreciated its currency since the exit multiple times over the years in order to keep a competitive currency and has sought to move to a market-determined exchange rate. The most interesting thing about Mauritania is due to these reforms, coupled with a booming iron ore sector and remittances inflows, the country has had strong poverty reduction. From 2000 to 2015, the poverty rate (national poverty line) fell from more than 50% to close to 30%. In 2019, Mauritania had a higher GNI per capita than Senegal.

[1] The Guinea example is interesting. When Guinea under Sekou Toure exited the CFA in 1960, French secret services inundated its economy with counterfeit banknotes and also damaged electrical wires. Since those days much has changed, and the country has had an inconsistent performance.

A. Zafar, *The CFA Franc Zone*,
https://doi.org/10.1007/978-3-030-71006-4_18

Then you have the Morocco story. It was once a French colony but became independent in 1956, but still maintains very strong trade and investment relations with France. The country is uniquely situated as a bridge between Sub-Saharan Africa and Europe. For many years, the country had a fixed exchange rate pegged to the euro (80%) and dollar (20%), under which the dirham could only be traded within a narrow range above and below the established exchange rate. In January 2018, the Moroccan central bank (Bank Al-Maghrib) started a process to gradually transition to a new regime and liberalize the exchange rate to improve the currency's flexibility to external shocks. After the first phase of reforms, Morocco kept the dirham pegged to the euro (60%) and the US dollar (40%). A subsequent phase has allowed the dirham to fluctuate over a wider 2.5% range in either direction compared to 0.3% in either direction previously. The idea is to give more support to the tradable sectors while maintaining price stability.

Then you have the curious case of Vietnam, a former French colony. Vietnam shared a colonial history with France but left the currency arrangement in the postwar years. French Indochina had the silver standard until 1930, followed by a peg of the Indonchinese piastre which was pegged to the franc. In 1946, the North Vietnamese introduced the dong, which became pegged to the Soviet ruble in 1961. By 1978, the dong became the currency of a united Vietnam. For years after that, like China and other Asian economies, Vietnam maintained a de facto peg to the US dollar. The move was also part of an effort to create a strong link to the US economy, which was emerging as a growing trading partner. After 2015, the State Bank of Vietnam (SBV) has adopted a more managed float system to prevent sharp depreciation against the dollar and allowing the dong to trade within a 3% band. As the macroeconomy remains strong, there is no longer fear of devaluations or policy reversals. The exchange rate regime has helped support the growth process.

CHAPTER 19

Colonialism, Racism, and Black Lives

There has always been a residual racism in the discourse on the CFA, dating back to the postwar years. There has been the perception that African policymakers are incapable of managing their own monetary affairs. It was said that BEAC and BCEAO managers did not have the sophistication to have an independent monetary policy. For many, Africa has been perceived as a violent and fragile continent, and not amenable to economic logic. The general perception that African problems require outsider solutions ignores the many successful African responses to African problems. There was an unwritten perception that Black Africans in the CFA zone were not capable of operating an exchange rate. The rise of African public intellectuals, the mobilization of African civil society, and the development of local activism has shown a marked ascent in the last two decades as the CFA zone failed to deliver on some of the promises, including growth, jobs, and foreign investment.

However, given the proliferation of capable African technocrats over the years, the long years of economic management, and the many successful experiences of exchange rate management in Africa, the persistence of the idea is troubling. Why did an inertia of perception stay despite the changes in ground realities? Why wasn't there enough courage to bring into the debate the global experience? Were the stability benefits so important that there was never an assessment of the risks? Why were economists and intellectuals, who are supposed to be the providers of

A. Zafar, *The CFA Franc Zone*,
https://doi.org/10.1007/978-3-030-71006-4_19

public goods, so reluctant to speak truth to power on the CFA? There are many unexplored questions that must be asked of the zone. The relative silence of parts of the African diaspora on the CFA has been interesting, in contrast to many other ethnic diasporas, who have spawned a vigorous debate on their respective regions.

The prevailing mindset was that external technocrats would be better at depoliticizing exchange rate management than African bureaucrats. While this perspective was ironically adapted by some of the African elite themselves, the growing experience of East Asian macroeconomic management has shown that technics trumped nationality when it came to exchange rate management. In East Asia, a competitive exchange rate had been central to the Japanese, Chinese, and Korean industrialization strategies.

There has never a strong attempt to bring in Asian voices, from countries like Vietnam, China, and Bangladesh, which had successful experience in exchange rate management and succeeded in unleashing the forces of light manufacturing. The African voices were not heard enough, and the few voices that were heard tended to replicate the European and French perspective. There was never a sustained reaching out to African think tanks and research outfits. Dissent grew in the margins but never in the mainstream.

Until recently, there was not a lot of consultation with domestic entrepreneurs, farmer associations, or civil society. A "bubble" mindset prevented many from understanding the complexities of the zone. Many of the countries were perceived as unsafe, and a few genuinely were at certain times in their history. But the gap between perception and reality was even more than for other parts of Sub-Saharan Africa. Conversations with entrepreneurs, journalists, and civil society were frequently not done. Africa was seen through foreign filters, without understanding the local context. This was not unique to the CFA zone, but to much of Sub-Saharan Africa. In the CFA zone, questions about the legitimacy of the system were considered heretical.

CHAPTER 20

The Winds of Change

However, over time these taboos have been changed. By the late 2010s, in terms of CFA, there was a constellation of factors that were leading to change.

First, there was a significant change in France. For many years, France was a central pillar of the CFA regime and the financial and intellectual anchor. Inheriting a policy from De Gaulle, successive French governments worked to preserve the parity and the relationships with the African political elite in the Francophone countries. The emphasis was on stability of exchange rate and a safe environment for investments. However, over the years, the French position has evolved and transformed. In a world of greater transparency and information flows, the opaque political economy of oil and resource management became harder to sustain. French frustration with poor governance, especially in CEMAC, played a role. French leaders signaled a shift a mindset, especially Francois Hollande, who affirmed that the French are open to all concrete proposals that come from African leaders.

Some French leaders were more interested in developing a global vision and felt that the CFA zone arrangements were a relic of the past. Several members of the French elite became aware of the past mistakes, and they wanted to move forward on a new path. The famous ELF Scandal in 1994, where there was a network of government employees laundering African oil money through the country's public oil company,

A. Zafar, *The CFA Franc Zone*,
https://doi.org/10.1007/978-3-030-71006-4_20

Elf Aquitaine, became fodder for journalists. However, that criticism took a few decades to evolve into a policy shift.

The ascent of Emmanuel Macron also represented a generational shift in French politics. Macron was the first French president born after the African independence, not beholden to the historical relationship and sensitive to a growing chorus of African protests, began in earnest to reform the system in line with his vision of a stronger and more equal French–African dialogue. Not inheriting any emotional or ideological baggage, Macron pledged to continue the reform momentum of his predecessor Francois Hollande who had wanted a new phase of Franco-African relations. Together with Alassane Ouattara, president of the Ivory Coast, a technocratic leader who was intent on modernizing the political and financial systems, they set out to reform the system. Macron lamented the history of colonialism and pointed out the faults of the republic. Stressing the need to rebuild bridges with a new generation of African youth, he wanted to turn a page on the past. He was less beholden to the views of the French Treasury than his predecessors, and he was more interested in forging a pragmatic move forward. Listening to a growing body of intellectuals as well as experts at the French Development Agency (AFD) concerned with African development, Macron has forged a path forward.

Beginning in the 1980s, there was a growing criticism in France regarding parts of the relationship between Africa and France. A new generation of French elites and youth became aware of the past mistakes, and they wanted to move forward on a new path.

Parallel to the change in France, there has been a change in African leadership and a growing vision for a ECOWAS common currency. Many African economies have emerged in the last two decades. A new generation of African leaders has demanded more sovereignty in the management of their economies. Supported by high oil prices and an ambitious reform agenda, the rise of Nigeria under President Buhari in recent years has been noteworthy. Fuelled by rising oil prices and political reform, Nigeria is the largest economy in West Africa and represents more than 70% of total ECOWAS GDP, and it dwarves the UEMOA Francophone countries. There has been a strong push under ECOWAS to have a single currency (eco) and foster greater intraregional trade in

West Africa and support the development of a market of more than 400 million consumers.

The global institutional architecture on African issues is changing, and there is the strong emergence of African voices. The African Development Bank has emerged as one of the centers of excellence and has articulated an African perspective on African development. It has focused on five key pillars: light up and power Africa; feed Africa; industrialize Africa; integrate Africa; and improve the quality of life for the people of Africa. There is the ascent of African billionaire entrepreneurs like Aliko Dangote, who is using his platform as Africa's richest man to spur the continent to become more self-sufficient in rice, in fertilizer, and in cement.

In 2015, Chadian President Idriss Deby stressed the importance of severing the CFA cord that in his judgment, was preventing development in Africa. Recently, Benin President Patrice Talon has said that it is not good that the current model continues in terms of sovereignty and managing one's own money. In Niger, President Issoufou has asked for an independent common ECOWAS currency.

However, it is important to note that there have been different points of view from some of the CFA leadership. There has also been support for the CFA among some African leaders, including Macky Sall of Senegal, who perceives CFA and the peg to the euro as a source of economic stability. Some of the CEMAC leaders in Cameroon and the Republic of Congo have expressed support for the system and the stability it provides.

There was a growing chorus of criticism, who found challenges with fixed exchange rates in a changing world. There were several strands of criticism, both popular and academic. Some of the criticism was well-conceived, while some of the critiques were not fully aware of the macroeconomics and institutional arrangements of the CFA zone. Anti-CFA demonstrations have been organized in several African and European cities to protect what they perceive to be a colonial currency. There has been criticism on the grounds of national sovereignty. Since the Operations Account with the pooled African reserves was in Paris, and France holds a de facto veto on the boards of the two central banks, the perception was that the countries did not exert full monetary sovereignty. Second, as will be seen later, there was criticism in terms of growth and development outcomes. According to the analysis, the CFA system hinders the industrialization and structural transformation of these economies.

In a seminal paper, Devarajan and Rodrik (1991), using a simple formal framework to clarify the trade-offs involved in the choice between a fixed and flexible exchange rate system, find that fixed exchange rates have been, on the whole, a bad bargain for the CFA member countries, and that under reasonable output-inflation trade-offs, the output costs of maintaining a fixed exchange rate have outweighed the benefits of lower inflation for the CFA zone. From the IMF perspective, Duttagupta et al. (2006) find that as economies mature and become more closely tied with international financial markets, the benefits of exchange rate flexibility appear to increase. They note increases in flexible regimes in countries including Brazil, Chile, Israel, and Poland.

On top of this, shifts in the global economic environment have led to changes in the CFA economies. The COVID pandemic has led to capital flight among other things and a decline in resources among emerging markets. Unable to diversify into manufacturing despite the resource windfalls from the commodity boom, the countries of the CFA zone will need to find new opportunities and new engines of growth. In recent years, as globalization has expanded and shocks have multiplied, the CFA zone has managed to survive in its original form. However, the validity of the zone is increasingly being questioned because the zone is facing greater shocks among economies that are only superficially linked.

With reference to the CEMAC zone, Agbor (2012) poses the problem in stark terms:

> A total of 80 currency boards have come into existence at some point since the mid-19th century, but to date only about 15 of them still exist, among which is the CFA franc monetary zone. The future sustainability of the CFA franc zone, to which the CEMAC CFA franc belongs, is increasingly questioned in the light of increasing asymmetries in exposure to external shocks, differential speeds of adjustment of the real exchange rate following shocks, differential impacts in economic fundamentals, and low intraregional trade and financial flows between the CEMAC and the WAEMU.[1]

The interesting test case on the CFA and CEMAC has come with the case of the Republic of Congo. Due to the collapse in oil prices, Congo has had escalating debt levels that reached close to 120% by 2017. Discussions

[1] https://www.brookings.edu/research/the-future-of-the-cemac-cfa-franc/.

with the IMF dragged on for several years. After the Greece controversy, the IMF has asked that Congo ensure the long-term sustainability of its debt as a precondition for a three-year extended credit facility program. The challenge for Congo was that some portion of its debt was bilateral debt to China. At more than $2.5 billion, it was not an insignificant sum. US Treasury had developed a principle whereby World Bank and IMF resources were not to be used to provide debt payments to China. IMF staff found the exchange rate to be overvalued by 15–20%, which would require a currency correction in normal circumstances.

However, given that Congo was part of CEMAC and for some, it is one of the weaker links, especially due to its dependence on oil and on oil-backed loan agreements. The decision was made to not just adjust the currency but to negotiate a complex restructuring arrangement. By the agreement, China will not give a haircut to Congo and reduce the amount of principal owed. It represents a new set of countries, some of which are natural resource economies, that have to address unsustainable debt due to commercial borrowing (much of which is borrowed at high interest) as well and non-Paris Club (China) borrowing. Due to COVID, the situation has worsened to some extent, and the Republic of Congo is now at a high debt overhang with a debt/GDP ratio of more than 100 percent.

In light of all these multiple challenges, there has been growing criticism in Africa by academics, policymakers, and civil society on the importance of gaining sovereignty and exerting control on monetary policy. This growing chorus sees the CFA franc as a colonial currency. Former Togolese Minister Kako Nubukpo and academic Ndongo Samba Sylla find that the CFA franc is a colonial relic and impeding African management of the economy and preventing economic development. In his critique of the CFA, Sylla argues:

> The CFA franc is a good currency for those who benefit from it: the major French and overseas corporations, the executives of the zone's central banks, the elites wishing to repatriate wealth acquired legally or otherwise.[2]

[2] https://www.insideover.com/economy/monetary-independence-looms-for-west-and-central-africa.html.

The Cameroonian economist Joseph Tchundjang Pouemi has spoken of CFA Africa's monetary servitude.[3] A new generation of African youth has emerged, who felt that the system was directly responsible for their low employment prospects. Given that close to 50% of Africans are born after the 1994 devaluation, the social landscape has changed. The most noteworthy is Kemi Saba, a civil society activist, who burned a CFA franc in protest in Dakar, and asked for the colonial currency to be changed and for outsiders to stop profiting from the continent. He was detained after a complaint by the Central Bank of West African States (BCEAO) and charged of "destroying a banknote" but was eventually released. This acquired a lot of media attention. In January 2019, Italian economy minister Luigi di Maio accused France of manipulating the economies of African countries that use the CFA franc and preventing their economic development. He also linked this issue to migration of refugees and provoked a rebuke from the French government. The discussions have become polemical and political.

The more conventional view of the CFA has come from the IMF as seen by Gulde and Tsangaridies (2008):

> Academics and policymakers generally see the experience with the operation of the CFA franc system as positive, noting the benefits of the arrangement for macroeconomic stability, in particular low and stable inflation, and the way it has stimulated institutional development. Still, there is continuing debate about the potential costs of rigidities associated with a fixed exchange rate system, given that most member countries are susceptible to major shocks, such as the current fall in cotton prices.

However, over time the debate has opened. In 2018, in an interview with the Africa Report, Dominique Strass Khan, the former head of IMF, put the matter very candidly:

> It is difficult to claim to be interested in the development of Africa – particularly French-speaking Africa – without asking oneself the question of its monetary system, especially when it is the subject of criticism, sometimes justified and sometimes a little less so. It seemed to me that the time had come to try to calm and broaden the debate. This concerns the link between the CFA franc and the euro. The subject should therefore concern

[3] https://www.thekraal.co/history/poemi-and-franc-cfa.

> all Europeans, and not just the French. One way or another, we had to get involved and take a stand.... Some consider that the CFA franc has harmed African countries and that it must disappear. I think they're exaggerating. Others believe, on the contrary, that it has played a formidable role. I think they are also exaggerating. The reality is that it has had advantages and disadvantages, but the important thing now is to ask what is best for the future. And that is above all for Africans to decide.[4]

Jean Michel Severino the former head of the French Development Agency AFD has this to say:

> The CFA franc has been strong over the past decade and one can imagine that countries with floating currencies have adjusted better than those using the common currency. Whilst it is not favorable to exports, it is not the strength of the CFA that is under the spotlight, but rather the disconnect of the development of a monetary system outside its African conjuncture. It will require African leaders to reflect on what mechanisms to put in place rather than completely halting the regional monetary union or cutting links between the euro and the CFA franc.[5]

Carlos Lopes, the Assistant-Secretary-General of the United Nations who is also the Executive Secretary of the United Nations Economic Commission for Africa, has said that the currencies used by 14 African states need to be adapted and reviewed to the international standards and that no country in the world should have a currency that hasn't been revised in more than 50 years:

> The optics are so bad I don't think it is sustainable for France to continue this arrangement. There's such a strong demand from African youth to take back their monetary independence...the political costs may be outweighing the economic gains.[6]

[4] https://www.theafricareport.com/14317/dominique-strauss-kahn-and-the-cfa-franc-the-current-system-has-to-be-seriously-cleaned-up/.

[5] https://www.theafricareport.com/7810/africa-why-francophones-are-lagging-behind-anglophones/.

[6] https://www.insideover.com/economy/monetary-independence-looms-for-west-and-central-africa.html.

According to Kako Nubukpo, one of the academics and former Togolese minister more critical of the CFA:

> The CFA Franc is a problematic currency: colonial and post-colonial heritage, its compatibility with the process of emergence of the 14 African economies that use it, is a real economic question…The social movements that it has been triggering for some years among African youths and diasporas are undoubtedly the question of the demand for emancipation of young people, caught between the massive unemployment of which they are the first victims and the lack of space for political and societal expression… It also undermines the export price competitiveness of the economies that use it…More serious, its perpetuation can also be seen as a voluntary servitude of African leaders found in the characteristics of this institutional arrangement..a convenient way of not being proactive in the monetary governance of their states, and a vehicle for accumulating wealth outside the African continent. The Franc Zone and the CFA Franc deserve serious dusting, given the demographic dynamics of Africa, which makes it more urgent than ever to create massive jobs on the continent.[7]

Finally, there is John Ashbourne, an iconoclastic financial analyst:

> The CFA zone is essentially a laughably ill-suited and dysfunctional and loveless marriage that's being held together for lack of a better option… it has spared the CFA franc-zone from the sort of violent, unpredictable inflation spikes seen in other countries.[8]

References

Agbor, Julius Agbor. 2012. The Future of the CEMAC CFA Franc. Global Views Policy Paper 2012–06 (December). Brookings Institution, Washington, DC.

Devarajan, Shantayanan, and Dani Rodrik. 1991. Do the Benefits of Fixed Exchange Rates Outweigh Their Costs? The Franc Zone in Africa. NBER Working Papers 3727. National Bureau of Economic Research, Inc.

[7] https://www.kapitalafrik.com/2019/02/05/the-franc-zone-and-the-cfa-franc-deserve-a-serious-dedusting/.

[8] https://www.africanglobe.net/business/west-africa-rebels-cfa-franc-currency-linked-colonial-france/.

Duttagupta, Rupa, Cem Karacadag, and Gilda C. Fernandez. 2006. Moving to a Flexible Exchange Rate: How, When, and How Fast? IMF Economic Issues 38. International Monetary Fund.

Gulde, Anne, and Charalambos Tsangarides. 2008. *The CFA Franc Zone: Common Currency, Uncommon Challenges*. International Monetary Fund.

PART IV

Why the Fixed Exchange Arrangement and Overvalued Currency Impede Development

CHAPTER 21

Competitiveness Challenges for the Private Sector

The world of the 2020s is the world of COVID, of open media, of trade integration, of volatile capital flows. The architects of the CFA lived in the world of the 1940s, which was very different from the world of the 2020s. For Macron and Ouattara, it was important to change the structure of the CFA to adopt to a changing world. Even the most prominent supporters of the current CFA system at the IMF recognize the importance of reform, although the discussion has never focused on the exchange rate mechanism itself. Gulde and Tsangarides (2008) note that in an environment of increasing financial globalization, volatile oil and raw materials prices, and some difficult regional security problems, the CFA franc is facing deeper challenges and will need some degree of structural reform.

The world has been facing increasing shocks and volatility, and Sub-Saharan Africa is much more integrated into the world economy than in the days of the 1940s. A shock in Wuhan has had a ripple effect on the world economy as trade and financial markets are more integrated, and supply chains are global in nature. From the financial crisis the covid shocks, commodity prices have been under siege. The roller-coaster ride of oil prices seems like it will continue into the future given the competing dynamics of Russian–Saudi rivalry, US shale surge, demand shocks due to COVID, and other parameters. The commodity boom that has fueled the CFA zone since the early 2000s, especially oil in the CEMAC and

A. Zafar, *The CFA Franc Zone*,
https://doi.org/10.1007/978-3-030-71006-4_21

agriculture and mining in the WAEMU, can no longer be the unique driver of growth given the pandemic and the global slowdown. Oil in CEMAC, cocoa in Cote d'Ivoire, and cotton in the Sahel have seen significant declines. For the first decade of the 2000s, growth in the CFA zone was part of a general rebound in Africa. The region's growth has been driven by rising mineral prices and discoveries, rising commodity prices, and fewer mistakes in economic management (Arbache and Page 2008). But those days are changing. However, in a world of Covid, there will be a need to modernize the macroeconomic framework to improve growth and competitiveness prospects.

The CFA arrangement should evolve to help support the emerging domestic private sector in the CFA countries. It should reflect a changing global environment of greater competition from lower wage emerging economies such as Bangladesh and Vietnam. Countries of the CFA zone will have to step up to compete in a broad range of sectors, increasing the importance of a competitive currency and a supportive industrial policy. As wages in China rise, there is increased risk of greater South–South competition for lucrative export markets in North America and Western Europe. The recent successes of Rwanda, Kenya, and Mauritius in targeting European export markets while maintaining a flexible currency can provide a good example for CFA economies. The CFA zone has a tremendous amount to learn from the East Asian experience. Monetary and fiscal frameworks were consistently updated to reflect changing macroeconomic realities. After the challenges of the Maoist era, Deng created special economic zones and opened the doors for private commerce. After the financial crisis, East Asian economies decided to accumulate reserves as self-insurance for a rainy day.

The evidence is increasingly clear that the output and competitiveness costs of maintaining a fixed exchange rate are challenging the benefits of lower inflation for the CFA zone. For BCEAO and BEAC, being tied to the euro means being tied to the objectives and goals of the European monetary authorities. The intellectual anchor of the euro remains the German Bundesbank, which has been haunted by the hyperinflation chaos of Weimar Germany, and has targeted a goal over the medium term of an inflation rate of 2%. While this may make sense in advanced economies, in the poorer economies of the CFA, employment and joblessness are major concerns. Moreover, there is no empirical consensus in the macroeconomics literature on the threshold beyond which inflation has pernicious effects on economic growth. Finally, the structural determinants of inflation in Europe are quite different from those in Sub-Saharan Africa.

The major issue with the CFA exchange rate is it impedes private sector competitiveness due to a tendency to be chronically overvalued given its link to the euro, which has tended to be a strong currency. The covid-related shocks have exacerbated the overvaluation of the CFA as the CFA has been hit with negative terms of trade shocks, but no currency adjustment. From a theoretical standpoint, an overvalued currency acts as a subsidy on imports and a tax on exports, leading to current account imbalances. The degree of overvaluation is not as high as it was pre-1994, but especially in CEMAC it has increased a lot due to the collapse in oil prices. Both the parity and the rigidity of the exchange rate merit reflection.

The importance of a competitive exchange rate is well-documented in the empirical literature. The IMF (2016) finds that prior to 2000, there was not much of a per capita growth differential among countries with various types of regimes. But since around 2000, countries with more flexible exchange rate arrangements in Sub-Saharan Africa have enjoyed 1–2 percentage points higher annual output per capita growth rates than pegs. Such a growth differential is not evident in other developing economies. McMillan and Rodrik (2011) find that countries experiencing growth-enhancing structural changes tend to maintain competitive or undervalued currencies. Freund and Pierola (2008) find strong links between undervalued currencies and export growth, and other scholars have pointed to political economy considerations. Finally, Rodrik (2008) shows how the undervaluation of the currency (a high real exchange rate) stimulates economic growth, especially for developing countries in that it affects the size of the tradable sector (especially industry). These results suggest that tradables suffer disproportionately from the government or market failures that keep poor countries from converging toward countries with higher incomes. In sum, an overvalued real exchange rate hinders structural transformation.

Both international and domestic experience show the advantages of adjustment to shocks to maintain competitiveness. When the CFA has in the past adjusted to trade shocks, the impact has been positive. The case of the 1994 CFA devaluation to adjust to an overvalued currency is well-known and documented. Cossé et al (1996) find that the CFA countries broadly achieved their program results in terms of economic growth, inflation, and improvement in the current account in the aftermath of the devaluation. Nominal wages were kept firmly under control, and inflation reduced sharply after initial price corrections. Competitiveness was strong in sectors where the share of labor in total costs was high, such as agriculture and light manufacturing. Gross domestic savings increased by more than 8 percentage points. The IMF (2017) finds that exchange rate adjustment in Latin America in the wake of commodity price declines led to a small boost to exports and a stronger reduction in imports than in the past, with demand shifting toward locally produced goods, alleviating the burden on domestic demand. Many Latin American countries stuck to their flexible exchange rate regimes and allowed their currencies to depreciate substantially. The currencies of Brazil, Chile, Colombia, and Mexico have lost about half their value against the US dollar.

One argument that has been used in the literature is the argument that elasticities in the CFA zone are low and that farmers and manufacturers do not respond to price incentives. However, after the 1994 devaluation, there was a significant increase in livestock exports from Sahelian countries that replaced European imports. In a seminal piece reviewing the empirical evidence after the 1994 CFA devaluation and applicable to the post-COVID era, Pritchett and Ghei (1999) reject the three pessimisms: (1) import demand pessimism—LDC import structure is such that most if not all inputs are required for output and that there is a low elasticity of substitution between imports and domestic production; (2) export supply pessimism—LDC exports are concentrated around a few products with low supply response and that changes in relative prices will not impact farmers; (3) export demand pessimism—world demand for products of LDC countries is inelastic in respect to income and prices. The research presents the empirical evidence:

- Import price elasticity in the CFA zone can be substantial. Expenditure switching should lead to imports with an elasticity between 0.8 and 1, implying a 30% devaluation can reduce equilibrium import volumes for a given output by between 25 and 30%.
- Supply pessimism of traditional exports is correct in the short to medium run, as exports of coffee, cocoa, and oil have output responses between 0.2 and 0.5
- Analysis of export growth in non-traditional products suggests that supply pessimism is not generally true and that farmers respond significantly to incentives. Chile's export of food items doubled

between 1985 and 1990, Kenya's horticulture industry grew by leaps and bounds in less than a decade, and

- The extremely rapid growth of non-traditional exports (Brazil in 1967, Mexico in 1982, and Turkey in 1980) was preceded by trade reforms that included a large adjustment of the real exchange rate. This is a necessary but not sufficient condition for export diversification.
- The very small size of current CFA exports suggests that general demand pessimism is misplaced as there is potential for enormous export expansion.

References

Arbache, Jorge Saba, and John Page. 2008. Hunting for Leopards: Long Run Country Income Dynamics in Africa. Policy Research Working Paper Series 4715, The World Bank.

Cossé, Stepahen, Johannes Mueller, Jean Le Dem, and Jean A. P. Clément. 1996. Aftermath of the CFA Franc Devaluation, IMF Occasional Papers 138, International Monetary Fund.

Freund, Caroline, and Martha Denisse Pierola. 2008. Export Surges: The Power of a Competitive Currency. Policy Research Working Paper 4750. Washington, DC: World Bank.

Gulde, Ann Marie, and Charalambos Tsangarides. 2008. *The CFA Franc Zone: Common Currency, Uncommon Challenges*. Washington, DC: IMF.

IMF. 2016. Regional Economic Outlook: Sub-Saharan Africa, April.

IMF. 2017. Western Hemisphere Regional Economic Outlook: Tale of Two Adjustments. Washington, DC, April.

McMillan, Margaret S., and Dani Rodrik. 2011. Globalization, Structural Change, and Productivity Growth. NBER Working Paper 17143. Cambridge, MA: National Bureau of Economic Research.

Pritchett, Lant, and Nita Ghei. 1999. The Three Pessimisms: Exchange Rates and Trade Flows in the Franc Zone. In *Exchange Rate Misalignment: Concepts and Measurement for Developing Countries*, ed. L. Hinkle and P. Montiel. A World Bank Research Publication and Oxford University Press.

Rodrik, Dani. 2008. The Real Exchange Rate and Economic Growth. *Brookings Papers on Economic Activity* 39 (2): 365–439.

CHAPTER 22

Political Economy of Urban Bias Against Rural Poor

One of the interesting features of the CFA arrangements is the complex political economy dimension. Every exchange rate arrangement has its own considerations, and the CFA is no exception. Countries design their exchange regimes in line with their political and economic objectives. Stasavage (1997) argues that the fiscal failures of the two subzones can be attributed to problems of institutional design involving the setup of the two CFA zone central banks, the monetary rules under which the central banks operate, and the relationship between the CFA states and France. He also argues that, in the 1980s and 1990s, political interests in France and Africa were more important in the CFA zone's failure to promote fiscal discipline in the sense that these interests affected the design of rules and institutions during periods of reform.

Van de Walle (1991) finds that the CFA zone has two unique features which affect their development policies: urban social base and patrimonial roots of the political system. There are specific features in the CFA system whereby the urban elite, who favors cheaper imports, has more clout than rural producers, who benefit from a cheaper exchange rate. Historically, the beneficiaries of an overvalued currency have been the formal sector in the CFA zone, the government civil service, and the state-owned enterprises. The leading enterprises, especially those that are very import-dependent and protected from competition by tariffs and preferential credit policy, tend to benefit from the status quo. There tend

A. Zafar, *The CFA Franc Zone*,
https://doi.org/10.1007/978-3-030-71006-4_22

to be close relationships between the government bureaucracy, the state enterprise owners, and the state. Even the middle-income urban groups in Dakar, Yaounde, and Abidjan have links to the government elite. They are the lobbying forces for a cheap food policy and generally cheap imports.

By contrast, the farmers and the smaller scale traders would benefit from a more market-based currency.[1] These farmers in the CFA zone are far from the cities and lack a strong cooperative or lobbying movement. However, as in other parts of Africa, more than 50% of the population of Sub-Saharan Africa are smallholder farmers. They usually own land less than five acres, have lower access to technology and inputs than their Asian counterparts, and are unable to finance expensive inputs. They also do not have a history of farmer aggregation through cooperatives and have not been able to tap into the political elite. In the political economy of the CFA, the farmers are the weak link, and they are perceived as subsistence farmers rather than as potentially commercially viable agricultural operators who can increase productivity and reduce risk. In many respects, the CFA zone is different from countries like Japan, where the rice farmers have clout, of France, where the agricultural lobby has strong power to influence decision-making. Given the French legacy, the civil service has very strong economic and political power in the Francophone zone, and its interests are divergent from the agriculturalists in the short-term but convergent in the longer term. A parity adjustment will free resources from some of the non-tradable and inefficient sectors and allow them to move to the more competitive tradable sector.

Agriculture is the most important sector in the CFA zone, more so in UEMOA than CEMAC, with more than a fifth of GDP coming from agriculture and accounting for the majority of employment. Many of the West African CFA economies are agriculture-based, but unfortunately suffer from low yields and significant post-harvest losses. Moreover, low fertilizer use, poor quality seeds, and weak water management affect the success of agriculture. On top of that, the policy regime, in terms of regulation, taxation, and public investment, has been less than optimal.

Senegal is an interesting example of a country with a huge agricultural potential since more than 70% of the population engages in farming, and

[1] One technical point is that from a microeconomic standpoint, a net food seller and producer gains more from a devaluation than a net food buyer. Also, the intensity of import use is another parameter to assess the impact of an exchange rate adjustment on farmers.

peanuts (groundnuts), rice, and horticulture accounting for most of the agricultural output. Blessed by geography and climate, land availability, and lower labor cost, the sector has been unfortunately stagnant for much of Senegal's history, with farmer productivity levels more than one-fifth of the levels in the rest of the economy. Since 2010, the sector has grown benefiting from a combination of rainfall, export demand, and subsidies.

Fisheries, which should be Senegal's comparative advantage has been in crisis due to overfishing. The sector has large untapped potential, especially in agro-processing, with only an estimated 5% of total horticultural production transformed domestically in 2019. It is the second-largest exporter of cherry tomatoes to the EU after Israel, with the support of a leading multinational GDS. FAO (2006) estimates that Senegalese cherry tomato and mango exports to Europe still account for a mere 2–3% of their domestic production4 (FAO 2006). Moreover, there are very few examples of the industrial use of domestic agricultural products.

The sector can benefit much more from greater private sector participation and investment. Currently, there are a few large firms and many small producers who have neither the scale nor the technology to expand output. Financing for the sector is difficult. It has received only 2% of banking financing in Senegal, which is a fraction of its needs. On top of that the country faces constraints linked to logistics, marketing, and provision of inputs. Although it has a favorable endowment, Senegal is a net food importer, particularly for rice. While Cote d'Ivoire has a stronger agricultural sector, due to the initial support from President Boigny, it too suffers from a lack of agricultural processing and most of the cocoa is exported in raw form. It imported rice of close to $600 million in 2020. Cocoa generated more than US$5bn in revenues for Côte d'Ivoire in 2015, and with some further cocoa processing, that figure can double or triple. Cameroon exports oil, cotton, and cocoa. Conspicuously absent in its export basket is manufactured or agro-processing. East African countries have done better in agriculture by several metrics. For example, Kenya exported in 2019 close to $2 billion in tea, coffee, horticulture, and flowers.

The overvalued currency in the CFA zone acts as a disincentive to commercial agriculture. A wide body of economic theory and empirical evidence demonstrates, trade and exchange rate policy influence production incentives, and resource flows between sectors. The CFA exchange rate impacts the competitiveness of the agriculture sector by affecting the prices of agriculture products and inputs and farmer profits. A devaluation leads to an increase in local currency terms of farmer producer prices, assuming the government does not try to prevent the price rise through controls. An overvalued currency in the CFA one has been a contributing factor to the large dependence on food imports. According to FAO data, between 1980 and 2007 Africa's net food imports in real terms grew at an average 3.4% per year. The President of the African Development Bank (AfDB), Akinwumi Adesina has expressed concern that Africa was spending 35 billion dollars annually on food imports and has been pushing for Africa to develop strong food self-sufficiency and provide incentives for faster commercialization.

Another good example of the effects of exchange rate on agriculture is for the cotton sector, which is especially significant to CFA countries. Benin, Burkina Faso, Côte d'Ivoire, and Mali account for about 80% of cotton production in West Africa and 90% of cotton production in francophone West Africa. Burkina Faso is now the largest West African producer of cotton and an important player in cotton in Sub-Saharan Africa. Its production expanded by an average 10% a year in 2000–2020, when more than 500,000 metric tons of seed cotton were produced. Many thousands of lives are linked to the success of the large vertically integrated cotton chains in Central and West Africa. Subsidies, mostly from the United States, have depressed world market prices and increased poverty among African cotton farmers. In the cotton sector, the costs are in local currency and the outputs are in dollar terms. The 1994 devaluation led to a strong supply response and impact on the subsector, boosting both cotton production and cotton company profits. Regional cotton production increased from 573,000 tons in 1993–1994 (the year before devaluation) to 921,000 tons in four years (Tschirley et al. 2009).

Cotton is similar to airlines in many ways. Airbus and Boeing are competitors in the dualistic airline but while the outputs (airplanes) are priced in dollars, the costs are in the respective currencies. For Airbus, which is a European initiative based in Toulouse, the costs are in euros, while for Boeing, the costs are in dollars. So for any ten-cent slide in the exchange rate with dollar falling to the euro, Airbus is projected to be losing $1 billion. Exchange rates matter for companies and producers. For cotton, the revenues are in dollars, but the costs are in local currency. As the euro strengthens, cotton farmer's profitability margins are eroded. After the devaluation of the CFA in 1994, the fixed price procurement price for farmers increased from 85 CFA per kg to 125 CFA per kg. After devaluation and with a higher price of cotton, the net income for cotton farmers increased by 36–44%, depending on the type of farming, after adjustments were made for the increased cost of imported inputs. This was also applicable to other rural producers and commodities. Similarly, in Senegal, fruits and vegetables for export have done well since the 1994 devaluation of the CFA franc.

The real exchange rate overvaluation can be a disadvantage to the poor. The empirical literature is mixed on the impact of currency depreciation on the poor. A devaluation helps the rural poor in three ways: by spurring economic growth in the economy, by helping producers of tradables in the economy, and by favoring producers of tradable goods (exports and import substitutes) and consumers of non-tradables. However, devaluation can also be contractionary as it erodes the cost of food imports and disproportionately affects the welfare of urban households. It can also have inflationary consequences depending on the nature of the pass-through to domestic prices, as well as the response of macro aggregates such as imports, exports, and gross domestic production. Dorosh and Sahn (2000) find that since African poor rural farmers are net producers of tradables, they gain from a devaluation, since devaluation increases the relative price of tradables, while urban poor, who tend to be net consumers of tradables, usually do not gain from a devaluation. However, they note that macroeconomic policy reform alone will not be sufficient in the short-run to reduce poverty in Africa. Many poor tend to be in low-level government jobs or in urban informal sectors. However, in practice, there are many other parameters that affect the impact, including the integration and distance from export markets and the nature of government pricing policy.

Bourguignon et al. (1989) find that devaluation that is oriented toward trade helps the poor in the low-income countries as it encourages export-oriented industries, which employ more workers and can create jobs.

In a recent paper, Elbadawi and Refaat (2015) develop a theoretical model to analyze how a real exchange rate undervaluation can be pro-poor and to assess the poverty impact of the real exchange rate and estimate the response of average household wage and non-wage incomes. Estimating the model using national-level panel data from the Egyptian Central Agency for Public Mobilization and Statistics, he finds robust evidence suggesting that strategic real currency depreciation/undervaluation at the macroeconomic level promotes pro-poor income growth at the household level by allocating resources toward agriculture, industry, and tradable services, raising incomes to people in these sectors.

Box 22.1 Case Study of Cote d'Ivoire and Ghana in the 1990s
In a study on the relationship between macroeconomic adjustment and poverty, Demery and Squire (1996), in the aftermath of the CFA devaluation, find a significant impact of macroeconomic variables on micro data. Comparing Cote d'Ivoire and Ghana, both large, coastal West African neighbors with predominant rural populations and both dominating the world cocoa market, the analysis finds that the two countries have coped with external shocks in significantly different ways, with dramatic differences in outcomes. While in both countries, poverty is predominantly rural, much of it occurring among small-scale farmers and among the self-employed, the differential impacts to declines in the international cocoa prices were noticeable.

Several interesting observations come out from the analysis. First, both countries were destabilized by external shocks, but Ghana adjusted promptly, as early as 1983, with its Economic Recovery Program (ERP), including a sharp depreciation in the exchange rate combined with trade liberalization. Although inflation continued to be present during the adjustment effort, the real exchange rate depreciated throughout the decade. The results were good, with growth restored and maintained at around 5% a year in real terms for much of the 1984–1994 period. Moreover, real per capita private consumption has also grown steadily, although more slowly. By contrast, in Cote d'Ivoire, due to the fixed exchange rate system, the authorities pursued an internal adjustment strategy, which led to a deterioration in living standards for all groups. According to Demery and Squire, in Ghana, most groups appear to have benefited from the ERP-induced recovery. All groups in Ghana among the rural poor appear to have benefited most, in direct contrast to their counterparts in Cote d'lvoire. The majority (around 85%) of the poor—food-crop farmers, export-crop farmers, and the self-employed all improved. In Ghana the poverty fell by 5% in general for all groups, while in Cote d'lvoire, all groups experienced a serious decline in living standards between 1985 and 1988 with increases in the incidence of poverty of at least 15%. This shows the significant link between macroeconomic policy and poverty outcomes.

On top of the exchange rate effects against commercial agriculture is excessive taxation of the sector in the CFA countries, although the numbers vary by country. Empirical work to Togo shows that when using average effective tax rates (corporate taxes, local taxes, labor and input taxes, and unreimbursed VATs) and using data from a representative sample of Togolese formal (micro, small, medium, and large firms), the estimated tax wedge averages over 90% of pretax profits based on 2014 figures.[2] It is such a distortion that the wedge reduces a healthy average return on assets (ROA) of 146% (excluding all taxes except import duties) to approximately 14% after tax. In a study on Ivory Coast, Abbott (2007) finds that Cote d'Ivoire has managed to maintain and grow exports of its leading export in spite of heavy taxation. From 1961 to 2004 the nominal rate of assistance (NRA) applied to cocoa showed an average effective 44% taxation of this crop, compared with average taxes on coffee of 55% over this period and on cotton of 29%. In sum, on top of the wrong incentives from a misaligned currency are the incentives from excessive taxation of the sector.

In this regard, the CFA zone can learn from the experience of Asian countries like China, Vietnam, and Bangladesh that had dramatic improvements in agricultural productivity at the onset of their economic reforms. China began its economic reforms with reform of agriculture and the introduction of household responsibility system and producer incentives to sell surplus crops to the market. Under Doi Moi reforms of the 1980s, the Vietnamese liberalized agricultural markets, provided incentives to farmers, and dismantled collectives. There was a sharp depreciation of the exchange rate to make Vietnamese exports more competitive, and agriculture was not taxed but supported. Tuan (2010) finds that reforms unleashed an entrepreneurial spirit in Vietnam, and farmers intensified rice production and diversified into new crops such as coffee and cashews. The results were very spectacular. By stimulating agricultural and overall economic growth, the reforms helped reduce rural poverty in just five years—from 1993 to 1998—by 21%.

In Bangladesh, the country became self-sufficient in food production a few decades after independence. The country progressively involved the private sector and avoided taxing the sector. There were two waves of agricultural reform in the 1980s–mid-1990s (Kabir et al. 2011). First, the subsidies on inputs were cut back, and domestic trading of inputs was liberalized, and after the mid-1980s till the mid 1990s, public distribution

[2] http://documents1.worldbank.org/curated/en/179631474899157168/pdf/Togo-SCD-Final-2016-09222016.pdf.

of grains was reduced and private trading in grain markets locally and internationally increased supplemented. Also, in terms of exchange rate policy, in 1979, the country moved from a fixed exchange rate to a flexible exchange rate, linking the taka to a basket of currencies of the country's major trading partners. The extent of overvaluation had dropped from 28% during the1970s to 8% during the early 1990s and remained around 5–7% in the mid-90s.

Despite natural calamities like cyclones, flood and drought, and diminishing agriculture land due to urbanization and population pressures, the country has been very successful in agriculture production. This is especially remarkable in a country which has been haunted by famine. The growth rate in food grains from independence to the present is close to 3% per year. The country is now self-sufficient in rice and fish production. A dynamic ecosystem has been built connecting private sector farmers and markets. Close to 16 million families make their livelihood from agriculture. The country has now several power agro-processing companies that are transforming raw products and converting them to processed dairy, poultry, and vegetable outputs. The country has a large production of rice, potato, onion, jute, garlic, fish, vegetables, and fruits. Bangladesh can teach the CFA zone that a competitively managed exchange rate, a strong private-public interface, and a very low taxation of agriculture can help avert the shadow of famine.

Another interesting parallel for the CFA zone is the case of Japan. Japan emerged from the ashes of World War II and became the second-largest economy in the world. During the 1980s, there was the perception that Japan would eclipse the United States. It developed a strong manufacturing base and export strength in a few decades. While its automotive and other exports are known, not many observers know the political economy in Japan and the power of agricultural groups. The 2 million rice farmers in Japan have strong lobbying with the leading political parties, leading to very strong support and even protectionism for the sector. Rice is considered sacred to Japanese culture and is a central part of the Japanese diet. The sector is supported by high prices paid by consumers, which have been more than ten times border prices. Despite being in a diminishing sector. Japanese rice farmers, contrary to CFA farmers, have been able to influence the political system.

Or take the example of the European Common Agriculture Policy of the European Union, driven mostly by French farming groups. First introduced in the early 1960s, it was part of the architecture of the EU from the earliest stages and reflected the substantial lobbying of farmers. It is a policy of agricultural subsidies, income support programs, and rural development measures for farmers. While the program has evolved and diminished in size, it still is a very important program for farmers, especially French farmers, with the total size at more than 60 million euros in 2019. While the policy has both supporters and critics (concerned about costs and efficiency), the important and relevant message is that French farmers have succeeded in obtaining policies that help their production.

Box 22.2 Exchange Rates and Agriculture: Evidence from the 1994 Devaluation

One way of understanding the role of exchange rates is to take a historical perspective and assess the impact of the 1994 devaluation on agriculture. Interesting empirical work at Michigan State University by Yade et al. (1999) conducts a detailed analysis of the effects of the change in parity on the agricultural sector using disaggregated sectoral and subsectoral data. The main finding is that the devaluation appears to have reversed the decline in GNP per capita in the Franc zone countries and stimulated an increase in the level of agricultural value-added as well as the agricultural sector's share in GDP. It is noteworthy that post-devaluation, food imports as a share of total agricultural exports declined for all countries in the UEMOA but Senegal, where agricultural exports fell significantly after the devaluation. The authors show that there has been an increase in food production for items which were previously heavily imported from outside, and that there has been an increase in regional trade in food products. However, in certain cases, there was an increase in local prices and decline in food consumption. The authors find an effect of increased producer prices in rice having a strong effect on rice production in Niger, Burkina, and Cote d'Ivoire. In the former, at the microeconomic level, there was strong growth in both production and productivity, while for the latter there were similar effects, although the rice was used for domestic consumption. Similarly, there was an increase in horticultural production in the region and intraregional trade in horticultural products and imports from the world market for many countries. The greatest increase in regional trade was found in the livestock (beef cattle) subsector following the devaluation, where the coastal countries substituted Sahelian production for European imports. The analysis demonstrates that exchange rate changes affect the incentives of agricultural producers.

References

Abbott, Philip. 2007. Distortions to Agricultural Incentives in Cote d'Ivoire. Agricultural Distortions Working Paper 46, December 2007, Washington, DC.

Bourguignon, F., J. de Melo, and A. Suwa. 1989. Distributional Effects of Adjustment Policies: Simulations for Two Archetype Economies. World Bank (Background Paper for 1990 World Development Report).

Demery, Lionel, and Lyn Squire. 1996. Macroeconomic Adjustment and Poverty in Africa: An Emerging Picture. *World Bank Research Observer* 11 (1): 39–59.

Dorosh, Paul A., and David E. Sahn. 2000. A General Equilibrium Analysis of the Effect of Macroeconomic Adjustment on Poverty in Africa. *Journal of Policy Modeling* 22 (6): 753–776.

Elbadawi, Ibrahim, and Eman Refaat. 2015. Competitive Real Exchange Rates are Good for the Poor: Evidence from Egyptian Household Surveys. Working Papers 966, Economic Research Forum, Revised November 2015.

FAO. 2006. *Indicateurs de l'Alimentation et de l'Agriculture—Pays: Sénégal.* www.fao.org/es/ESS/fr/compendium_2006/pdf/SEN_ESS_F.pdf.

Kabir, Golam, Najmul Hossain, and Moutushi Rahman. 2011. Liberalization of the Bangladesh's Agriculture Sector: Lessons Learned from the 1980s and the 1990s. Research report, December 2011.

Nguyen Do Anh Tuan. 2010. Vietnam's Agrarian Reform, Rural Livelihood and Policy Issues. http://www.rimisp.org/wp-content/uploads/2010/05/Paper_Nguyen_Do_Anh_Tuan.pdf.

Stasavage, David. 1997. The CFA Franc Zone and Fiscal Discipline. *Journal of African Economies* 6 (1): 132–167.

Tschirley, David Lawrence, Colin Poulton, and Patrick Labaste. 2009. *Organization and Performance of Cotton Sectors in Africa: Learning from Reform Experience*. Washington, DC: World Bank.

Van de Walle, Nicholas. 1991. The Decline of the Franc Zone: Monetary Politics in Francophone Africa. *African Affairs* 90 (360) (March): 383–405.

Yade, Mbaye, Anne Chohin-Kuper, Valerie Kelly, John M. Staatz, and James Tefft. 1999. The Role of Regional Trade in Agricultural Transformation: The Case of West Africa Following the Devaluation of the CFA Franc, Michigan State University, Lansing, Staff Paper 99. 28 June 27–30.

CHAPTER 23

Coping with Shocks: Growing Debt and Erratic Public Investment

A related challenge with the CFA zone is the inability to adjust to terms of trade shocks and the corresponding impact on debt and public investment. If the exchange rate is rigid, the country can either borrow and increase debt or undertake a costly fiscal consolidation via an internal adjustment strategy. In the CFA, historically, the risks of fiscal consolidation in the face of widening deficits in many countries have led to a cutback in public investment, which tends to be easier to cut than wages and salaries.

One approach from the CFA zone has been to borrow more to respond to a crisis. In an analysis of the response of Gabon, one of the more representative CEMAC oil economies, to terms of trade shocks, Zafar (2004) uses a quantitative methodology to decompose responses to shocks from 1980 to 2000 and finds a weak response in terms of import intensity, economic compression, and non-oil export promotion. Gabonese policymakers postponed adjustment by resorting to considerable borrowing during this period. This excessive borrowing had ripple effects on the debt. The government borrowed from commercial banks and donors, causing its external debt/GDP ratio to increase from 30% of GDP in 1970–1976 to 80% in 1999.

A second policy response has been to reduce public investment. Empirical work shows that public investment in the CFA zone tends to be

A. Zafar, *The CFA Franc Zone*,
https://doi.org/10.1007/978-3-030-71006-4_23

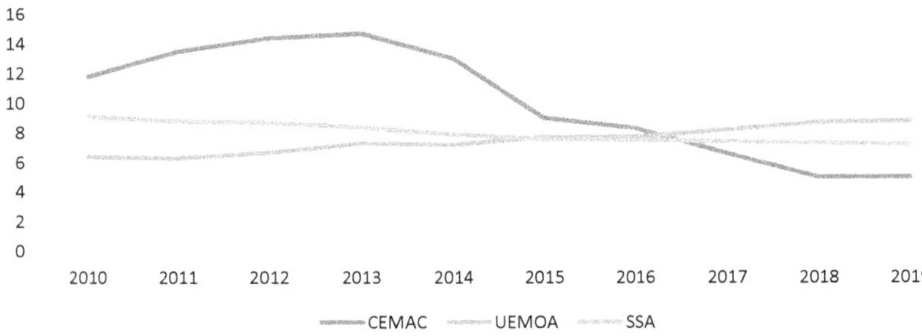

Fig. 23.1 Public investment in CFA Zone 2010–2019 (% of GDP) (*Source* World Bank, IMF)

procyclical. The adjustment to shocks entails a reduction in public investment, which is deleterious for longer term growth. Yilmaz et al. (2016) examine the cyclicality of public investment in African countries using panel data for the 1996–2012 period and analyze public investment in country subgroups, including WAEMU and ECOWAS. They find that both CEMAC and UEMOA had procyclical public investment, and that over the period public investment as a percent of GDP was lower in both the CFA zones than in Sub-Saharan Africa as a whole. South Asian Development Community (SADC) has the highest public investment. In a study, Dessus and Varoudakis (2013), using evidence from a large panel of low-income and lower middle-income countries over 1995–2012, find that, unlike other countries, public investment in the WAEMU has been procyclical. Thus, public investment shrinks more in bad times than it increases in good times and appears to have become procyclical since the introduction of the fiscal convergence criteria in 1994.

Public investment in CEMAC has declined between 2010 and 2019 in the wake of the oil price declines, while in UEMOA it has remained steadier. CEMAC had overtaken the SSA average but has recently fallen below (Fig. 23.1). During the 2016–2018 period in CEAMC under the IMF programs, public investment was cut from 6% of GDP to 5% in a response to the oil shock. The challenge for fiscal management in CEMAC is that the public investment program bears the burden of adjustment. Projects develop a "stop and go" execution rhythm based on initial budget allocations and are stopped arbitrarily based on revenue shortfalls. Work is started and then it is abruptly reduced given paucity of funds.

Without a more stable public infrastructure investment, it becomes more challenging for CEMAC to make the necessary investments in infrastructure to boost productivity and close the infrastructure gap. On top of that, in terms of efficiency of public investment, the CFA zone is among the weaker performers in Africa in terms of quality of expenditure. Finally, while the CFA countries are far from regional leaders like Ethiopia, which has had public investment as 15–20% of GDP, the CFA zone, especially CEMAC, has been closer to the SSA mean. For UEMOA, the public investment story is different, as there has been an increase in Eurobond financed public investment in both Senegal and Cote d'Ivoire and this has helped the two leading economies have a higher growth rate than a decade earlier. There has been important work on bridges, roads, and airports in these countries. Capitalizing on its falling debt price, Senegal plans to sell as much as 800 million euros ($880 million) of offshore bonds in 2020 to fund new infrastructure, but the covid pandemic has led to a delay. However, in UEMOA, there is a risk that expensive Eurobonds is generating additional debt without attractive returns.

References

Dessus, Sébastien, and Aristomene Varoudakis. 2013. Protecting Public Investment Against Shocks in the West African Economic and Monetary Union: Options for Fiscal Rules and Risk Sharing. Policy Research Working Paper 6562, World Bank, Washington, DC.

Yilmaz, Serdar, Abdoulaye Ouedraogo, and Mehmet Serkan Tosun. 2016. Cyclicality of Public Investment in Africa. *International Journal of Public Policy* 12 (3/4/5/6): 378.

Zafar, Ali. 2004. What Happens When a Country Does Not Adjust to Terms of Trade Shocks? The Case of Oil-Rich Gabon? World Bank Policy Research Working Paper No. 3403, World Bank, Washington, DC.

CHAPTER 24

Lack of Independent Monetary Policy and Credit Rationing

One of the central problems of the CFA zone is the different context of monetary policy in Europe and monetary policy in Francophone Africa. While the former consists of industrialized countries, the latter consists of many poorer countries at different stages of development. The ECB has set an inflation target of 2% and works through the interest rate and through open market operations to influence that target. In the CFA zone, the inflation dynamics is somewhat different. Boccara and Devarajan (1993) develop a model of inflation differentials for CFA franc zone countries, and identify two effects: a monetary effect (where commodity booms lead to a surge in reserves, which if unsterilized, lead to inflation) and a fiscal effect (where higher government revenues lead to higher spending, which is inflationary). Thus, the fact that BCEAO and BEAC borrow the ECB inflation target seems inappropriate for the circumstances in their country, leading to a mismatch of monetary policies.

Monetary policy has a unique capacity to play a countercyclical role during boom times and a supportive role during bust times. There are now many countries, including in Africa, who have successfully managed their exchange rates and used monetary policy to support economic growth as well as price stability. Many countries in Africa are using inflation-targeting frameworks, whereby the central bank commits to publicly targeted inflation target ranges. Some of these countries include

A. Zafar, *The CFA Franc Zone*,
https://doi.org/10.1007/978-3-030-71006-4_24

those with managed float regimes, such as Ghana and South Africa. The fundamental point of monetary policy is to create a bridge between the financial sector and the real economy.

Unfortunately, in a fixed exchange rate such as the CFA, monetary policy just has one job—to support the peg and there is little space for discretion or creative tools by central banks. While the CFA zone has succeeded in preventing the central banks from financing runaway fiscal deficits and anchored some discipline in monetary policy, its rigidity has prevented it from supporting development in the economy. Even in terms of inflation management, Khan and Senhadji (2000) identify the threshold point at which inflation reduces economic growth at 1–3% for developed economies, but the threshold point for developing countries is between 11 and 12%. The implications of this finding are significant. Moreover, there are ways that countries with more flexibility have been able to keep a lid on inflation. Exchange rate flexibility is not synonymous with runaway inflation. As Stephen O' Connell (2012) has argued:

> The majority of non-CFA central banks now operate reserve-money frameworks that are the direct descendants of IMF conditionality programs and retain severe limits on central bank finance to government. These frameworks target inflation in the well-defined sense that benchmarks for reserve-money growth are derived from projections of inflation-consistent growth in money demand; in most cases the central bank announces a desired range for inflation.

Financial sectors in SSA countries remain among the shallowest in the world and, within Sub-Saharan Africa, financial depth in the CFA franc zone is even more limited. In 2014, credit to the private sector amounted, on average, for 16% of the GDP for low-income SSA countries compared to a level of 32% of the GDP observed, on average, in low-income countries from other regions, although the two groups of countries had a similar financial development level in the early 1990s. On average, in 2019, credit to the private sector in terms of GDP amounted to about below 19% for the countries that are members of the CFA franc zone, compared to about 23% for the rest of Sub-Saharan Africa (excluding South Africa) (Fig. 24.1), although UEMOA has a higher level than CEMAC.

There are four reasons for this. First, there is the inescapable fact the fixed exchange rates limit the scope for monetary policy and domestic

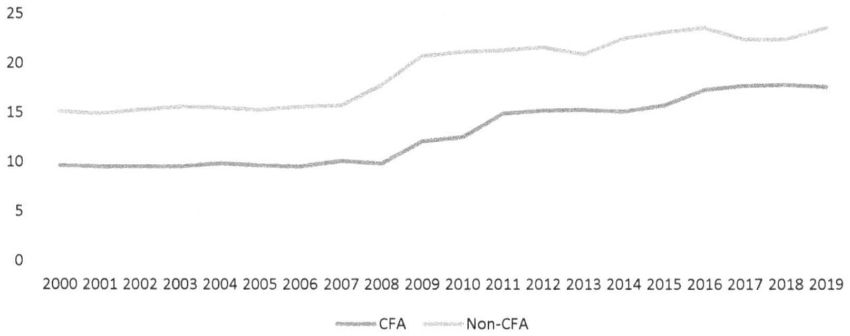

Fig. 24.1 Credit to the private sector 2000–2019 (% of GDP) (*Source* World Bank dataset)

credit growth. Second, there are high capital requirements for setting up new banks, given the very tight prudential standards of BEAC and BCEAO. Third, many of the banks are foreign banks (more than 80% banking assets including many French and Moroccan banks) or their subsidiaries with large liquidity buffers and with tendency to lend on a short-term basis at relatively high interest rates to some large corporates in a few special sectors. They are not open to SME financing that requires excessive due diligence and credit review. These banks tend to be sitting on high liquidity, but they tend to invest in government debt. So most government debt in UEMOA and CEMAC is held by local banks, and there is a lack of cross-border holdings, impeding regional financial integration.

Ghura et al. (2009) conduct an empirical investigation of factors that may explain why financial depth in the CFA franc zone is shallower than in the rest of SSA using panel data for a sample of 40 countries for 1992–2006. They find that gap in financial development between the CFA franc zone countries and the rest of SSA can be explained by differences in institutional quality (e.g., availability of credit information, and strength and enforcement of property rights), variables that policymakers can influence. Given this, there is ample scope for CFA countries to rethink some of the institutional arrangements that put a low prominence on monetary policy independence and financial intermediation.

In a review of financial integration in UEMOA, Amadou Sy (2006) finds that excess liquidity and its distribution in the system are obstacles to a regional monetary policy; financial depth in WAEMU is still low when compared to non-SSA developing countries because access to banking services remains limited; the WAEMU interbank market is thin and activity is limited to intragroup transactions. The CFA zone has a curious paradox. There are banks that have excess liquidity, there are large differentials between central bank policy lending rates and commercial rates, and there are many firms and businesses not able to obtain capital. Countries in the CFA zone are relying on sovereign debt issuance to finance their spending. By 2019, the outstanding value of West African CFA regional securities has been more than 15% of GDP.

In a post-COVID world, it is important for monetary policy to support the economic recovery and deepen financial intermediation. In their review of inflation-targeting regimes in Africa, Heintz and Ndikumana (2011) find that a strict rules-based approach to monetary policy, including inflation targeting, is not desirable for the countries of sub-Saharan Africa, given inflation dynamics and structural realities and that any monetary policy should include scope for discretion to allow the central bank to respond to shocks, especially those originating from the supply side. Over time, monetary policy should be part of the arsenal of CFA central banks, and an inflation targeting approach can be developed that fits in with the economic context in CEMAC and UEMOA.

References

Boccara, Bruno, and Shanta Devarajan. 1993. Determinants of Inflation in Franc Zone Countries in Africa. World Bank Policy Research Working Paper 1197, Washington, DC.

Ghura, Dhaneshwar, Kangni R. Kpodar, and Raju J. Singh. 2009. Financial Deepening in the CFA Franc Zone; The Role of Institutions, IMF Working Papers 09/113, International Monetary Fund.

Heintz, James, and Leonce Ndikumana. 2011. Is There a Case for Formal Inflation Targeting in Sub-Saharan Africa? *Journal of African Economies* 20 (2): 67–103.

Khan, Mohsin, and Abdelhak S. Senhadji. 2000. Financial Development and Economic Growth; An Overview, IMF Working Papers 00/209, International Monetary Fund.

O'Connell, Stephen A. 2012. Inflation Targeting in Africa. *Oxford Companion to The Economics of Africa*. 359–364. https://works.swarthmore.edu/fac-economics/256.

Sy, Amadou Nicolas Racine. 2006. Financial Integration in the West African Economic and Monetary Union (September 2006). IMF Working Paper, 1–25.

CHAPTER 25

An Alternative: Flexible Exchange Rates and Post-Pandemic Recovery

Flexible exchange rates help cushion economies from macro shocks. And in the post-COVID-19 world, once there is the resumption of growth, they can play an important policy role. They can help a country adjust to economic dislocations, by providing more export support and monetary flexibility to authorities to address the shocks. Monetary authorities can also work on using tools to manage the exchange well to avoid sharp increases in imported inflation depending on the extent of exchange rate pass-through.[1]

In early 2020, the COVID-19 pandemic struck the world with expected deadliness, leading to a global pandemic crisis. Starting in Wuhan, the pandemic spread to Europe and the United States and affected the global economy. Declared a pandemic by the World Health Organization on March 11, 2020, the virus has led to close to more than 135 million cases by end of March 2021. There have been close to 3,000,000 global deaths, while no continent, except for Antarctica, has been spared. In February, Nigeria became the first country in Africa to officially register a case of COVID. Other countries have fallen suit. Countries have responded with ambitious and intensive lockdown efforts. The epidemiological impact had an immediate economic impact leading

[1] Exchange rate pass-through is defined as the responsiveness of international prices to changes in exchange rates. It tends to be lower in CFA countries and can be addressed via monetary measures.

A. Zafar, *The CFA Franc Zone*,
https://doi.org/10.1007/978-3-030-71006-4_25

to global recession and growth challenges. For the government, the crisis represents a severe test to support fragile economies. For many ordinary citizens, it has felt that the world has stopped.

As of March 2021, Africa is doing better than every other continent in terms of the number of cases and the number of deaths. So far coronavirus has been contained in capital cities, but there has been some spread to the rural areas. Governments in Africa have reacted quickly by imposing lockdowns, especially in countries like Senegal and South Africa. The hope is that Africa's young demography, climate, and vaccination history may help to reduce the tide of the pandemic. Since Africa has not been at the center of the pandemic, the direct impact on lives has been less muted there, but the economic impact has already been felt amidst a world of disrupted supply chains and collapsing growth.

There are fears that things may get worse, but they have not materialized so far. The Economic Commission for Africa (ECA), found that more than 300,000 Africans could potentially lose their lives due to COVID-19. International Food Policy Research Institute (IFPRI) estimates the impact globally and finds that over 140 million additional people could fall into extreme poverty in 2020, including 80 million in Africa and 42 million in South Asia. According to the International Labor Organization (ILO), more than 200 million workers can be thrown into unemployment. Some experts fear that the deaths can be much less, due to the seasonality of the virus and other factors. Various models have come out with diverse estimates. Speculation and uncertainty grip the world's imagination as it tries to fathom the scale and impact of this pandemic.

For Africa, the fear is that the pandemic will damage the continent's recent economic recovery where growth is expected to slow down from 3.2% to 1.8% in a best-case scenario (ECA 2020). Perhaps more than 25 million people will fall into extreme poverty. The pressure on the continent's fragile health infrastructure can be immense. There will be strong pressure on fiscal policy due to the projected increases in stimulus packages and social safety nets. The worry is what happens to the pandemic when it reaches countries which do not have the capacity to control it and lack adequate public health standards. Vera Songwe, the UN Under-Secretary-General and Executive Secretary, Economic Commission for Africa, has asked for $100 billion to protect the continent and to urgently and immediately provide fiscal space to all countries to help address urgent safety net needs.

Another risk to Africa is the ramifications of the pandemic from the macroeconomic to the micro. Global growth reduction and disrupted trade links can lead to strong impacts on local food supply. This could cause price hikes and market panics. Food insecurity would rise along with poverty (Laborde et al. 2020). However, evidence from markets in Africa suggests that by March 2021 there has been no major impact of covid of prices in African markets. There are hopes that the virus reduces by the summer of 2021 due to vaccinations, demographics, and social distancing. However, there are concerns by the WHO that the vaccinations may be delayed in Africa due to supply shortages and delivery delays. Before covid, the CFA countries had an uncertain trajectory, but covid has amplified their growth challenges and led to a significant across-the-board contraction. It is also expected to weaken the challenging fiscal position of already vulnerable West and Central African economies.

As coronavirus reached the African continent, there was immediate response by the policymakers in the CFA countries to seal borders, institute lockdowns, and sensitize populations to the magnitude of the new pandemic. Given the previous experience with Ebola and other health hazards, the CFA zone has displayed strong resilience. As of March 2021, there have been more than 100,000 reported deaths in Africa, of which less than 5 percent in the CFA zone.

Two major decisions have been reached by the international financial community to help support African economies. First, the IMF has doubled its annual access limits for the Rapid Financing Instrument to USD 100 billion and revamped its Catastrophe Containment and Relief Trust (CCRT) to help 23 African countries through rapid debt service relief. Second, G20 Finance Ministers have agreed to freeze bilateral government loan repayments for low-income countries that request forbearance until the end of the year. They have asked private creditors to participate in the initiative on comparable terms, but investors have been more interested in a country-based approach. The EU and the WBG have also provided bailout and health sector support projects.

Although there have been some policy measures issued by the regional central banks, the scope for further fiscal expansion and countercyclical monetary policy is significant. The general BEAC and BCEAO reforms were constrained in their policy responses but still were able to deliver a stimulus.

- In UEMOA, besides the health measures taken to address the pandemic, the Governments allocated almost US$9 billion to alleviate the pandemic's impact on employment and production and temporarily suspended the "convergence, stability, growth and solidarity pact," which tries to limit debt and inflation in UEOMA.
- The central bank has pledged increased bank resources. There has been an increase of 340 CFA billion to the central bank weekly allocation to banks, reaching a total of 4.750 billion.
- There will be the creation of a special window with no ceiling for refinancing loans to small and medium-sized enterprises (SMEs /SMIs).
- The central bank has created a new framework inviting banks to accommodate demands from firms with COVID-19-related repayment difficulties to postpone for a three-month renewable period debt service falling due, without the need to classify such postponed claims as NPL;
- Central bank executives will negotiate with electronic money issuers to reduce transaction costs and encourage people to make greater use of digital payment methods to better limit contact and movement.
- The central bank also wants to supply banks with banknotes to enable them to ensure satisfactory operation of automatic teller machines (ATMs).

In parallel the CEMAC Commission and BEAC announced several policy measures:

- CEMAC allocated over $150 million to public health projects
- In March 2020, BEAC announced that it would make available to banks operating in the CEMAC zone a liquidity package of FCFA 500 million (approx. USD 829 million) to finance the needs of economic operators affected by COVID-19.
- On April 15, 2020, the BEAC announced a decrease in the costs of electronic transactions within CEMAC, with a view to promoting the use of digital payments.
- The monetary policy committee of BEAC has recommended that credit institutions guarantee the provision of services to their customers and strengthen remote banking operations.

References

European Commission for Africa. 2020. COVID-19: Protecting African Lives and Economies. Addis Ababa.

Laborde, David, Will Martin, and Rob Vos. 2020. Poverty and Food Insecurity Could Grow Dramatically as COVID-19 Spreads, IFPRI, Washington DC. https://www.ifpri.org/blog/poverty-and-food-insecurity-could-grow-dramatically-covid-19-spreads.

PART V

Macroeconomic Developments in the CFA Zone

CHAPTER 26

Impact of the COVID-19 Pandemic on the CFA Zone

COVID-19 has had a ripple effect on the world economy. The CFA Franc zone, while having fewer number of cases relative to many in Asia, Europe, and North America, has suffered a strong economic impact, which has outweighed the epidemiological impact.

In economic terms, government growth and fiscal prospects have worsened after multiple lockdowns in many of the CFA countries. Another effect has been on remittances to the CFA zone, which historically tend to be stable and anti-cyclical. Lack of income overseas has led to declining remittance flows back home. Foreign investment, which was promising has receded, especially in the extractive sectors. There is also a growing ripple effect on the financial sector, especially for SMEs facing liquidity constraints with anecdotal evidence from both UEMOA and CEMAC suggesting firm's liquidity constraints have widened. For the CFA zone, there are three silver linings from the tragedy. First, oil importers in WAEMU benefit from a much lower oil price. Second, the increased price of gold—considered a safe investment in risky times—has benefited Burkina and Mali. Third, the region is receiving large amounts of financial support from international creditors and donors. As there are signs of recovery in 2021, the evidence suggests that some of these negative trends may start to reverse.

A. Zafar, *The CFA Franc Zone*,
https://doi.org/10.1007/978-3-030-71006-4_26

Regional Convergence

The likely outcomes are that the pandemic will affect regional convergence and worsen pre-COVID fiscal balances, especially in CEMAC, where the reserves had already been depleting. The BEAC had been allowing statutory advances (known as monetizing the fiscal deficit), to extend credit from the monetary authority to the fiscal authority. In theory, there was a cap, but due to the pandemic, there will be increasing risks to macroeconomic convergence. CEMAC and UEMOA face the scepter of increasing fiscal and current account deficits. The risk is that the system is unsustainable, with growing pressures on the balance of payments requiring a currency adjustment.

CHAPTER 27

What Is Happening to Growth and Inflation?

COVID has amplified the shocks to the CFA economies. For the last decade, the overall macroeconomic performance of the zone has resulted in lower growth over a longer period than in the non-CFA economies in Africa, but also lower inflation. While the CFA zones have had markedly better records in managing inflation compared to the rest of Africa with levels reaching less than 2% in recent years, their growth record has not been strong over a longer term trajectory. Figure 27.1 shows the impact on GDP growth of COVID-19.

The COVID crisis has had a differential impact on different countries. First, all the countries are negatively impacted by COVID. Two, only five out of thirteen will have negative real GDP growth, while the rest have positive but low growth. Third, the oil producers, such as Equatorial Guinea and the Republic of Congo, which were already projected at negative growth in 2019, have suffered due to the global collapse in oil prices. Fourth, Benin, Cote d'Ivoire, and Senegal, all coastal economies, have managed to maintain resilience.

In regional terms, after a decade of weaker growth performance earlier, UEMOA's improvement has been curtailed, while after years of better performance earlier in a decade, COVID has amplified CEMAC growth's difficulties in recent years. CEMAC has had a growth collapse due to the oil price fall (Figs. 27.1 and 27.2). If one sets the time horizon at the last two decades, one may realize that economic growth in CEMAC

A. Zafar, *The CFA Franc Zone*,
https://doi.org/10.1007/978-3-030-71006-4_27

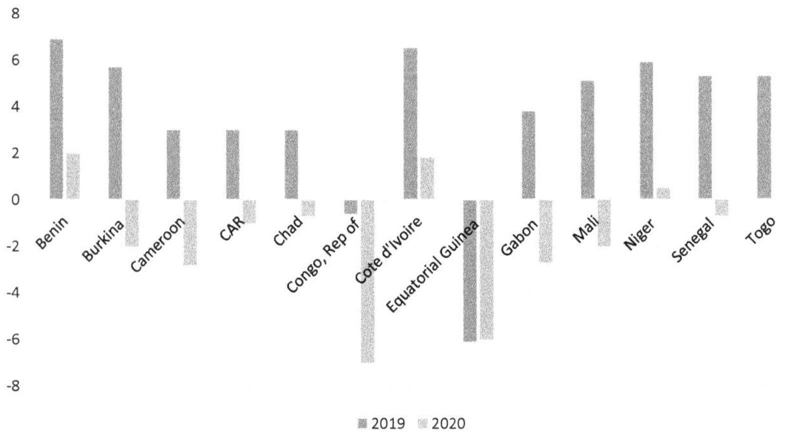

Fig. 27.1 Real GDP growth by CFA country (%) 2019–2020 (*Source* IMF [2020])

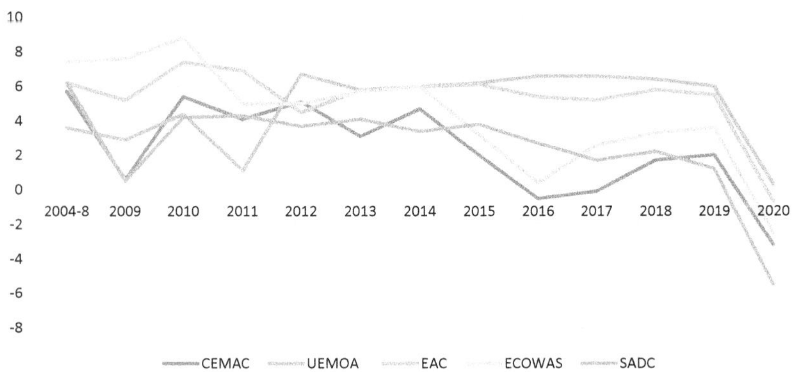

Fig. 27.2 Real GDP growth rate (%), CEMAC and WAEMU, 2004–2020 (*Source* IMF)

and WAEMU countries has been less vigorous than the growth in Asian countries or Sub-Saharan African countries more generally, while volatility has been high. The silver lining for the CFA zone has been low inflation during the pandemic (Fig. 27.3).

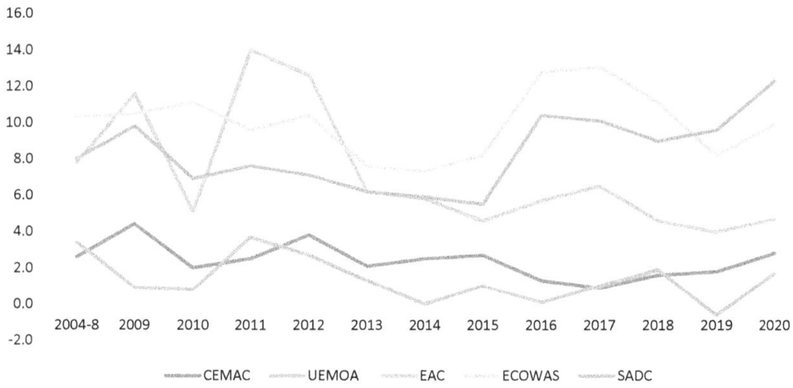

Fig. 27.3 Inflation (average annual), CFA zone, 2004–2020 (*Source* IMF)

The analysis is consistent with the recent IMF (2016) work comparing pegs and pegged exchanged rates in Sub-Saharan Africa. In a review of exchange rate performance, the IMF finds several patterns. First, Sub-Saharan African countries with pegged exchange rate regimes have had the best inflation performance with little apparent cost in terms of higher output volatility. The lower inflation stems from stronger monetary discipline and greater policy credibility under a pegged exchange rate regime. Second, the growth performance of countries with pegged regimes has, on average, been weaker than countries with non-pegged regimes during the second half of the sample period (2000–2014). Third, intermediate and floating regimes have, on average, enjoyed higher growth relative to countries with pegs, but this has come at a cost of higher inflation and, for (de jure) intermediate regimes, greater output volatility. Fiscal positions also tended to be weaker particularly during the 2001–2014 period, which was characterized by easier external liquidity conditions and market access for many of these countries. But the seemingly weaker fiscal discipline has not translated into sustained higher levels of debt relative to the size of the economy.

Reference

IMF. 2016. Regional Economic Outlook: Sub-Saharan Africa, April.

CHAPTER 28

Widening Twin Deficits in the Subzones

The two CFA subregions have experienced current account and fiscal deficits in recent years, mostly linked to adverse terms of trade shocks. These have been amplified in the wake of the pandemic. While overall macroeconomic management has improved, the current account deficit worsened in the CFA zone, especially after 2011, mostly because of the decline in commodity prices and the larger expansion in imports. For CEMAC, it is projected to reach −7.1% in 2020, while the fiscal deficit has reached −2.5% of GDP. The dramatic fall in oil to close to $30 a barrel in 2020 due to a combination of COVID-19 and price wars between Saudi Arabia and Russia have also worsened the CEMAC fiscal deficit. In the WAEMU, due to COVID impact on commodity prices, the export proceeds fell for other commodities, leading to a widening current account deficit of −5% of GDP and a fiscal deficit of −5.9% of GDP. These deficits led to stress on macroeconomic management (Fig. 28.1).

One challenge for the CFA zone has been fiscal discipline. In theory, fiscal discipline is an important adjustment tool in fixed exchange rate systems. However, in practice the evidence is unclear. There are some differences between the CFA zone and the non-CFA zone in relation to fiscal deficits but significant differences between countries in the CFA. Depending on the year, the fiscal balance in the CFA countries was better or worse than other sub-regions in Africa. The fiscal discipline that is supposed to be a hallmark of the Franc zone is not matched by the data.

A. Zafar, *The CFA Franc Zone*,
https://doi.org/10.1007/978-3-030-71006-4_28

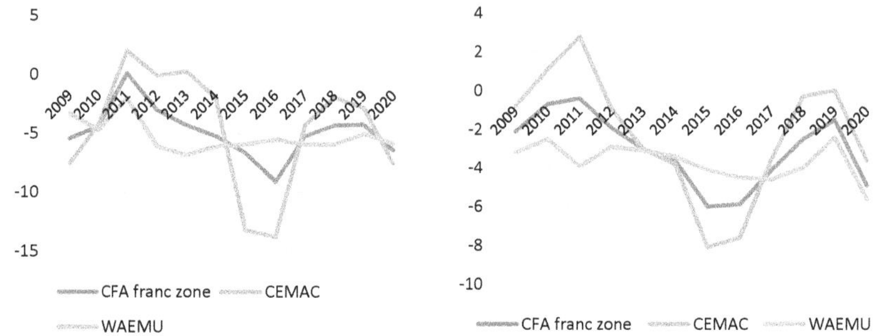

Fig. 28.1 Current account deficit (including grants) and fiscal deficit (including grants), CFA zone, 2009–2020 (*Source* IMF [2020])

In fact, Tornell and Velasco (2000) compare the experience of francophone countries that have pegged to the French franc versus the rest, and find that francophone African countries operating under that regime seem to have exhibited less fiscal discipline—defined as average deficits—after controlling for a host of factors, than their anglophone counterparts.

Reference

Tornell, Aaron, and Andres Velasco. 2000. Fixed Versus Flexible Exchange Rates: Which Provides More Fiscal Discipline? *Journal of Monetary Economics*, Elsevier 45 (April, 2): 399–436.

CHAPTER 29

Accelerating Public Debt

Due to the unprecedented shock, COVID-19 has led to a worsening debt situation for CFA economies. This has increased debt service costs. Already pre-covid, the debt as a percent of GDP was growing in many countries, including the Republic of Congo, Gabon, Senegal, and Togo (Fig. 29.1). Post-HIPC, the countries have borrowed heavily from international financial institutions as well as China to finance their infrastructure development and to address the balance of payments deficits. There has been a move by monetary authorities in UEMOA to rely on more market-based sources of finance while in CEMAC there has been more borrowing from China. However, the issuance of Eurobonds in CEMAC has been increasing in recent years. Gabon, one of the lowest rated sovereigns in Africa, issued a $750 million bond in 2020, marketing 10-year dollar securities with a yield of 7%.

Chinese lending, which was low in recent years, has increased considerably, especially for natural-resource economies, such as the Republic of Congo. Some of the Chinese deals have been hard to understand as the terms have been opaque and non-transparent. Some loans were simple transactions in which loans were received in exchange for oil. While much of the information is difficult to find, there is some evidence to suggest foreign currency debt percent in both CEMAC and UEMOA ranges from 30 to 50% and Chinese debt is a lesser percent.

A. Zafar, *The CFA Franc Zone*,
https://doi.org/10.1007/978-3-030-71006-4_29

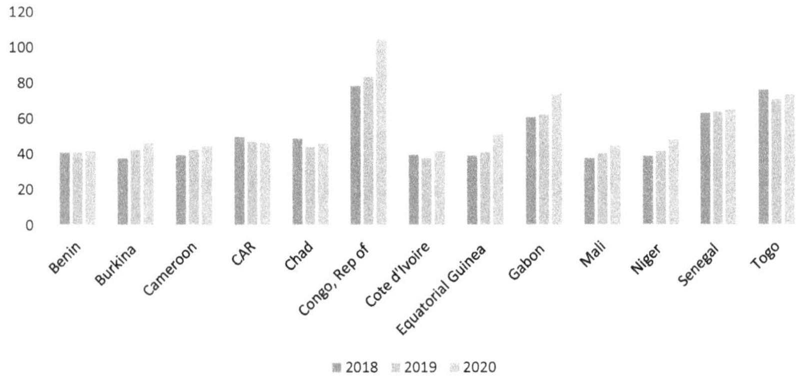

Fig. 29.1 Government debt 2018–2020 (% of GDP) (*Source* IMF [2020])

In terms of debt, the situation is different in UEMOA than CEMAC, and the situation has been evolving in recent years. In UEMOA, debt has built up in recent years and reached almost 50% of GDP by 2019. Increased borrowing from multilateral institutions as well as from boom in Eurobond issuance across the country has led to an increase in debt. Much of it has been dollar-denominated raising concerns about exchange rate risk. Countries as diverse as Côte d'Ivoire, Benin, and Senegal have borrowed foreign currency from international capital markets, mostly through various Eurobonds issuances. Much of the money has been used to finance infrastructure. CEMAC had a buildup of external debt due to the collapse in oil prices but much of it got restructured in the wake of IMF programs. At some point, the Republic of Congo had a debt of close to 110% of GDP, or close to $10 billion. In the wake of pandemic, these debt numbers will increase until there is some debt restructuring.[1]

In terms of investment, CEMAC and UEMOA generally remain below the levels of low-income African economies, although UEMOA has been increasing slightly in recent years. Most investment is private investment, which accounts for two-thirds of investment in the CFA zone. In response to the mid-2020s oil price shock, CEMAC cut the public investment from 6.3% of GDP in 2016 to 4.8% in 2018. UEMOA has moved in

[1] One of the key sticking points in the multi-year negotiations between the Republic of Congo and the IMF between 2016 and 2019 has been on the debt restructuring of large Congolese debts owed to China and other investors.

the opposite direction with greater public investment in the same time period. Nevertheless, the danger is that the covid pandemic will lead to an expansion of debt and a decrease in investment, but it is too early to make a more precise assessment.

Linked to debt and its long-term servicing is income growth and convergence. One interesting feature of economic zones is the potential for income convergence across countries over time. The dream has been for the richer countries to help catalyze the development of the poorer ones. The idea follows from neoclassical growth models which assume that poor countries grow faster than rich ones due to diminished returns to capital in richer countries and poorer countries have advantage of technologies and practices from more experienced countries. This has been one of the key rationales behind the formation of customs unions and common currency areas and its expansion to newer members. This was one of the rationales for the accession of the European Union to eastern and southern states. Convergence can mean two things. It can mean that poor economies tend to grow faster than rich ones, or it can mean that countries in a group have a reduced dispersion of their real per capita GDP levels over time.

In practice, it is harder for convergence due to happen because of barriers to capital flows or technology transfers. Many developing countries attract FDI, but sometimes it is FDI in extractive industries and there is an absence of knowledge or technology transfer. Movement of capital to poorer countries is also impeded by regulatory limits, banking restrictions, foreign exchange controls, and other legislation that prevents development from happening on an equal playing field. Many of the East Asian economies, such as Korea, were quite successful at converging with richer country income levels, but the country managed to build a strong economic base. In the European Union, there has been some convergence towards the EU average of the level of income across EU regions and member states.

Using Angus Maddison dataset spanning more than 60 years, one finds no pattern of economic convergence in the UEMOA zone (Fig. 29.2). A couple of patterns are visible. First, the strongest performers are the coastal economies, and the weaker performers are the landlocked ones. Second, there is the dominant role of Cote d'Ivoire, but its growth trajectory has been quite bumpy until the last decade. Third, Senegal has a similar per capita income to what it had at independence. Fourth, although many of the poorer countries, such as Mali, Burkina, and Niger,

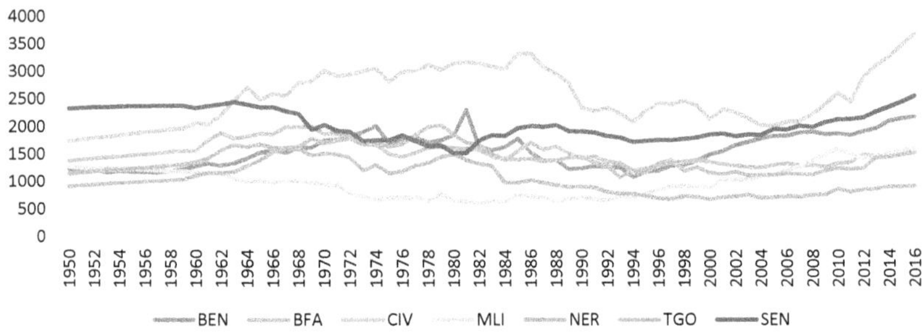

Fig. 29.2 UEMOA GDP per capita 1950–2016 (%)

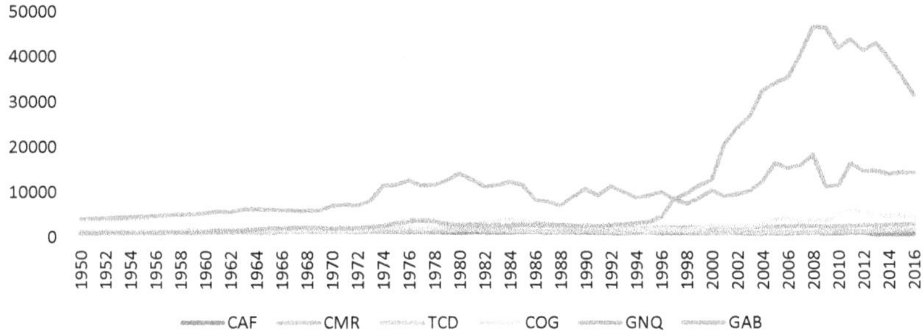

Fig. 29.3 CEMAC GDP per capita (%) (*Source* Maddison dataset)

have had gains, these gains have not led to any meaningful catch-up phenomenon. Finally, initial conditions have had an impact on later developments. Country rankings in per capita income have not changed much in UEMOA over the life cycle of the zone.

The patterns are similar in CEMAC. First, the leader, Cameroon, has not been the leader in per capita income. Secondly, the small oil-rich economies, Gabon, Equatorial Guinea, and the Republic of Congo, have had significant income rises, which are linked to oil windfalls. Even though there is significant poverty in these countries, on a per capita basis the countries have become richer. The per capita income trajectories of the oil economies follow the boom and bust cycles in the oil market. Finally, the Central African Republic and Chad show no signs of income convergence with the zone's richer members (Fig. 29.3).

Reference

International Monetary Fund. 2020. Regional Economic Outlook: Sub-Saharan Africa, October. Washington, DC.

PART VI

Exchange Rate Dynamics in the CFA Zone

CHAPTER 30

Misalignment and Its Consequences

The recent COVID-19-related shocks have amplified pressures on the exchange rate, especially in CEMAC. This has been a perpetual problem for the CFA zone, especially since the introduction of the euro in 1999, risking further loss of export competitiveness. Given the COVID-19 pandemic, there has been a decline in prices of key CFA commodities, especially oil, cocoa, cotton, and others, resulting in growing pressure on the balance of payments and reserves, especially in CEMAC. Gold, which one of the main exports of Burkina, is the only export commodity that has seen price increase. The international ratings agencies have also noted the challenges for the CEMAC zone. According to Fitch, there is evidence of growing liquidity strain, with BEAC gross external assets, worth USD8.5 billion end-February 2020 (around 3.5 months of 2019 estimated regional imports), possibly halving in 2020, without an increase in external official financing above 2019 levels, and even assuming no drawdown from the three other smaller member countries. Considering this, it is important to assess the impact of COVID-19 on exchange rate misalignment. The concept is quite simple, but the measurement of misalignment is complex and must address a host of methodological and empirical issues. There are four methodologies (Table 30.1).

Purchasing Power Parity. For the CFA zone, a PPP analysis of the real effective exchange rate (REER) for 1994–2020 reveals a growing appreciation of the REER following the introduction of the euro

A. Zafar, *The CFA Franc Zone*,
https://doi.org/10.1007/978-3-030-71006-4_30

Table 30.1 Exchange rate misalignment: methodologies

There are in general four approaches in the academic literature to measuring exchange rate misalignment: purchasing power parity (PPP) estimates, behavioral equilibrium exchange rate (BEER) time-series econometric approach, macroeconomic balance and trade elasticities method, and the computable general equilibrium models. All these four methodologies try to develop a view of the equilibrium real exchange rate and its relationship to the actual real exchange rate to provide an analytical base for good macroeconomic management. The methodologies are described below according to the seminal work by Hinkle and Montiel (1999)

- **Purchasing power parity**. This is the most common approach. Using the PPP-based method and using CPI as the price index, the long-run equilibrium level of the real exchange rate is estimated using the value of the RER during some base year as the "PPP base-year." This approach calculates misalignment by plotting the real exchange rate over time and comparing its value during the period of interest to the corresponding value in the base year in which the real exchange rate was judged to be at its long-run equilibrium value. Macroeconomists like to think of the real exchange rate as the ratio of the price of non-tradables, which are domestically determined, over tradables, which are determined by foreign prices. One version of the PPP is the Big Mac index created by the Economist in 1986
- **BEER and equilibrium**. This time-series econometric approach is a general approach to modeling equilibrium exchange rate, and there are many versions of this method. In the work of Clark and MacDonald (1999), the specified theoretical exchange model is used to obtain a measure of the equilibrium exchange rate and compared with the actual real exchange rate to measure the degree of misalignment. As opposed to PPP, the BEER analyzes the equilibrium exchange rate as a vector of fundamentals and works from the assumption that real factors are the key explanation for the slow mean reversion to PPP observed in the data. These factors can include government spending, openness, productivity changes, trade price changes, and other variables
- **The macroeconomic balance and trade elasticities**. This approach works from a broader macroeconomic perspective and estimates a current account "norm." The exchange rate misalignment is the amount of real exchange rate adjustment that is needed to correct the imbalance and to move towards a more sustainable current account position. The method uses a formula based on the elasticities of imports and exports and their link to the current account. The higher the overvaluation and the departure from the norm, the greater the adjustment that is required

- **DLR and computable general equilibrium**. Developed in the early 1990s, the DLR belongs to the class of open economy macro-models that assess the impact of shocks on equilibrium exchange rates. It is different from a PPP approach, as well as the BEER, in that it uses a three-good framework: exports, imports, and domestic goods. The different feature of this approach is that it analyzes how the long-run equilibrium real exchange rate is affected by changes in the relative prices of imports and exports. The DLR method is based on three equations: one linking the exports–GDP ratio to the relative price of exports in terms of domestic goods, one relating the imports–GDP ratio to the relative price of imports in terms of domestic goods, and an identity deriving the resource balance–GDP ratio from the export and import ratios. Since it focuses on shocks, the DLR approach generally leads to higher estimates of misalignment than the more conventional approaches

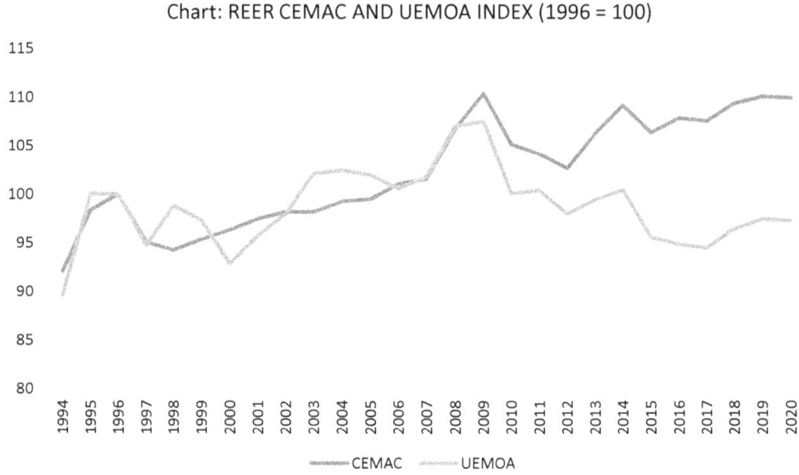

Fig. 30.1 Real effective exchange rate index (1996 = 100) (*Source* BCEAO, BEAC, author calculations)

(Fig. 30.1). The 1994 devaluation corrected the exchange rate misalignment of the CFA. Post-devaluation, the real effective exchange rate started appreciating gradually. By 2012, there was a cumulative appreciation of the REER of close to 15% in PPP terms in the CEMAC and 5% in the WAEMU. Between 2010 and 2019, the paths of UEMOA and CEMAC diverged reflecting the different nature of the two economies. Since 2010, the CEMAC REER has appreciated more than 7%, while the UEMOA REER has depreciated less than 5%. The major drivers for CFA continue to be the strength of the euro.

While the 1994 devaluation of the CFA franc improved the competitiveness of these economies and allowed countries to maintain external competitiveness gains for a couple of years, the steady appreciation of the REER in the immediate post-devaluation years—illustrated by the upward trend in the REER until the end of 2009—reflected the erosion of price competitiveness in the countries. However, from the PPP results, the assessments of the equilibrium exchange rate in both zones show that a significant art of the competitiveness gains from the 1994 devaluation has disappeared. Coulibaly (2014) finds that while the appreciation of

Table 30.2 Exchange rate misalignment in CFA zone (2010–2020)

	PPP	*DLR*
Chad	−5.0	44.6
Cameroon	−3.3	27.5
Gabon	2.6	34.7
EQ Guinea	2.0	25.6
Congo, Rep of	1.9	31.7
Central African Republic	27.3	18.0
CEMAC	4.3	30.4
Côte d'Ivoire	−6.5	19.1
Benin	−13.1	16.1
Burkina Faso	−6.5	18.8
Mali	−8.0	19.3
Niger	−11.0	17.8
Senegal	−9.8	22.9
Togo	−6.3	26.4
UEMOA	−8.7	20.1

Source Author calculations; PPP estimates from IMF REO (October, 2020) and are from 2010 to 2019. A negative sign indicates undervaluation

the euro in the last decade did not translate into strong and generalized currency overvaluations—except in Central African Republic, Benin, and Equatorial Guinea—it had however strongly reduced the extent of real undervaluation induced by the 1994 devaluation of the CFA franc (Table 30.1).

Devarajan, Lewis, Robinson (DLR). However, using the simple computable general equilibrium model, the misalignment of the CFA between 2010 and 2020 is considered to be 30.4% and that in UEMOA is 20.1%. The DLR analysis shows that the CFA franc is overvalued and would need a significant correction to achieve more adjustable trade balances, especially in CEMAC. Fiscal consolidation may not suffice to adjust the current account imbalances. Given the magnitude of trade shocks, the CEMAC CFA is perceived to be more overvalued than in UEMOA. There is significant heterogeneity across countries, with the Republic of Congo being quite overvalued while Cote d'Ivoire is closer to equilibrium (Table 30.2).

This is in line with the recent IMF analysis, but of a higher magnitude than IMF estimates. IMF also provided an official assessment of the overvaluation of the CFA franc, with a higher rate in CEMAC and a lower rate in UEMOA (IMF 2019a, b). According to the IMF assessments, the 2019 current account and real effective exchange rate (REER) suggest an overvaluation and a weaker external position than implied by fundamentals and desirable policies. This has been a departure from the IMF position, which generally found the CFA aligned with fundamentals. This approach is from the IMF's "EBA-Lite's" Current Account (CA) model, which compares the underlying current account balance with the model-estimated current account norm, suggesting an overvaluation in CEMAC of 11.4% with the 2019 current account deficit estimated at 2.5% of GDP against a norm of 0.3% GDP surplus. For UEMOA, the EBA's Current Account model, indicates an overvaluation of 5.0%.

Trade and Intraregional Trade

The COVID-19 pandemic has impacted global trade. According to World Trade Organization economists, world trade is expected to fall by between 13 and 32% in 2020 as the COVID 19 pandemic disrupts normal economic activity. There has been a reduction in global trade as demand orders have slowed down and supply chains have been disrupted. CFA exports, such as cotton from Niger, Mali, and Burkina Faso, oil from the CEMAC countries, and cocoa from Cote d'Ivoire, have faced decreased demand and lower prices in world markets. CFA countries, which depend on capital imports for public investment, have suffered. Under the optimistic scenario, the recovery will be strong enough to bring trade close to its pre-pandemic trend, while the pessimistic scenario only envisages a partial recovery. UEMOA will have less of a trade shock than CEMAC because its economies have different commodity mixes, and the shock to them has been less severe than to oil.

Another area where COVID could have a potential impact is in intraregional trade among CEMAC and WAEMU countries. The table shows that the share of intraregional trade among CEMAC countries increased marginally from a rather low base of 2.78% over 1995–1999 to 3.31% during 2010–2014. While the analogous share for WAEMU countries was much higher (i.e., 11.49% during 1995–1999), it has hovered around that same level for the last twenty years or so. Indeed, all of the African RTAs have much lower levels of intraregional trade relative to the non-African RTAs. For example, the share of intraregional trade among CAN members has been around 8–9% while that among ECOWAS members has been around 9–10%. By contrast, the analogous share for ASEAN countries has averaged around 20–25% while those for NAFTA countries have been over 40%. It will be important to gather data to assess the COVID impact on trade by the end of 2020.

The low level of intraregional trade amongst CEMAC and WAEMU countries reflects not only the structural frictions that plague such trade but also the fact that none of the member countries of WAEMU has a large local market (like the United States in NAFTA and Brazil in MERCOSUR). Furthermore, countries in the region have comparative advantage in relatively similar products so that one would not expect to see a great deal of trade among them. By contrast, the pattern of comparative advantage of the United States is quite distinct from that of Mexico and this difference generates a natural rationale for trade. By contrast, such is not the case for CEMAC and WAEMU countries. Thus, in addition to impediments, scale and comparative advantage considerations also lie behind the relatively small amount of trade amongst members of the two African RTAs. Even accounting for the relatively similar economic structure of countries within the CEMAC and WAEMU, the level of trade between them has remained relatively low for a long period of time. Apart from supply-side limitations, the lack of growth in intraregional trade can be attributed to poor infrastructure (road, rail, and port networks), irregular supply of energy and its high cost, and the scarcity of trade financing.[1]

Finally, as the share of the CFA zone's trade with Europe has fallen from 50% to less than 25% in the last 15 years, as trade expands with Asia. The CFA zone is trading with many other partners and economies, including Turkey, Morocco, and Korea. This is leading to asymmetric shocks within the zone. The hopes of trade integration with neighbors are fading because, despite decades of development, intrazonal trade in the CEMAC and the WAEMU has remained low, at 3.3% and 11.4% respectively, relative to other customs unions elsewhere in the world (Table 30.3).

[1] The common external tariff (CET) of the CEMAC has five rates (zero, 5, 10, 20, and 30%), with an average applied tariff (over all goods) of 18.2%. As in UEMOA, agriculture continues to be the most protected sector (22.5%), followed by manufacturing (17.5%) and the extractive industries (11.2%).

Table 30.3 Share of intraregional trade, selected regional trade agreements, 1995–2020 percent

	2000–2004	*2005–2009*	*2010–2014*	*2015–2020*
CEMAC	2.55	3.03	3.31	3.28
WAEMU	12.46	11.62	11.36	11.43
Andean Community	9.56	8.63	7.91	7.80
Common Market for Eastern and Southern Africa	5.36	5.62	7.39	7.39
ECOWAS	10.87	9.98	9.19	9.28
Association of Southeast Asian Nations	23.59	25.23	24.56	24.57
Southern Cone Common Market	15.41	15.37	14.59	15.12
North American Free Trade Agreement	45.22	40.91	40.71	40.65

Source Data of the United Nations Conference on Trade and Development

References

Clark, Peter, and Ronald MacDonald. 1999. Exchange Rates and Economic Fundamentals: A Methodological Comparison of Beers and Feers. Recent Economic Thought Series, Springer.

Coulibaly, Issiaka. 2014. Competitiveness and Growth within the CFA Franc Zone: Does the Switch to the Euro Matter? *International Economics* 139: 1–18.

Hinkle, Lawrence E., and Peter J. Montiel. 1999. Exchange Rate Misalignment: Concepts and Measurement for Developing Countries. Washington, DC: World Bank.

IMF. 2019a. Central African Economic and Monetary Community (CEMAC): Staff Report on the Common Policies in Support of Member Countries Reform Programs, Washington, DC.

IMF. 2019b. West African Economic and Monetary Union (UEMOA): Staff Report on the Common Policies in Support of Member Countries Reform Programs, Washington, DC.

CHAPTER 31

Getting Out of the Impasse: Exchange Rate Options for the CFA Zone

Throughout the world, exchange rates must be designed to suit the concerns and objectives of a country or zone. The CFA is no exception. There is no magic formula for exchange rate management and there is not a universally suitable exchange rate regime for every country in the world. Moreover, the circumstances vary between different points in time even in one country. The general practice in Sub-Saharan Africa for the non-CFA countries, as has been the case globally, has been a shift to flexible exchange rates, with varying degrees of central bank intervention and inflation targeting. The floats have not ever been free but usually quite managed. African policymakers, like those in many emerging markets, have struggled between the desire for stability and the desire to adjust to shocks and preserve competitiveness. Central banks have evolved both in terms of institutional knowledge and in experience in managing exchange rates.

The choice of exchange rate has varied since the 1940s and 1950s. In the postwar period, with the rise of the Bretton Woods Agreement, the United States and other participating nations pegged their exchange rates and fixed the value of the US dollar to the price of gold. The general tendency in the international monetary system was to peg the exchange rate and avoid volatility. By the 1960s pressure was building in the system as the United States did not have enough gold to cover the dollar volume. By 1971, Nixon abandoned the gold standard and the era of fixed

A. Zafar, *The CFA Franc Zone*,
https://doi.org/10.1007/978-3-030-71006-4_31

exchange rates of developed countries started to unravel. Many developing country currencies started floating against some major currencies and also shifting from single currency pegs to basket pegs. As developing country central banks gained experience and as foreign exchange markets developed, there was a push toward more flexible exchange rate arrangements. While in early 1970, more than four-fifths of developing countries had fixed pegs, by the mid-1990s, only about a half of these countries maintained them.

As the world became more volatile in the 1970s, and the world dealt with the OPEC oil crisis, the debt crisis, growth slowdowns, increased and volatile capital flows, developing country policymakers adapted their exchange rate regimes to deal more ably with shocks. In an environment of more global macroeconomic uncertainty, political and monetary authorities tried to keep more policy independence. As the East Asian examples show, developing countries also tried to use exchange rates to promote manufactured exports and seek greater integration with the global trading system. Also, with the support of the IMF and the World Bank, many developing countries sought to devalue their currencies to overcome balance of payments difficulties and growing black-market currency premia.

By the mid-1990s, there was a partial reversal, as some countries became aware of the "fear of floating." Excessive volatility and the resurgence of inflation, especially in Latin America and parts of Africa, led central banks to intervene in the form of a managed float. The dollar moved a lot during this period. Policymakers sought to prevent excessive volatility and attempted to reduce inflationary pressures, which had mushroomed in many countries. However, while some countries such as Argentina moved back to more rigid currency board arrangements due to dealing with hyperinflation, most developing countries continued to maintain a degree of flexibility. Hard pegs became restricted to currencies with weak credibility among policymakers and those where it was difficult to manage inflation.

By the 2000s and 2010s, the trend toward more intermediate regimes continued. While many developing countries did not have fully floating regimes, only a minority were pegged. The regime became a function of the policymakers' attempts to address inflation, capital flows, and competitiveness considerations. The nature of shocks economies faced became parameters for managing monetary policy. Pegged exchange rates were favored in countries where there were monetary shocks, while flexible exchange rates were favored where there were more real shocks.

Many East Asian economies used to be pegged to the dollar, but after the 1997 Asian financial crisis, there was a move toward greater flexibility. While some of the smaller countries like Hong Kong, Bhutan, and Myanmar kept hard pegs, many others, including Indonesia, Philippines, and Thailand became much more oriented to having managed float regimes with inflation-targeting frameworks. Turkey is interesting as it has had every kind of exchange rate regime over the last 30 years but it transitioned to a floating regime after the 2001 banking crisis, where the Turkish authorities tried to prevent speculative attacks against the Turkish lira by freely floating the currency. However, as opposed to the CFA economies, Turkey suffers the opposite problem—excess volatility.

Historical experience in advanced, emerging market and developing economies suggests that exchange rate movements typically have sizable effects on export and import volumes. The boost to exports associated with currency depreciation is found to be the largest in countries with initial economic slack and with domestic financial systems that are operating normally.

Regarding the CFA, there is growing concern about the viability of the fixed exchange rate peg. For CEMAC, Agbor (2012) finds that oil resource depletion in the somewhat near future is one of the greatest risks to the sustainability of the current peg linking the CEMAC CFA franc to the euro and sees the stagnating growth performance in CEMAC's non-oil GDP coupled with continuing volatility in global financial markets posing additional threats to the fixed exchange regime. In a survey of the CFA zone and future arrangements. Tchatchouang (2015) finds that some future scenarios may require an exit from the fixed peg to the euro, and asks also if French convertibility can be guaranteed without a fixed peg to the euro. In a more general way, Guzman et al. (2018) find that real exchange policies can contribute to economic development, and that a stable and competitive RER policy can support tradable sector development. However, they argue the impact of RER policies is increased when they are complemented by traditional industrial policies that increase the elasticity of the aggregate supply to the RER, including interventions in the foreign exchange market and regulation of capital flows. The consensus among macroeconomists is that a fixed exchange rate regime facing declines in net foreign assets over time will have to adjust its parity accordingly. For the CFA zone:

- It is important to understand the inflation-growth trade-off per the zone and examine the best option.
- The exchange rate should minimize the increase in the real effective exchange rate and minimize the adverse effects of competitiveness.
- It is vital to consider the degree of monetary policy independence needed to pursue the domestic inflation and output goals.
- The exchange rate architecture should reflect the degree of institutional strength at the regional level and the capacity to manage the system.
- The design of the zones should reflect the future terms of trade shocks that are likely to materialize as well as the commodity price projections.
- The degree of integration with the world economy and the pattern of trade will also influence the exchange rate outcome.
- The degree of imported inflation and the capacity to manage it will be essential as well as understanding the monetary transmission mechanism in the two zones.
- There is a well-known "impossible trinity" in macroeconomics whereby a country cannot simultaneously maintain the trifecta of a fixed exchange rate, capital mobility, and a monetary policy dedicated to domestic goals. So a CFA reform where monetary policy is used for domestic ends will have to either have a more flexible exchange rate or significantly reduce capital mobility.

References

Agbor, Julius Agbor. 2012. The Future of the CEMAC CFA Franc. Global Views Policy Paper 2012–06 (December). Washington, DC: Brookings Institution.

Guzman, Martin, Jose Antonio Ocampo, and Joseph E. Stiglitz. 2018. Real Exchange Rate Policies for Economic Development. *World Development*, Elsevier 110 (C): 51–62.

Tchatchouang, Jean Claude. 2015. The CFA Franc Zone: A Biography. In *The Oxford Handbook of Africa and Economics: Volume 2: Policies and Practices*, ed. Célestin Monga and Justin Yifu Lin.

CHAPTER 32

Alternative Pegs for the CFA: Basket, Separate Pegs, Peg to Dollar

As CEMAC and UEMOA move forward in their reform agendas, it will be important to evaluate different options. These reforms should be anchored in growth objectives and be rooted in pragmatism. The Macron-Ouattara reform has changed the name from the CFA to the eco, kept the country configuration the same in UEMOA, continued the fixed parity to the euro, and ended the Operations Account at the French Treasury. The French convertibility guarantee is still unclear. The goal of this reform is to improve sovereignty while keeping the strong anchor to the euro, and hence retaining macroeconomic stability. So far, the approach is only for UEMOA.

However, the reform still maintains the rigidity of the current system and does not address the adverse impact on growth and competitiveness of the CFA (or eco). The reform has its main focus on maintaining low inflation through the peg. However, such a low inflation target can be revisited. In an important study using sophisticated econometric modeling, Tapsoba and Bicaba (2014) find that being a member of the WAEMU reduces the growth rate by 1.5% on average and that the optimal inflation target for the WAEMU ranges between 5 and 7.3% as opposed to the current 2%, and close to rates targeted by several central banks in other Sub-Saharan African countries.

A. Zafar, *The CFA Franc Zone*,
https://doi.org/10.1007/978-3-030-71006-4_32

Peg to a Basket

One of the most promising pegged regimes for the CFA zone is the basket peg, where the basket consists of two or more currencies. A basket peg is relevant to CEMAC because it has greater trade shocks linked to one commodity—oil—compared to UEMOA. A basket peg is fundamental for UEMOA given the different shocks faced in West Africa and the changing trade patterns with Europe and Asia. In UEMOA, benefiting from international experience, the basket peg would provide both stability in terms of currency anchor and flexibility.

A basket peg would be a good opportunity for CEMAC to maintain some of the anchor properties of the exchange rate peg, while moving towards greater flexibility. The countries can reduce the volatility in both the nominal and effective exchange rates and provide better stability for oil exporters. Given the large magnitudes in oil swings affecting the Republic of Congo, Equatorial Guinea, Gabon, and Chad (Fig. 32.1), such a system would help manage these shocks. Pegging to a basket will require the involvement of a central bank with institutional independence.

The precise design of the peg is tailored to country circumstances, but normally the peg is weighted according to a country's trading partners or according to a currency composition. Jeffrey Frankel (2005) has argued that oil-exporting economies should peg their currencies to the price of oil. Alternatively, the best design for CEMAC could be an exchange rate

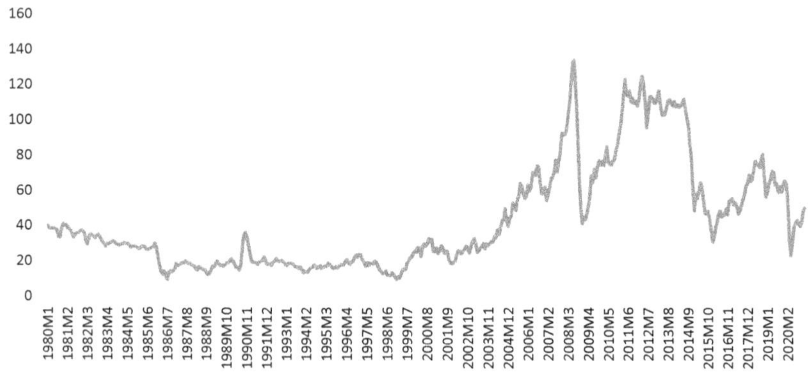

Fig. 32.1 Oil Price ($/barrel) 1980–2020 (*Source* IMF commodity series, World Bank dataset)

system, which has a basket based on three parameters: the euro, the dollar, and the price of oil. That would help ensure a stable element with the current system and a variable element, which includes the volatile price of oil.

For CEMAC, one possible model is to follow the Kuwaiti model, where in 2007 the exchange rate was pegged to a basket of international currencies of Kuwait's major trade and financial partner countries. The actual weighting has been kept confidential. The peg was an attempt by the Kuwaiti authorities to protect the currency from the adverse effects of US Dollar depreciation at the time. Currently, the Kuwaitis are maintaining their peg and currency parity, even during the pandemic.

There are several challenges for a peg to a basket. First this peg can be challenging in a country where the fiscal policy is not well-managed. However, in CEMAC, the institutions have strengthened after more than two decades of macroeconomic surveillance and institutional coordination. Moreover, a peg to a basket may end up leading to loss of French support. In operational terms the BEAC will have to have transparent formula and a clear and strong communication strategy.

Separate Pegs for CEMAC and WAEMU

Another option would be to separate peg for each subregion assuming an optimal currency area. Under this regime, the currencies will be pegged at different parities, but they will still both continue to be pegged to the euro. The advantage of this approach is two-fold: recognition of the asymmetric shocks that make the CEMAC and WAEMU different, especially because of oil, and the maintenance of the strengths of the current system.

However, it fails to recognize the costly internal adjustments that are needed to adjust to oil shocks in CEMAC. And it assumes that the zones are optimal currency areas. For a truly optimal currency area, the losses from higher adjustment costs are equal to the gains to members from using fewer currencies. Asymmetric shocks should be managed by labor mobility, capital mobility, flexible price or monetary wages, and fiscal federalism. In a currency union, there should be a currency risk-sharing or fiscal mechanism to share risk across countries in the OCA, especially from surplus to deficit countries. However, in CEMAC and UEMOA, the restrictions in labor mobility, the lack of capital mobility, and the absence of fiscal transfers from coastal to landlocked areas is noticeable.

Pegging to the Dollar

Another option for the CFA zone, especially CEMAC, would be to peg to the dollar. There would be several advantages to this approach but many disadvantages. First, the CFA zone would be anchored to the most powerful economy in the world. Second, there would be less overvaluation than pegged to the euro, as the dollar tends to be lower in value. Third, for oil economies, like CEMAC, there would be no mismatch between the revenues in dollars and anchor in dollars. Agbor (2012) argues that a dollar peg allows CEMAC zone countries access to US capital market instruments and would ensure stability of the single CEMAC francs in the event of the depletion of oil resources and foreign reserves. Moreover, it can ensure the stability of income flows from abroad, considering that almost all CEMAC exports are denominated in US dollars and access to US financial instruments through the dollar peg might be instrumental in hedging against dollar-related exchange rate risks.

However, replacing one expensive peg with another would make CFA economics inherit the interest rate policy of the Fed rather than the European Central Bank. Moreover, adjustment to shocks would be still a challenge. Also, most important, it is unclear what would be the approach of the French Government in CEMAC, which may not guarantee convertibility or support if the dollar replaces the euro as the nominal anchor.

An oil economy that has a dollar peg is Saudi Arabia. This currency peg has been decided by the Saudi Arabian Monetary Authority (SAMA) as a strategic choice to anchor monetary and financial stability that has supported economic growth in Saudi Arabia for several decades. Given that Saudi Arabia has enormous forex reserves at close to four years of imports and strong oil reserves, the anchor has been successful.

References

Agbor, Julius Agbor. 2012. The Future of the CEMAC CFA Franc. Global Views Policy Paper 2012–06 (December). Washington, DC: Brookings Institution.

Frankel, Jeffrey A. 2005. Peg the Export Price Index: A Proposed Monetary Regime for Small Countries. *Journal of Policy Modeling*, Elsevier 27 (June, 4): 495–508.

Tapsoba, Rene, and Zorobabel Bicaba. 2014. Low Inflation Luxury. Lindau Nobel Laureate Meetings.

CHAPTER 33

Floating Arrangements for the CFA: Managed and Free-Floating

Managed Float

Another good option for both CEMAC and UEMOA is to have a managed float system. Occupying a middle position between fixed and flexible exchange rates, a managed float is a system whereby the exchange rate fluctuates according to the market demand but is managed by the central bank. A region's central bank may occasionally intervene in adjust the country's currency value in a certain direction according to parameters. The nature of the interventions will depend on how strictly the central bank needs to intervene to correct short-term volatility. One option is for countries to adjust exchange rates based on the balance of payments position. In operational terms, managed float systems allow for a varying degree of central bank intervention based on the use of the interest rate.

The advantage of the managed float system is that it can be used as a longer term policy. If the float is tightly managed, it can provide a nominal anchor and help to stabilize exchange rates and expectations concerning exchange rates and inflation. In many parts of the world, a combination of intermediate and floating regimes have delivered results. In a review of the international experience of exchange rate management for oil and other commodity economies, Setser (2007) at the Peterson Institute of International Economics, finds that exchange rate flexibility has helped advanced commodity-exporting economies manage commodity price fluctuations,

A. Zafar, *The CFA Franc Zone*,
https://doi.org/10.1007/978-3-030-71006-4_33

and finds that countries as diverse as Australia, Norway, Canada, South Africa, and Brazil allow substantially more flexibility than the norm for many large oil exporters.

Another use of managed floats is to prevent countries from balance of payments difficulties and to shield countries from painful devaluations later. More and more countries are adopting managed floats to protect their currencies from increased volatility in foreign exchange markets. One way that countries can manage the exchange rate is through forwards and other financially sophisticated tools.[1]

There are significant disadvantages to manage floats. A managed float regime in a monetary union requires tremendous political consensus, institutional strength, and fiscal risk-sharing. In practical terms, countries may disagree on whether the currency should be allowed to appreciate or depreciate. CAR and Cameroon may have a different perspective, as may Senegal and Niger. First in operational terms, it is hard for central banks to know in practice the timing of intervention. While authorities have a general view on the path of the exchange rate, they are not bound by any intervention rule. Second, managed float regimes can be subject to market pressures and volatility of capital flows. Finally, following Calvo and Reinhart (2000), many countries that say they allow their exchange rate to float mostly do not. In order to address excessive volatility, monetary authorities may overreact and intervene too frequently in the markets.

As the countries can move toward a managed float in the long run, they will have to target inflation given the risks of greater exchange rate pass-through. Few Sub-Saharan African countries have a formal framework, but many central banks try to target inflation. Under this framework, the central bank commits to a publicly announced numerical range for inflation and then provides institutional commitments through a set of mechanisms that emphasize transparency for outcomes. In the last decade, the number of central banks in Africa practicing full-fledged inflation targeting has risen to more than 20, with South Africa becoming SSA's first adopter in 2000, and in 2007 Ghana was the first low-income country in the world to adopt the framework. For the CFA zone, a switch to inflation targeting, by allowing zone-wide exchange rate flexibility, could produce a superior balance of constraint and discretion than

[1] By definition, a forward contract or forwards is a type of derivative security, which are agreements to buy or sell an asset, at a fixed price and date. These help companies manage exchange rate risk.

the current system. Inflation targeting is done by putting limits on central bank finance to government and ensuring deficits are not monetized.

Free-Floating

A final option is a freely floating exchange rate that is market-determined with very little central bank intervention. While in theory many countries adopt it, in practice very few countries practice it. The advantage of a freely floating exchange rate is that it is not controlled by governments. Moreover, there is no need for capital flow restrictions as macroeconomic fundamentals will determine currency demand and supply. It also allows quick flexibility to external shocks.

The disadvantage is that it is hard to maintain in practice and operationalize. The biggest risk of a freely floating system is the exchange rate volatility that could hurt trade and investment. There are concerns about the open forex market and currency viability that motivate central bankers to intervene. Empirical research shows that most countries have a "fear of floating" and manage their exchange rates, even those that declare a floating regime to the IMF.

Another problem with a float is that there is a risk of exchange rate overshooting, as was noted by the late macroeconomist Rudiger Dornbusch. In countries such Brazil, Russia, Thailand, and Indonesia, there has been a strong overshooting of the exchange rate beyond its equilibrium and protracted turmoil in the currency markets. Due to sticky prices and flexible currencies, adjustment lags in one part of the economy can lead to more volatility in another part. This leads to a situation where the short-run effect is greater than the long-term effect.

Breakup of Unions and Rise of National Currencies

A final option is to breakup the zones and bring in national currencies. Of all the options, this one appears the worst and least likely to lead to a positive outcome. The big advantage would be a victory for national sovereignty and government choice on the exchange rate. Each country can manage the exchange rate in a way that is congruent with its policy objectives. Many economies have left the CFA zone, such as Morocco,

Tunisia, and Algeria, and have done quite well and are stronger economically than any user of the CFA. However, others that have had flexible currencies, such as Guinea, have not fared as well.

However, there is the risk of not capitalizing on economies of scale as many of the economies are simply too small. The administrative and fiscal cost of issuing and managing a new currency will difficult. Countries will need to set up a national central bank and provide the staffing and legislation to manage the monetary policy, putting pressure on national capacity. The gains from cross-country collaboration and the institutional development that have occurred will be lost. This can fuel conflict among some of the nations as the peg has helped bring them together. Despite the lack of fiscal transfers, the CFA arrangement still allows the landlocked countries a policy dialogue and coordination framework with coastal economies.

Table 33.1 presents the advantages and disadvantages of the various exchange rate options.

Table 33.1 Exchange rate options, CFA zone

Nature of regime	*Option*	*Advantage*	*Disadvantage*
Pegged regime	Status quo: business as usual	Anchor for low inflation and some macroeconomic stability Historical legacy Guarantee unlimited convertibility of the exchange rate has helped predictability	Low per capita income growth Inability to adjust to terms of trade shocks Overvalued currency leading to erosion of competitiveness Rigid system with inflexible reserve management Conservative monetary policy and disconnect between financial sector and real economy Current system does not address growing CFA trade with non-EU members, including Asia
Pegged regime	Pegging to a basket	Allows more flexibility and helps macroeconomic stability by minimizing changes in the REER Better likelihood of a non-overvalued currency	The system requires choices of basket and decision to be publicly announced or not Central bank will need to be more interventionist and demonstrate oversight Implication on reserves will need to be addressed

(continued)

Table 33.1 (continued)

Nature of regime	*Option*	*Advantage*	*Disadvantage*
Pegged regime	Optimal currency area for each subregion	Maintains the stability of the current system Recognizes asymmetric shocks that make the CEMAC and WAEMU different, especially because of oil	None of the two zones is an optimal currency area New system remains inflexible and does not adjust to shocks In relation to CEMAC, the current system means that oil price shocks will require costly and risky internal adjustments
Pegged regime	Peg to the dollar	Allows the CFA zone to follow many emerging economies, which peg to the dollar May lead to less overvaluation of the currency	Still unable to adjust to terms of trade shock French convertibility guarantee unlikely Dollar peg presents its own set of challenges, which means CFA monetary policy is decided by the US Federal Reserve
Intermediate regime	Managed float	Adjust the exchange rate to shocks Prevents overvaluation and helps competitiveness Restore sovereignty in management of exchange rates	Open capital markets make it challenging for countries to manage a soft peg Convertibility guarantee may end Central bank will have to decide the band of adjustment

Nature of regime	*Option*	*Advantage*	*Disadvantage*
Floating regime	Free float	Adjust the exchange rate based on the balance of payments position Market-determined exchange rate	Excessive volatility can damage economies Fear of floating: unpredictable investment climate Central banks will need to set up auctions and elements of the foreign exchange market

References

Calvo, Guillermo A., and Carmen M. Reinhart. 2000. Fear of Floating. Working Paper 7993, November 2000.

Setser, Brad. 2007. The Case for Exchange Rate Flexibility in Oil-Exporting Economies. Policy Briefs PB07-8. Peterson Institute for International Economics.

PART VII

The Road Ahead and Reform Roadmap

CHAPTER 34

Ten-Step Exchange Rate Reform for a Post-Pandemic World

In light of this, it is important for the CFA zone to replace the peg with the euro with a more flexible approach. This chapter outlines a ten-step reform roadmap. The long-term impact of the COVID pandemic is still unclear as it plays out. Some elements of the world economic system may go back to normal, but some parts may change fundamentally. The collapse in shipping and travel may take years to recover. The role of China as a hub of global manufacturing may change as buyers move to other emerging markets. The ugly scepter of protectionism, voluntary export restrictions, and economic nationalism may raise its head.

The lack of multilateralism in the global economy is also an important factor. The United States, long the dominant hegemon, may increase its focus on national interests and not devote as much attention to international institution-building and problem-solving. The European Union is looking inward to decide its future in the era of Brexit. Other countries have national preoccupations. Tensions between the US and China, the two dominant economies, preclude an international solution to global problems. The economy in a way resembles the world before World War II where countries have sought to protect themselves in an era of crisis. China seeks to rebuild its economy and its image in the aftermath of the pandemic. Other economies are forging the best solutions according to their circumstance.

A. Zafar, *The CFA Franc Zone*,
https://doi.org/10.1007/978-3-030-71006-4_34

For Africa, the COVID crisis represents both a tragedy and an opportunity. In terms of immediate measures, African governments will need to follow up on their successful lockdowns and set up systems of contact tracing and monitoring, as well as stocking up on health equipment, ventilators, and oxygen. In parallel, funding for front-line health care workers will need to increase, and public investment in hospitals, equipment, and health infrastructure should go up to revert neglect for the health sector. The advantage in Africa may have been the experience with Ebola and other diseases, coupled with a younger demography, a warmer climate, lack of large travel links, a history of vaccinations, and an ability to be resilient during crises. But COVID-19 may have paradoxically increased African unity and spur domestic solutions. In May 2020 the current African Union Chair South African President Cyril Ramaphosa has called on the continent to use the global crisis as an opportunity to reimagine a new Africa.[1] Commentators and policymakers are together looking at ways in which Africa can successfully emerge from the pandemic. Inadequate fiscal buffers, together with unpredictable aid inflows, will make the defense of the euro peg increasingly costly for the CFA zone in a post-pandemic world.

Considering the differing exchange rate arrangements, attached is a suggested Ten-Step Plan for Reform of CFA.

1. **CEMAC and UEMOA. Separation of CEMAC from UEMOA into different zones**

    - The CFA reform can start the reform once the **post-pandemic recovery** is in place. In an environment of **output collapse**, the reform should be started where there is some resumption of normalcy and a sustained period of analysis.
    - It does not make economic sense to have **oil exporters and oil importers** in the same zone. The differential impact of volatile oil prices and the different structures of the two zones mean that the two zones share few structural similarities but just the same parity to the euro. The economic and institutional links between the two zones remain shallow. Both of the zones are better connected to France than to each other.

[1] https://www.tralac.org/news/article/14627-covid-19-must-enable-a-new-africa-president-ramaphosa.html.

- There seems **little justification for both zones to have the same parity to the euro**. Given the magnitude of the recent oil shocks, it is likely that the parity for CEMAC will be more variable than the parity for UEMOA. The **parity should reflect the fundamentals** of the economy and the terms of trade shocks that they face.
- **Neither of the two zones is an optimal currency area**, with little intra-zone trade (10% in UEMOA and less than 5% in CEMAC). Factor mobility is significantly higher in UEMOA than in CEMAC. Capital mobility faces administrative hurdles.
- The terms of the **French convertibility guarantee** for UEMOA must be clarified. The French guarantee appears to be tied to the euro parity and the pooling of reserves. It may be difficult for the French Government to want to guarantee a CEMAC new currency whose exchange rate will fluctuate according to the oil prices.
- At the same time, it will be sensible for the regional authorities to revise the **multilateral surveillance mechanism** which has established fiscal and debt rules to ensure prudent fiscal policy. The **convergence criteria have to be modernized** focusing on fiscal balances, debt, inflation, and non-accumulation. Inflation threshold can be increased to 5%, a level closer to the ECOWAS convergence criterion of 10%, the fiscal deficit can be amended to provide more short-term fiscal space in the Sahel and reflect non-oil balances in CEMAC, and the debt limits can be amended to reflect the shock.
- For CEMAC, **a new currency pegged to a basket in the near future** and for a **UEMOA a new managed float regime** can help improving growth, fiscal and current accounts.
- One challenge for both zones will be to address **foreign currency-denominated debt** held by the public or private sector through **debt restructuring or debt cancellation with international creditors**. Public debt in UEMOA and in CEMAC increased due to the pandemic, but the risk of **debt distress** is higher in CEMAC given the fall in oil prices. The UEMOA economies, as well as some CEMAC economies, have been successful in tapping the **Eurobond market**, which

remains an alternative source of financing, but which is now expensive due to the risk premium.

- There is a body of **international experience** that the CFA countries can tap into when designing their exchange rate regimes. Many of the countries, especially in East Asia, have a long history with flexible exchange rate management and managed float regimes.
- The different pegs must reflect the **differing political economies** of the two zones as each zone has its own governance, its own history, and its own nuances. CEMAC will need to evolve in institutional strength as it takes over the management of the currency. The experience of **oil economies** such as Kuwait, Russia, and Nigeria will be very important as models for the CEMAC countries.
- Back of thumb calculations based on 1994 parameters and trade elasticities find that a 10% slide in the CFA can lead to at least a 1% gain in CFA growth, but the effect can be larger. The **fiscal deficit will decrease** with a CFA devaluation, as was demonstrated during the earlier 1994 devaluation.
- Impact on **trade balance** of a CFA currency with a lower parity is unclear. Non-oil growth in CEMAC is stagnant, but capital and consumer goods are key imports. Exports of primary commodities have low elasticity, but non-traditional exports are responsive.
- The impact on **inflation** of CFA devaluation is slight. Existing literature finds incomplete pass-through in Sub-Saharan Africa, with average elasticity estimated at about 0.4 (Razafimahefa 2012).
- **Impact of 1994 devaluation on UEMOA**. Growth resumed and inflation declined within two years after the devaluation. However, one of the lessons from the 1994 devaluation was that fiscal and wage policies prevent the emergence of wage-price spiral and that contractionary fiscal policy in terms of freezing government nominal wages would be important. The reform can be accompanied by a credible macro-fiscal package. Monetary policy also can be used to reduce the inflation gain immediately after the new currency is introduced. As a result, within two years, inflation returned to almost pre-devaluation levels.

2. **CEMAC. Issues a new currency with new name and move from a fixed parity to the euro toward an intermediate peg to a basket for CEMAC in the medium term.**

    - CEMAC should **adjust to a new long-term shock** in oil market given that the situation in the medium-term is **unsustainable**. Combination of US shale, Russia–Saudi price war, COVID, rise of renewables, and other factors means that oil price will be on an average less than $50 in the medium term. Moreover, long-term decline in CEMAC output means that CEMAC will have to eventually adjust the exchange rate.
    - As the CFA franc in WAEMU is being changed to eco, **a new currency in CEMAC** can be set up with **a new name**.
    - **A basket peg in CEMAC** is a good way to solve the chronic overvaluation of the CFA and to help CEMAC monetary authorities adjust to oil price declines. In this CEMAC will be following the international good practices, such as the case of Russia and Chile.
    - CEMAC can follow the example of Kuwait and adopt a formula in the medium-term towards **an intermediate basket** in CEMAC. This will minimize the fluctuations of CEMAC against all currencies.
    - It can have a **tripartite formula with equal weight to euro, dollar, and oil price** rather than a peg to the euro. While some countries use a basket based on trade shares, for CEMAC it makes more sense to be linked to the key commodity and the key anchor currencies in the world economy and for the exchange rate to vary.
    - The formula will provide a disciplining mechanism to ensure central bank compliance and **prevent major policy mistakes**.
    - The authorities can **intervene in the market** and buy and sell to keep the currency **within a certain band** and prevent speculators, especially in cases where the formula is not known
    - The new currency will **depreciate or appreciate depending on oil price and euro and dollar movements** to a new level, exerting an impact on GDP growth, the fiscal position, and the current account.
    - The monetary authorities will have a bit more flexibility to define the **long-run inflation path** in the choice and weights

of a basket, compared to the peg with the euro, where the inflation is determined by the region of the anchor currency.

- It should set **a clear timeline with an orderly transition** for movement toward that peg that allows the institutions to emerge and be ready for the transition.
- Government can also make a **transparent formula** and have a regular **communication** strategy.
- The CEMAC authorities **can renegotiate and clarify with France** the terms and conditions of the French convertibility guarantee. **A swap line with the ECB** may be a better alternative.
- CEMAC can put in place a system of **fiscal rules** in order to better manage reserves. These rules can impose some degree of constraint on fiscal policy with numerical limits on the deficit, or non-oil deficit, or some other indicator of public expenditure. Monetary policy should not be submitted to fiscal imperatives and political goals.
- Fiscal policy will have to **manage domestic government spending**. Fiscal policy becomes even more important. Fiscal expansion can be used to support post-pandemic recovery to be followed by a return to sustainability.
- CEMAC will have to manage a **risky debt trajectory** and avoid a repeat of recent history. A political economy of untargeted spending, coupled with a dependence on opaque loans may increase the debt spiral and lead to greater pressures on the exchange rate.
- CEMAC should develop the capacity to **clear trade invoices** in currencies other than the dollar given the forex challenges and the dollar rationing.
- The **regional banking commission COBAC** should modernize its approach and propose ways to reduce excess liquidity in the banking system through measures to provide financial intermediation to creditworthy companies

3. **Move toward a basket peg in the medium term for the UEMOA CFA zone**

- In the medium-term, UEMOA should move to a parity that is pegged to a basket of currencies reflecting its changing international trade. Such an intermediate regime should combine both stability with flexibility.[2] One possibility is a tripartite formula based on euro, dollars, and renmimbi that would better reflect the changing trade patterns while giving the system credibility and legitimacy, but there may be other relevant formulas.

- UEMOA can move in the long-term to a **managed float regime with daily variations** that is a flexible currency, but which allows central bank intervention regularly in the foreign exchange market. The degree of the **band of intervention** will be agreed by the BCEAO, based on its policy objectives. Most important, there will have to be a deep consensus on fiscal policy rules which will underwrite the stability of the managed float regime together with policies to address asymmetric shocks and ensure cohesion of the monetary union. As has been seen in the case of the euro, the absence of a fiscal union presents a challenge.
- UEMOA can use a flexible exchange rate for **growth and development** goals to help increase per capita income growth in the subregion by supporting productive tradable activities and by import substitution.
- As opposed to CEMAC, UEMOA is **less overvalued**, and it is not uniquely dependent on one commodity.
- This arrangement can also help **fix the balance of payments disequilibria** in excessively volatile periods.
- Excess reserves, which are beyond the 3-month threshold of pooled reserves, can also be used to build emergency funds, especially for Sahelian countries, who will suffer from low domestic revenue mobilization and inadequate aid inflows during the recovery period.
- The UEMOA eco should be managed by the BCEAO with **an inflation-targeting lite regime adapted to the regional context**.

[2] As of 2019, UEMOA imports close to 40 percent from Europe, 35 percent from Asia (mostly China), close to 8 percent from the US, and the remaining from within Africa. It exports close to 47 percent to Europe, 24 percent to Asia, 7 percent to the US, and the remaining to other African countries.

- **BCEAO's current model** for inflation forecasting should be strengthened, where the current model is intended for forecasting inflation by components, such as underlying inflation plus energy and agriculture components.
- Operating a managed float in the long run will require a liquid and **efficient foreign exchange and interbank market** that allows market participants to gather experience.
- Exit to a managed float in the long-term should be accompanied by **exchange controls to reduce overshooting** of the exchange rate and **possible temporary capital controls**.

4. **Continue discussions between UEMOA and ECOWAS on a common currency**

- Given that there is a push for a common currency in West Africa and renewed momentum under the leadership of Nigeria, the discussions between the Francophone and Anglophone UEMOA countries should be held regularly, in parallel with the revisions of **ECOWAS and UEMOA macroeconomic convergence criteria** post-pandemic.
- By pursuing a basket peg, the CFA zone can expand to the smaller Anglophone countries such as Ghana. Ghana has indicated little interest in a euro peg, and the French Treasury will not provide guarantees to ECOWAS Anglophone countries.
- However, with **Nigeria** leadership, the work will still involve building the institutional foundations for the common currency. The problem with the **ECOWAS single currency** is that the political will has to be there, and a technical solution has to be found of putting a major oil exporter in the same parity as many oil importers.
- Pursue **African Continental Free Trade Area** (AfCFTA) worth over $3.3 trillion in terms of trade as a long-term goal. This can be a major catalyst for intraregional trade as many private businessmen and investors will no longer face exchange rate risk of navigating in countries with different exchange rate regimes. However, the process will take time.
- Pursue **ECOWAS single currency** with strategy but with right institutional pillars, technical analysis, and consensus among countries. A well-functioning monetary union requires fiscal institutions and rules that can be enforced to help

members respond to asymmetric shocks. Under the leadership of the ECOWAS Commission, it will be important to accelerate the implementation of the Roadmap of the single currency program. It will be key to articulate a set of convergence criteria for adherence by expected members.

5. **Revamp reserve management policy in both zones**

- The CFA zone can rethink its **reserves adequacy framework** in light of the changes announced in UEMOA. It will be important to measure the optimal reserve size, given the managed float and the number of months of imports. Given UEMOA long history as an independent central bank, reserve management will not be complex and could also benefit from foreign technical assistance.
- Either they keep them as a form of **self-insurance and precaution** to "save for a rainy day" at a time of shocks, or they keep them to defend the exchange rate amidst speculative pressures or they keep them for nationalist or mercantilist reasons as proxy for country economic power. Countries can keep reserves in a sovereign wealth fund or public investment fund.
- In 2019, **CEMAC's reserves have reached a bit above three months of imports**, which is below the levels needed in many emerging markets and for many resource-rich economies. In the last few years, CEMAC has been supported by large flows of exceptional financing. Post-pandemic aid will be important financing, especially for CEMAC.
- For UEMOA, the IMF (2019) finds that at end of 2018, **external reserves** covered 4.3 months of prospective extra-regional imports of goods and services. Under the baseline scenario of fiscal consolidation—where member states meet the regional fiscal deficit convergence criterion of 3% of GDP from 2019 onwards and external competitiveness improves in the medium-term—the reserve import cover is projected to reach 4.8 months by 2023. However, these estimates were made before the pandemic.
- There are several changes that can occur for CEMAC. After the deal between Macron and Ouattara, BCEAO reserves can be moved from the French Treasury most likely to the

BCEAO account at the Bank of International Settlements and/or invested elsewhere. Both central banks should also invest reserves in other profitable assets with higher returns. The pooling of reserves can still be done with a managed float.

- CEMAC can learn from the **Russian experience in managing oil windfalls**. The Russians floated the currency in, with no pre-established targets for its exchange rate. Ruble has adapted to oil price movement and where a fiscal rule moves revenue from oil to above $40 a barrel to a National Wealth Fund (NWF).
- CEMAC can adopt **macroprudential policies** that strengthen the regional economy and its financial system and reduce the need for foreign exchange reserves as a precautionary countercyclical capital buffer. Oil price hedging and indexation of government bonds to oil prices can be used.

6. **Maintain the same institutional set up and configuration of countries in CEMAC and UEMOA but devise systems of fiscal transfers to the poorer countries in the zone**.

    - Years of institutional coordination have created **strong working collaboration at the technical levels** in CEMAC and UEMOA. In ASEAN in East Asia, the technical discussions among customs officials predated the political decisions.
    - Develop a mechanism of **fiscal transfers/insurance**, especially from the **coastal to the landlocked countries**. This should compensate countries facing asymmetric shocks. Under the EU project, the Commission set up structural funds, linked to initiatives, and cohesion funds, which were to be used to increase the growth capacity of the poorer member states in southern Europe.
    - An **early warning and surveillance system using good technology for monitoring food security and climate change** impact on a monthly basis must be set up in **UEMOA Commission** and **CEMAC Secretariat**. This can manage and monitor food security. Especially useful for UEMOA, such a system should alert regional authorities to food-deficit areas in the respective countries and encourage national authorities to create a system of food stocks and distribution systems.

7. **Establish a clear swap line providing emergency finance and liquidity to CEMAC** .

    - Several central banks in developed economies, including the and the European Central Bank, have for decades maintained **bilateral swap facilities**, which help in situations of market stress and liquidity crisis. Swap facilities would allow a supply of currency available for overnight and short-term lending only.
    - CEMAC can develop **a swap line with the US FED or ECB** enabling the regional bank to access foreign currency liquidity. This agreement can complement or replace the French guarantee arrangement and help mitigate domestic financial instability during any transition to a new exchange rate regime.
    - **A swap facility**, that would be multilateral in nature, overseen by the IMF could ensure a similar safety net for developing country central banks. Recent example: Qatar has offered **financial support** to Turkey's central bank, expanding a currency-swap agreement to $15 billion.

8. **Establish currency printing facilities in CEMAC and UEMOA**

    - It would be good from a **sovereignty perspective** to start printing denominations of the new currency in Francophone Africa. It will increase the currency's prestige domestically.
    - The faces on the notes could represent national heroes from UEMOA and CEMAC history.
    - There will be **seignorage** (profit made by BCEAO or BEAC by issuing currency, in terms of the difference between the face value of coins and their production costs).
    - It will be good to issue many **smaller denomination notes** as money will be seen by the common person and support their aspirational vision.

9. **Develop an annual forum for central bank cooperation**.

    - There should be **regular meetings** between BCEAO, BEAC, and regional African Banks, especially Morocco, Egypt, Nigeria, and South Africa.

- There should also be **regular meetings with Asian central banks**. These meetings can be a great opportunity for Asian bankers to share the operational and practical experience of moving from fixed exchange rates to managed floats and the challenges in forex management especially in times of volatile capital flows. BEAC and BCEAO can benefit from the best international expertise in the developing and emerging world.

10. **Develop a long-term capital market**.

- BCEAO and BEAC can learn from the experience of other countries on ways to develop the **interbank market** and **longer term capital market** to be able to create more financial depth. At present, the model is bank-centric and focused on sovereign bond issuance. Government borrowing in UEMOA and CEMAC is crowding out lending to the private sector.
- It will be important to assess the regulatory legislation and **streamline approval processes for corporate bond issuance** in CEMAC and UEMOA.
- There can be discussions on developing a corporate bond market by **bringing together corporates, institutional investors, and regulators**.

References

International Monetary Fund. 2019. West African Economic and Monetary Union (UEMOA): Staff Report on the Common Policies in Support of Member Countries Reform Programs. Washington, DC.

Razafimahefa, Ivohasina. 2012. Exchange Rate Pass-Through in Sub-Saharan African Economies and Its Determinants. IMF Working Papers 12/141, International Monetary Fund.

CHAPTER 35

Restructure CFA Zone Debt

Another important challenge during the post-recovery in the CFA zone will be to address the rising debt levels. These have been accelerated since the pandemic. The large government spending to invest in public healthcare as well as stimulate the economies will push public debt to nearly 100% of global economic output in 2020. The combination of larger fiscal deficits, exchange rate depreciations, and the lower GDP growth path is having a ripple effect on debt-to-GDP globally. The concern in CEMAC and UEMOA, together with other parts of the developing world, is a risk of growing debt distress and potential sovereign debt defaults.

In the CFA zone, external debt increased from 29.1% of GDP in 2019 to 34.1% of GDP in 2020, with CEMAC increasing from 29.1% of GDP to 36.1% of GDP, and UEMOA going from 29.0 to 33.0% in the same time period (IMF 2020). According to the IMF analysis, government revenue in 2020 is expected to fall below pre-COVID-19 projections by about 2.3 percentage points of GDP; the combined effects of revenue shortfall and higher debt service is increasing the debt service-to-revenue ratio from about 22% under pre-COVID-19 projections to about 27% under current projections. The problem is especially serious for oil exporters.

According to IMF–World Bank debt sustainability analyses, many of the low-income countries in the world at risk of debt distress, while 11 Sub-Saharan African countries are currently at high risk of debt distress.

A. Zafar, *The CFA Franc Zone*,
https://doi.org/10.1007/978-3-030-71006-4_35

In CEMAC, the problem is more serious, with the Republic of Congo in clear debt distress, while countries like Cameroon, Chad, and the Central African Republic remain at high risk. In UEMOA, the countries are at more moderate risk of debt distress, including Senegal and Cote d'Ivoire. Several of the CFA countries—especially Senegal, Cote d'Ivoire, and Cameroon—have issued expensive foreign currency bonds and face challenges repaying them.[1] In spite of very low global interest rates, the borrowing costs for most developing countries have risen with credit spreads on emerging market sovereign bonds more than doubling to more than 500 basis points. The CFA countries face expensive repayments on bonds to investors, frequently paying interest rates between 8 and 9% recently.

Another factor that has changed compared to previous debt crises is the changing role of China, which now accounts for more than 60% of global bilateral debt. Zafar (2007) has noted a strong and growing relationship between China and Sub-Saharan Africa in terms of macroeconomic, trade, investment, and aid links, partly fueled by Chinese search for natural resources to support its industrialization, especially oil. China's economic ascendance over the past two decades has generated ripple effects in Sub-Saharan Africa. In the first systematic evaluation of Chinese lending, a recent dataset comprising 100 Chinese loan contracts with 24 low and middle-income countries, a Center for Global Development Study (2021) finds confidentiality clauses that prevent the borrower from revealing the term of the loan; informal collateral arrangements that benefit Chinese lenders over other creditors; and significant leeway for China to cancel loans and accelerate repayments. Given Chinese increased exposure, especially in the Republic of Congo, this debt situation will be difficult to manage multilaterally.

Horn, Reinhart, and Trebesch (2020) argue that in a world of recession, depressed commodity prices, collapsing cross-border trade, and a flight to safety in financial markets, there is the possibility of a replay of

[1] Senegal had financed infrastructure development by issuing Eurobonds, but which are financed at rates between 5 and 10%, significantly above other emerging markets. Olabisi and Stern (2015) find that sovereigns in Sub-Saharan Africa paid a premium of 2.9 percentage points over the rest of the world, or an extra $2.2 billion between 2006 and 2014. This has been considered by some to be the African premium as African countries are perceived to be riskier borrowers even though almost all African borrowers have made timely payments on their Eurobonds.

the 1930s and 1980s debt crises. Developing a comprehensive and transparent new dataset on China's overseas lending, they show that many developing countries are much more indebted to China than previously known and that Chinese loans have three characteristics. First, almost all of China's overseas lending is official, making China by far the world's largest official creditor. Second, most of China's lending is on commercial terms, with average interest rates close to those in private capital markets. Third, debt to China has been accumulating at a rapid pace in these countries. In some countries, such as the Republic of Congo, Chinese debt at more than $2 billion is close to one-third of total external debt. More than 50% of Chinese lending is "hidden," with implications on policy surveillance, risk pricing, and debt sustainability analysis.

Policy Response

In light of the crisis, there has been a flurry of international activities centered on ways to reduce international debt. Under the G20's Debt Service Suspension Initiative, the participating institutions announced the first temporary suspension of debt payments, with 43 countries out of 73 that are eligible signed up. These partial debt service suspensions were offered to low-income developing countries eligible to the World Bank's International Development Association (IDA), and ambitious bailout packages were sent. There is also an ongoing debate on the extension of a freeze in debt service payments offered by G20 countries to the poorest nations to go into next year.

However, there have been four challenges in the discussion. First, multilateral and commercial debt is excluded from debt service suspension for all countries. Secondly, many middle-income countries at risk are excluded from the initiative. Third, some countries did not participate in the discussions because they were concerned that ratings agencies and bond markets would penalize them with ratings downgrade. Finally, some countries have been reluctant to transparently open all their books to the global creditor community, including the full stock of the debt to China. The discussion has also been shifting from debt suspension to debt cancellation, but there has been some reluctance of both China and private creditors to favor debt haircuts. In April 2021, the IMF has discussed a possible $650 billion SDR allocation to member countries to address the debt problems worsened by the pandemic. In this context, there are several paths forward for debt restructuring.

- The countries should update their debt sustainability analyses in coordination with the international financial institutions.
- They can continue to negotiate with both official and private-sector creditors on restructuring their debt service payments.
- The countries must continue to negotiate with China, which is emerging as one of the largest bilateral creditors to the CFA zone.
- The countries should sequence their exchange rate reforms in parallel with the debt restructuring so that a depreciation of the currency does not lead to an increase in interest payments.

References

Horn, Sebastian, Carmen Reinhart, and Christoph Trebesch. 2020. China's Overseas Lending. Kiel Institute for the World Economy ISSN 1862–1155.

International Monetary Fund. 2020, October. Regional Economic Outlook: Sub-Saharan Africa, Washington, DC.

Olabisi, Michael, and Howard Stein. 2015. Sovereign Bond Issues: Do African Countries Pay More to Borrow? *Journal of African Trade* 2 (2015): 87–109.

Zafar, Ali. 2007. The Growing Relationship Between China and Sub-Saharan Africa Macroeconomic, Trade, Investment and Aid Links. *The World Bank Research Observer* 22: 103–130.

CHAPTER 36

Strengthen Supply Chains and Reduce Transport Costs

One of the main impacts of the pandemic has been a challenge to global supply chains. Firms have been reluctant to venture out from their borders at least in the short term. It has been hard for many countries to procure raw materials due to the restrictions and shutdowns. Covid has exposed the fragilities and vulnerability of global supply chains and accentuated the overdependence on China, including for items such as masks, gloves, and PPPE outfits.

In an interview, Carmen Reinhart, Chief Economist of the World Bank has recently called the pandemic "another nail in the coffin of globalization" and argued that the pandemic will create challenges:

> Globalization took two strikes with the 2008-09 crisis — Brexit and the US-China trade war. The pandemic has thrown a third. People will be more mistrustful of crossing national borders, many firms are reorienting their global supply chains inward, and global investors may increase their home bias as debt difficulties among sovereigns increase. Unfortunately, the clear commitment by governments to seek international co-operation (or, at least, co-ordination) needed to stem the tide of de-globalization is lacking at the moment.[1]

[1] https://www.bloomberg.com/news/articles/2020-05-21/reinhart-says-pandemic-is-last-nail-in-globalization-s-coffin.

A. Zafar, *The CFA Franc Zone*,
https://doi.org/10.1007/978-3-030-71006-4_36

The World Bank's World Development Report 2020 notes that international trade has expanded rapidly after 1990, powered by the rise of global value chains (GVCs) and fragmentation of production across countries, leading to poor countries gaining from trade. However, since the global financial crisis of 2008, the growth of trade has been sluggish, and the expansion of GVCs has slowed, also threatened by the rise in automation and growing conflict and protectionist sentiment in larger countries. With the pandemic, there is evidence of further splintering in GVCs due to the suspension in international trade and the potential movement away from China as many firms relocate production.

Paradoxically, the disruption in international trade and global supply chains could help catalyze regional and continent-wide integration efforts in Sub-Saharan Africa, including the CFA zone. For many years, Africa has had fragmented markets and high transit costs. However, in a major move, in March 2018, 44 African heads of framework to establish a single continental market for goods and services, with free movement of capital and business travelers. This framework came to be known as the African Continental Free Trade Area (AfCFTA).

The declaration was noteworthy for four reasons. First, it was the first pan-African initiative of its type. Second, it was a significant effort at resolving the barriers that are preventing goods and services from moving across national borders. The Chief Economist of Africa Exim Bank, one of the rising financial institutions in Sub-Saharan Africa, notes that the continental free trade area will establish a market of 1.2 billion people with a combined GDP of $2.5 trillion and combined consumer and business spending of more than $4 trillion, making the continent a global player. Besides increasing market efficiency and reducing costs of doing business, the AfCFTA can ease trade and investment flows and shift the composition and direction of foreign investment (Fofack 2018).

The freeing of the CFA exchange rate in UEMOA and CEMAC and delinking from euro will allow the zone to increase trade with its neighbors and reduce expensive transit costs (Fig. 36.1). Since Nigeria is 75% of regional West African GDP ($397 billion in Nigeria compared to $43 billion in Cote d'Ivoire), the smaller countries of the CFA can move toward a more flexible currency to increase trade flows with the Anglophone countries, all of whom have a managed float regime. CEMAC can improve links with East Africa and capitalize on the growing dynamism there. There is already a significant cross-border inflow of goods from the CFA zone into Nigeria, much of which is not recorded in official data

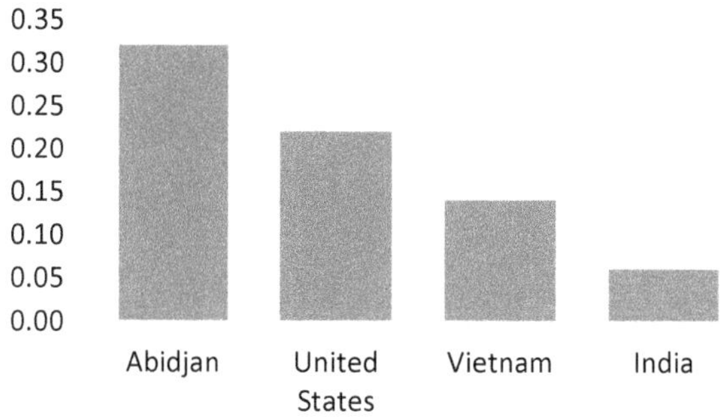

Fig. 36.1 Container transport cost (cents per ton-kilometer) 2019 (*Source* IFC [2020])

sources. Given the large number of Francophone landlocked economies, it will be important for these economies to get more integrated in the regional markets.

In this context, the CFA policymakers must undertake all necessary reforms to reduce trade barriers and administrative hurdles and help move toward a freer economic and trading space. Key reforms include:

- Rationalization of tariffs according to the common external tariff (TEC)
- Harmonization of tariff and tax rates across the UEMOA and CEMAC economic space
- Reduction of administrative hurdles for traders and reduction in checkpoints along key regional corridors
- Limiting tariff exemptions and phasing out surcharges,
- Stronger customs administration with better monitoring of products and rules of origin
- Improve data collection on trade flows and country regulations.

References

Fofack, Hippolyte. 2018. A Competitive Africa, Finance and Development, IMF, December, 55(4). Washington, DC.

International Finance Corporation. 2020. Creating Markets in Cote d'Ivoire: Mobilizing the Private Sector in Support of Economic Transformation in Côte d'Ivoire. Washington, DC.

CHAPTER 37

Support Small and Medium-Sized Enterprises and Gender-Sensitive Policies

The CFA countries can provide a more supportive environment for firms. All the leading firms of the CFA zone have been impacted by the crisis, but it is the small and medium enterprises (SME's) in the CFA zone that have less than few months in cash reserves. Before the pandemic, according to Enterprise Surveys, more than 22% of SSA firms list access to finance as the principal obstacle to their expansion (Fig. 37.1). This is followed by electricity, informal competition, and political instability. During the recovery, the SME's can play a role as they account for more than 90% of the firms in the CFA zone and close to three-quarters of the jobs.

A recent survey of firms by the Inter-Patronal Grouping of Cameroon (Gicam), conducted in April 2020 on a sample of 100 local companies presents some interesting insights.[1] The key findings are:

- 92% of the sampled companies declared that the COVID-19 pandemic has had a very negative (52%) or negative (40%) impact on their activities.

[1] https://www.businessincameroon.com/economy/2704-10244-cameroon-coronavirus-has-a-very-negative-impact-on-61-of-smes-and-27-of-large-enterprises-gicam.

A. Zafar, *The CFA Franc Zone*,
https://doi.org/10.1007/978-3-030-71006-4_37

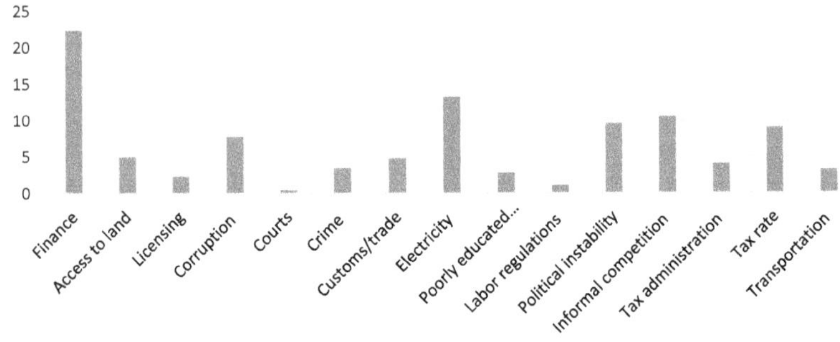

Fig. 37.1 Obstacles for Firms in Sub-Saharan Africa (2010–2019) (*Source* World Bank dataset, Enterprise Surveys, author calculations)

- SMEs and service companies have been the most affected. The proportion of SMEs reporting a very negative impact is higher (61%) than that of large companies (27%).
- Similarly, 58% of service companies reported being very negatively impacted by the pandemic compared to 38% of industrial companies.
- 40% of the companies declared that their production is directly affected by the pandemic, but the proportion conceals strong disparities.
- For large companies, 50% claim their production is directly affected, compared with 36% of SMEs.

In the CFA zone, large firms have access to international financing at low rates, including from parent companies or large foreign banks. SME's by contrast, whether in Cameroon, or Senegal, or Mali, obtain their investment from self-financing or family or network loans. In the CFA zone, many financial institutions appear hesitant to lend to smaller manufacturing enterprises and retail traders due to lack of familiarity with these firms; stringent regulations of the BCEAO and BEAC; the lack of a credit bureau; collateral requirements in an environment with insecure land tenure arrangements; and the high cost of using notaries to secure asset guarantees.

Moreover, there is a limited capacity among entrepreneurs to pull together bankable projects for presentation to financial institutions. Some

SMEs are very well-managed and have shown strong flexibility and adaptability during the crisis, while others have not had the right vision or cash to survive. Anecdotal evidence reveals stories of heroic entrepreneurs who have interesting innovations, including PPE equipment and testing solutions. Domestic funding for start-ups and new ideas was absent. The well-known Institute Pasteur of Dakar received seed funding for its COVID-19 testing kit was obtained not from the BCEAO but from the UK government and the Gates Foundation.

The banks in both CFA zones frequently suffer from excess liquidity as they are profitable and invest in either large and successful companies or they profit from holding domestic and regional government debt. As BCEAO and BEAC are trying to converge to Basel II and Basel III prudential frameworks to strengthen banking sector resilience, the interest in SME lending is not a high priority. However, over time, the Central Banks will have to develop a more coordinated SME policy, including supporting collateral registries, credit scoring, training for entrepreneurs, and financial innovations.

However, there are multiple SME financing schemes and guarantee funds. International Finance Corporation partnered with ECOBANK in 2015 to create a $110 million risk-sharing facility to provide finance for small- and medium-sized enterprises in fragile and conflict-affected states in West and Central Africa. Based on a model of equal risk-sharing, IFC and ECOBANK have started supporting many of the SMEs that were bypassed by the big banks.

Another challenge in the CFA zone is the gender dimension. Women have been hit particularly hard by the pandemic, given they disproportionately work in high risk sectors, with 740 million women in the informal sector (ILO 2020). There is a lack of capital for female entrepreneurs and women businesses in the CFA zone as there is in much of Sub-Saharan Africa, and there is a large unmet need for finance. In the CFA zone, less than 25% of females have access to a bank account. The innovative entrepreneurialism in East Africa—especially Kenya and Zambia—is less pronounced in the CFA zone, according to both anecdotal evidence and small surveys. Of the top 100 countries in the World Economic Forum Gender Gap Report 2015, only Senegal and Cameroon are in the top 100, compared to many of the Anglophone countries. Rwanda (6), South Africa (17), and Kenya (48) are significantly better than the best Francophone performer, Senegal (72). Other problems:

- The COVID-19 pandemic has hit women around the globe hard. In Francophone Africa, more than 90% of firms are SMEs, and more than 50% of the workers are female, women have borne a disproportionate share.
- Women are absent in the nascent technology space. In 2018, only 5% of the $1.2 billion raised for tech start-ups in Africa went to French-speaking countries, with Senegal leading. It has been following Tunisia to legislate a start-up act—a law providing tax breaks to innovative new businesses in areas from agriculture to mobile banking, with a particular targeting of young women to help them develop as tech entrepreneurs.[2]

One possibility is to use fintech lenders to promote new lending models considering the advances in financial technology that target women. Given the advanced analytics at their disposal, many new fintech companies can provide credit scoring and due to necessary due diligence on company creditworthiness in a fraction of time that has been used by traditional banks. The experience of MyBank in China which uses digital technology and sophisticated algorithms to target businesses that are bypassed by banks may be a usable model.

Reference

International Labor Organization (ILO). 2020. *The COVID-19 Response: Getting Gender Equality Right for a Better Future for Women at Work*. Geneva: ILO Policy Brief.

[2] https://www.weforum.org/agenda/2020/02/senegals-female-business-west-africa/.

CHAPTER 38

A More Climate Friendly CFA Zone

As the world moves toward a period of greater climate change, it will be important to put into place policies that address both climate mitigation and climate adaptation. It is clear that Africa will be one of the continents that is most vulnerable to the world's changing weather patterns. A new report, The State of the Climate in Africa 2019, a multi-agency publication coordinated by the World Meteorological Organization (WMO), notes that increasing temperatures and sea levels, changing precipitation patterns and more extreme weather are threatening human health and safety, food and water security and socioeconomic development in Africa.[1]

Climate-induced shocks can affect all dimensions of life—food supply, health, and livelihoods. A combination of longer dry seasons and shorter wet spells may alter the African ecosystem. Droughts, leading to food shortages and price hikes, may exacerbate food vulnerabilities. Since Africa is not a large producer of greenhouse gases, it will be more active in relation to climate adaptation rather than climate mitigation.

Several innovations and promising areas that can be used to address climate change include:

- Development of more sophisticated climate models that closely examine the impact of climate change on the CFA zone. Given

[1] Climate Change Is an Increasing Threat to Africa | UNFCCC.

A. Zafar, *The CFA Franc Zone*,
https://doi.org/10.1007/978-3-030-71006-4_38

the growing risk of Sahelian famines and turbulent thunderstorms across the Central African eco-forest, the models can provide more granularity and information for policymakers trying to plan for the future.

- Greater investment in relevant analytical work can help African policymakers plan for the future. Using ground measurements, a recent study has quantified groundwater recharge rates across the whole of Africa, averaged over a fifty-year period, which will help to identify the sustainability of water resources for African nations.
- Effective governance and investment decisions need to be informed by reliable data, not only about where groundwater exists, but also the rate at which groundwater is replenished.
- There is the promising Great Green Wall for the Sahara and the Sahel Initiative (GGWSSI), a pan-African program launched in 2008 by the UN and African Union (AU). This program has received close to $15 billion and is an attempt to restore degrading land in the Sahara, save biological diversity, create green jobs, and build resilience of the Sahelian people. It can also help boost food security and support local communities to adapt to climate change.
- Introduction of Israeli-style drip irrigation, which will help support small-scale agriculture, and replace the manual irrigation with a solar-powered pump that delivers water to drip irrigation systems from the rivers. The drip irrigation is envisaged to reduce water usage while increasing crop yield, quality, and consistency.
- The African Development Bank's desert-to-power initiative can help develop 10 gigawatts of solar energy and supply 250 million people with green, clean electricity by 2025. The idea is to turn the Sahel region into a renewable powerhouse and harness its solar potential to create the world's largest solar zone. The intended beneficiaries of the initiative are more than 250 million people across the Sahel. Solar power, which requires constant sunlight, abundant land, and good technical infrastructure, is promising in the Sahel.

Annex

See Fig. A.1 and Tables A.1 and A.2.

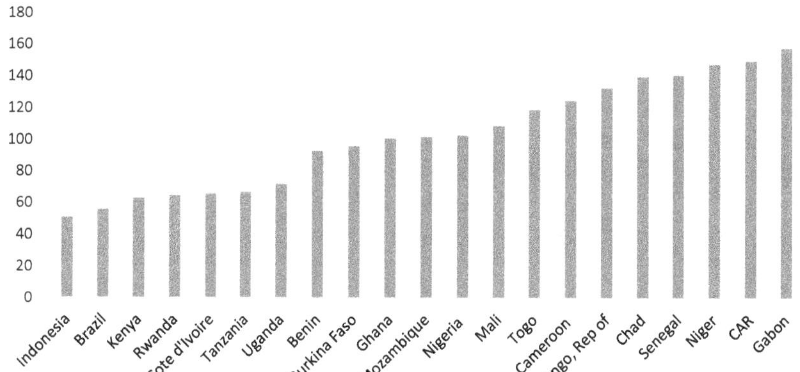

Fig. A.1 Logistics Performance Index (LPI) (*Source* World Bank)

A. Zafar, *The CFA Franc Zone*,
https://doi.org/10.1007/978-3-030-71006-4

Table A.1 Studies on the misalignment of the CFA Franc

Author	*Methodology*	*Key finding*
Zafar (2005b)	Purchasing power parity (PPP) and time-series econometrics using Engle-Granger and unit roots	Finds a modest appreciation using a relative PPP-based methodology to estimate the degree of misalignment of the CFA franc since the introduction of the euro in 1999. Between 1999 and 2005, the real effective exchange rate (REER) appreciated by close to 8% in the WAEMU and 7% in the CEMAC, influenced by the volatility in the euro–dollar bilateral exchange rate and the monetary policies in the two subzones
Abdih and Tsangaridies (2006)	Fundamental equilibrium exchange rate approach and the Johansen cointegration methodology	In both the CEMAC and the WAEMU, REERs were broadly in line with their long-run equilibrium values, and the fundamentals account for most of the fluctuation in the REERs, with clear relations between the exchange rate and the terms of trade, government consumption, and productivity improvements
Couharde et al. (2011)	Panel cointegration techniques and an error correction model	The real appreciation of effective exchange rates in the CFA zone in the 2000s had not translated, by 2007, into a real overvaluation comparable with that occurring before the devaluation of the CFA franc in 1994. However, some countries are exceptions, indicating a strong heterogeneity within the CFA zone

Author	*Methodology*	*Key finding*
Gnansounou and Verdier-Chouchane (2012)	Macroanalytical framework to calculate the equilibrium REER relative to the equilibrium value	In 2001–2011, there was a tendency toward overvaluation of the CFA franc; the misalignment curve of the CFA seems closely linked to the euro–dollar exchange rate except in the case of price increases in major commodities exported by each country. In 2011, half the CFA zone countries (Benin, Burkina Faso, the Republic of Congo, Equatorial Guinea, Guinea-Bissau, Mali, and Niger) were in a situation of real overvaluation
IMF (2015b)	The EBA-lite current account model	Compares the underlying current account balance with the model norm. This model shows 8.9% overvaluation of the REER in UEMOA in 2015 driven by productivity differences
IMF (2019a)	The EBA-lite current account model for CEMAC	This model suggests an overvaluation in CEMAC of 11.4% with the 2019 current account deficit estimated at 2.5% of GDP against a norm of 0.3% GDP surplus

Table A.2 CFA zone policies and COVD-19 pandemic

Policy Area	*Measure*	*Operational details*
Macroeconomic Policy	• Use IMF SDR allocation of another $1 trillion to bolster CEMAC and UEMOA reserves and obtain balance of payments support • Extend existing programs and WBG and AFDB can provide more budget support	Important for countries to leverage international assistance in ways to shield economies from macro and trade shocks
Fiscal Management	• Use fiscal policy to provide stimulus and emergency lifelines for firms and individuals • Increase fiscal allocations to the health sector • Support wages of workers	Focus on emergency relief, including for firms and individuals
Monetary Policy	• BEAC and BCEAO can ease countercyclical capital buffer and support liquidity for the economy • Support banks in continuing to finance households and corporates experiencing difficulties	Provision of liquidity needed to prevent firm collapse and support of private sector
Debt Environment	• Provide debt relief for CFA countries that are IDA • Encourage these countries to prepare a mid-term debt management strategy	Important to ensure that debt management reflects sustainability parameters
Health and epidemiology	• Increase budget allocation for health sector, including equipment, gloves, and PPEs • Provide financing for front-line health workers via supplemental budgets • Develop effective system of contact tracing	Work closely with international experts given the large experience in containing coronavirus

(continued)

Table A.2 (continued)

Policy Area	*Measure*	*Operational details*
Firm liquidity	• Support measures to promote liquidity for SMEs • Central Banks policy cuts can encourage interest rate subsidies to help firms • Encourage loan repayment deferrals • Support female entrepreneurs and women-run SMEs	Focus should be on firm survival, preventing bankruptcy, and avoiding worker layoffs
Social protection	• Identify priority list of workers and families most impacted by the crisis • Develop and strengthen social safety nets using fiscal transfers for vulnerable populations	It will be important to develop a strong administrative regime to ensure good governance of funds

Box A.1 The CFA and the Eurozone: Similarities and Differences

The CFA is pegged to the euro, which has a very interesting history, although the euro is a much younger currency. Before the euro, the CFA was pegged to the French Franc. The euro was created in 1992 by the Treaty of Maastricht (Netherlands), where the foundation of the European project of a common currency and cooperation framework was defined. The treaty was signed by 12 members (Belgium, Denmark, France, Germany, Greece, Ireland, Italy, Luxembourg, Netherlands, Portugal, Spain, and the United Kingdom). The euro was the culmination of a long process that began decades earlier with the creation of a customs union, led by France and Germany. The European Commission has pushed for the idea, but it took years to materialize.

The treaty defined the monetary arrangements of the zone. The Treaty established the European Central Bank (ECB) whose main mandate was to protect the currency and maintain price stability. In conception, the euro inherited from the Germans a strong focus on reining inflation. Germany has also always favored a rules-based approach, while France has opted for more flexibility. The tensions between these two approaches have characterized the euro debates until today.

The three stages of the Maastricht treaty were: introduction of free capital movements (1990–1993); increased cooperation between central banks and greater harmonization of policies (1994–1998); and gradual introduction of the euro (1999–present). The Maastricht Treaty established a set of rules of convergence criterion around inflation, public debt, interest rate, and exchange rate. It also provided for rules for new entrants. A Stability and Growth Pact was signed in 1997 to ensure that countries followed prudent fiscal and budgetary policies. The goal was a deep economic and political integration. However, the euro crisis, partly prompted by differences between the richer Northern countries and the relatively poorer Southern countries, has led to some delay in the European integration project and sparked populist resentment and demands for restoration of national sovereignty in some of the countries.

There are many similarities and differences between the euro and the CFA. First, they are both regional groups with a common currency between its members. The euro is pegged to no currency, while the CFA is pegged to the euro. Second, there are powerful countries and laggard countries in both arrangements. Third, there are associated institutions meant to provide greater political coordination between the countries. Fourth, there are few mechanisms for individual countries to adjust to terms of trade shocks. Fifth, interest rate policy is meant to keep inflation low. However, the CFA has much less intraregional trade, weaker coordinating institutions, and no system of fiscal transfers from the richer to the poorer countries.

References

Abbott, Philip. 2007. Distortions to Agricultural Incentives in Cote d'Ivoire, Agricultural Distortions Working Paper 46, December 2007, Washington, DC.

Abdih and Tsangaridies. 2006. FEER for the CFA Franc. IMF Working Paper WP/06/236, International Monetary Fund, Washington, DC.

African Development Bank. 2000. African Development Bank, Bank Group Policy on Good Governance Abidjan.

Africa Report. 2012. https://www.theafricareport.com/7810/africa-why-francophones-are-lagging-behind-anglophones/.

Agbor, Julius Agbor. 2012. The Future of the CEMAC CFA Franc. Global Views Policy Paper 2012–06 (December), Brookings Institution, Washington, DC.

Agenor, Pierre-Richard. 2005. The Macroeconomics of Poverty Reduction. *Manchester School* 73 (4): 369–434.

Akum, Fontch, and Zachary Donnerfeld. 2015. Gathering Storm Clouds: Political and Economic Uncertainty in Central Africa, Institute of Security Studies.

Alfani, Federica, Andrew Dabalen, Peter Fisker, and Vasco Molini. 2015. Can We Measure Resilience? A Proposed Method and Evidence from Countries in the Sahel. World Bank Policy Research Working Paper 7170.

Alfani, Federica, Andrew Dabalen, Peter Fisker, and Vasco Molini. 2019. Vulnerability to Stunting in the West African Sahel. *Food Policy*, Elsevier 83: 39–47.

Arbache, Jorge Saba, and John Page. 2008. Hunting for Leopards: Long Run Country Income Dynamics in Africa. Policy Research Working Paper Series 4715, The World Bank.

A. Zafar, *The CFA Franc Zone*,
https://doi.org/10.1007/978-3-030-71006-4

Boccara, Bruno, and Shanta Devarajan. 1993. Determinants of Inflation in Franc Zone Countries in Africa. World Bank Policy Research Working Paper 1197, Washington, DC.

Boughton, M. 1991. The CFA Franc Zone: Currency Union and Monetary Standard. IMF Working Paper (WP/91/133), Washington, DC.

Bourguignon, F., J. de Melo, and A. Suwa. 1989. Distributional Effects of Adjustment Policies: Simulations for Two Archetype Economies. World Bank (Background Paper for 1990 World Development Report.

Cabrillac, Bruno, and Emmanuel Rocher. 2013. Les Perspectives des Unions Monétaires Africaines. *Revue d'économie financière* 110 (2): 99.

Calvo, Guillermo A., and Carmen M. Reinhart, 2000. Fear of Floating. Working Paper 7993, November 2000.

Clark, Peter, and Ronald MacDonald. 1999. Exchange Rates and Economic Fundamentals: A Methodological Comparison of Beers and Feers. Recent Economic Thought Series, Springer.

Clingendael. 2020. Decentralisation and Inclusive Governance in Fragile Settings: Lessons for the Sahel, Netherlands Institute for International Relations, CRU Policy Brief.

Collier, Paul. 2007. *The Bottom Billion: Why the Poorest Countries Are Failing and What Can Be Done About It*. Oxford: Oxford University Press.

Cossé, Stepahen, Johannes Mueller, Jean Le Dem, and Jean A. P. Clément, 1996. Aftermath of the CFA Franc Devaluation. IMF Occasional Papers 138, International Monetary Fund.

Couharde, Cécile, Issiaka Coulibaly, and Olivier Damette. 2011. Misalignments and Dynamics of Real Exchange Rates in the CFA Franc Zone. Economix Working Paper 2011-28, Paris.

Coulibaly, Issiaka. 2014. Competitiveness and Growth within the CFA Franc Zone: Does the Switch to the Euro Matter? *International Economics* 139: 1–18.

Dell, Melissa, Benjamin Jones, and Benjamin Olken. 2012. Temperature Shocks and Economic Growth: Evidence from the Last Half Century. *American Economic Journal: Macroeconomics* 4 (3): 66–95.

Demery, Lionel, and Lyn Squire. 1996. Macroeconomic Adjustment and Poverty in Africa: An Emerging Picture. *World Bank Research Observer* 11 (1): 39–59.

Dessus, Sébastien, and Aristomene Varoudakis. 2013. Protecting Public Investment against Shocks in the West African Economic and Monetary Union: Options for Fiscal Rules and Risk Sharing. Policy Research Working Paper 6562, World Bank, Washington, DC.

Devarajan, Shanta. 1992. Preserving the Union: Lessons of History, Theory and Thirty Years of Experience, speech delivered at 30th Anniversary of UEMOA in Dakar, Senegal.

Devarajan, Shantayanan, and Jaime de Melo. 1987. Adjustment with a Fixed Exchange Rate: Cameroon, Cote d'Ivoire, and Senegal. *World Bank Economic Review* 1 (3): 447–487.

Devarajan, Shantayanan, and Dani Rodrik. 1991. Do the Benefits of Fixed Exchange Rates Outweigh Their Costs? The Franc Zone in Africa. NBER Working Papers 3727, National Bureau of Economic Research, Inc.

Devarajan, Shantayanan, and Raju Singh. 2012. Government Failure and Poverty Reduction in the CEMAC. In *Oil Wealth in Central Africa*, ed. Bernardin Akitoby and Sharmini Coorey. Washington, DC: IMF.

Diffenbaugh, Noah, and Marshall Burke. 2019. Global Warming Has Increased Global Economic Inequality. Proceedings of the National Academy of Sciences, edited by Ottmar Edenhofer, Potsdam Institute for Climate Impact Research, Potsdam, Germany, and accepted by Editorial Board Member Hans J. Schellnhuber March 22, 2019.

Dinh, Hinh, Jobs, 2017. Industrialization, and Globalization. OCP Policy Center, Morocco.

Dorosh, Paul A., and David E. Sahn. 2000. A General Equilibrium Analysis of the Effect of Macroeconomic Adjustment on Poverty in Africa. *Journal of Policy Modeling* 22 (6): 753–776.

Duttagupta, Rupa, Cem Karacadag, and Gilda C Fernandez. 2006. Moving to a Flexible Exchange Rate: How, When, and How Fast? IMF Economic Issues 38, International Monetary Fund.

Elbadawi, Ibrahim, and Eman Refaat. 2015. Competitive Real Exchange Rates are Good for the Poor: Evidence from Egyptian Household Surveys. Working Papers 966, Economic Research Forum, Revised November 2015.

Engelbrecht, F., Adegoke, J., Bopape, M.-J., Naidoo, M., Garland, R., Thatcher, M., McGregor,J., Katzfey,J.,Werner, M., and Ichoku, C. 2015. Projections of Rapidly Rising Surface Temperatures Over Africa Under Low Mitigation. *Environmental Research Letters* 10 (8). 085004. http://www.csir.co.za/nre/coupled_land_water_and_marine_ecosystems/pdfs/CCAM_African_temps.pdf.

European Commission for Africa. 2020. COVID-19: Protecting African Lives and Economies, Addis Ababa.

FAO. 2006. *Indicateurs de l'Alimentation et de l'Agriculture — Pays: Sénégal*. www.fao.org/es/ESS/fr/compendium_2006/pdf/SEN_ESS_F.pdf.

FAO. 2012. Why Has Africa Become a Net Food Importer? Explaining African Agricultural and Food Trade Deficits. In *FAO Trade and Markets Division*, ed. Manitra A. Rakotoarisoa, Massimo Iafrate, and Marianna Paschali. Rome.

Fofack, Hippolyte. 2018. A Competitive Africa, Finance and Development, IMF, December, 55(4). Washington, DC.

Frankel, Jeffrey A. 2005. Peg the Export Price Index: A Proposed Monetary Regime for Small Countries. *Journal of Policy Modeling, Elsevier* 27 (4): 495–508.

Frankel, Jeffrey, 2012. Choosing an Exchange Rate Regime. The Handbook of Exchange Rates.

Frankel, Jeffrey. 2017. Systematic Managed Floating. Harvard Kennedy School Paper Written for 4th Asian Monetary Policy Forum, Singapore.

Freund, Caroline, and Martha Denisse Pierola. 2008. Export Surges: The Power of a Competitive Currency. Policy Research Working Paper 4750, World Bank, Washington, DC.

Ghura, Dhaneshwar, Kangni R Kpodar, and Raju J Singh. 2009. Financial Deepening in the CFA Franc Zone; The Role of Institutions. IMF Working Papers 09/113, International Monetary Fund.

Gnansounou, S., and A. Verdier-Chouchane. 2012. Mésalignement du taux de change effectif réel: Quand faudra-t-il de nouveau dévaluer le franc CFA? Working paper series 166, December, African Development Bank, Tunis.

Golub, Stephen, and Ahmadou Aly Mbaye. 2020. Removing Impediments to Export-Led growth in Senegal: Groundnuts, Fishing, Textiles, Fruits, and Vegetables. Washington, DC. Brookings. https://www.brookings.edu/blog/africa-in-focus/2020/09/01/removing-impediments-to-export-led-growth-in-senegal-groundnuts-fishing-textiles-fruits-and-vegetables/.

Gulde, Anne, and Charalambos Tsangarides. 2008. *The CFA Franc Zone: Common Currency, Uncommon Challenges*. Washington, DC: International Monetary Fund.

Guzman, Martin, Jose Antonio Ocampo, and Joseph E. Stiglitz. 2018. Real Exchange Rate Policies for Economic Development. *World Development, Elsevier* 110: 51–62.

Guilllaumont, P., and Guillaumont Jeanneney, S. 2017. La Zone franc en perspective, Revue.Fin du franc CFA en Afrique de l'Ouest, quel avenir pour l'éco? FERDI.

Ha, Jongrim, M. Ayhan Kose, and Franziska L. Ohnsorge. 2019. Understanding Inflation in Emerging and Developing Economies. World Bank Policy Research Series 8761, Washington, DC.

Hadjimichael, Michael T., and Michel Galy. 1997. The CFA Franc Zone and the EMU. *IMF Working Papers* 97 (156): 1.

Heintz, James, and Leonce Ndikumana. 2011. Is There a Case for Formal Inflation Targeting in Sub-Saharan Africa? *Journal of African Economies* 20: ii67–ii103.

Hinkle, Lawrence E., and Peter J. Montiel. 1999. *Exchange Rate Misalignment: Concepts and Measurement for Developing Countries*. Washington, DC: World Bank.

Horn, Sebastian, Carmen Reinhart, and Christoph Trebesch. 2020. China's Overseas Lending. Kiel Institute for the World Economy ISSN 1862–1155.

IMF (International Monetary Fund). 2015a. Central African Economic and Monetary Community (CEMAC) Selected Issues. IMF Country Report No. 15/308, Washington, DC.

IMF. 2015b. West African Economic and Monetary Union Selected Issues. IMF Country Report No. 15/101, Washington, DC.

IMF. 2016, April. Regional Economic Outlook: Sub-Saharan Africa.

IMF. 2017, April. Western Hemisphere Regional Economic Outlook: Tale of Two Adjustments. Washington, DC.

IMF. 2019a. Central African Economic and Monetary Community (CEMAC): Staff Report on the Common Policies in Support of Member Countries Reform Programs. Washington, DC.

IMF. 2019b. West African Economic and Monetary Union (UEMOA): Staff Report on the Common Policies in Support of Member Countries Reform Programs. Washington, DC.

IMF. 2020, October. Regional Economic Outlook: Sub-Saharan Africa, Washington, DC.

Intergovernmental Panel on Climate Change. 2013. Fifth Assessment Report, United Nations.

International Budget Partnership. 2014. Are New PFM Reforms in the WAEMU and the CEMAC Working? Lessons from the Open Budget Survey, by Babacar Sarr, IBF Research Note.

International Finance Corporation. 2020. Creating Markets in Cote d'Ivoire: Mobilizing the Private Sector in Support of Economic Transformation in Côte d'Ivoire. Washington, DC.

International Labor Organization (ILO). 2020. *The COVID-19 Response: Getting Gender Equality Right for a Better Future for Women at Work*. Geneva: ILO Policy Brief.

Kabir, Golam, Najmul Hossain, and Moutushi Rahman. 2011. Liberalization of the Bangladesh's Agriculture Sector: Lessons Learned from the 1980s and the 1990s. Research report, December 2011.

Kasekende, Louis. 2011. The Evolving Nature of Macroeconomic Management in Sub-Saharan Africa and its Implications for IMF Programs Speech by Dr Louis Kasekende, Deputy Governor of the Bank of Uganda, Kampala, 26 January 2011.

Kavanagh, Michael. 2006. The 1994 Devaluation of the CFA Franc and the Changing Role of France in African Development. International Affairs Council, Working Paper Number 06-04, New Haven, CT.

Khan, Dominique Strauss. 2019. Breaking the Taboo. 'The Current System Has to Be Seriously Cleaned Up'. Interview with Africa Report. https://www.theafricareport.com/14317/dominique-strauss-kahn-and-the-cfa-franc-the-current-system-has-to-be-seriously-cleaned-up/.

Khan, Mohsin and Abdelhak S. Senhadji. 2000. Financial Development and Economic Growth; An Overview. IMF Working Papers 00/209, International Monetary Fund.

Konnert, Dirk. 1998. The Euro, a Blessing for Africa? Consequences of the peg of the African Franc CFA to the Euro, Munich. MPRA_paper_5777.pdf.

Kose, M. Ayhan, Franziska Ohnsorge, Peter Nagle, and Naotaka Sugawara. 2020. Caught by a Cresting Debt Wave, Finance and Development, June 2020, 57(2). Washington, DC.

Laborde, David, Will Martin, and Rob Vos. Poverty and Food Insecurity Could Grow Dramatically as COVID-19 Spreads. IFPRI, Washington, DC. https://www.ifpri.org/blog/poverty-and-food-insecurity-could-grow-dramatically-covid-19-spreads.

Levy, Brian, 2014. *Working with the Grain. Integrating Governance and Growth in Development Strategies*. Oxford: Oxford University Press.

Lopez, Carlos. 2016. Franc CFA Outdated. Interview with Africa News. https://www.africanews.com/2016/09/28/franc-cfa-outdated-un-assistant-secretary-carlos-lopez/.

Mbaye, A.A., S.S. Golub, and Phil English. 2015. Policies, Prices, and Poverty: The Sugar, Vegetable Oil, and Flour Industries in Senegal. World Bank Policy Research Working Paper 7286, Washington, DC.

McMillan, Margaret S., and Dani Rodrik, 2011. Globalization, Structural Change, and Productivity Growth. NBER Working Paper 17143, National Bureau of Economic Research, Cambridge, MA.

McMillan, Margaret, Dani Rodrik, and Íñigo Verduzco-Gallo. 2014. Globalization, Structural Change, and Productivity Growth, with an Update on Africa. *World Development* 63 (C): 11–32.

McMillan, Margaret, Dani Rodrik, and Claudia Sepulveda. 2017. Structural Change, Fundamentals and Growth: A Framework and Case Studies. NBER Working Paper No. 23378, May.

Mendelsohn, R., A. Dinar, and A. Dalfelt. 2000. *Climate Change Impacts on African Agriculture. Preliminary Analysis Prepared for the World Bank.* Washington, DC: World Bank.

Monga, Célestin, and Justin Yifu Lin (eds.). 2015. *The Oxford Handbook of Africa and Economics*, 2 vols. Oxford, UK: Oxford University Press.

Ndikumana, Leonce, and James K. Boyce. 2018. Capital Flight: Updated Methodology and New Estimates. Political Economy Research Institute (PERI), University of Massachusetts at Amherst.

Newfarmer, Richard S, John Page, and Finn Tarp, eds. 2018. *Industries Without Smokestacks: Industrialization in Africa Reconsidered*. Oxford: Oxford University Press.

Nguyen Do Anh Tuan. 2010. Vietnam's Agrarian Reform, Rural Livelihood and Policy Issues. http://www.rimisp.org/wp-content/uploads/2010/05/Paper_Nguyen_Do_Anh_Tuan.pdf.

Nubukpo, Kako, 2019. Which Future for the CFA? https://agridigitale.net/art-which_future_for_cfa_franc_.html.

Nubukpo, Kako. 2020. The ECO and the CFA Franc: Four Weddings and a Funeral. The Africa Report, January.

O'Connell, Stephen A. 2012. Inflation Targeting in Africa. *Oxford Companion to the Economics of Africa*, 359–364. Oxford: Oxford University Press.

Olabisi, Michael, and Howard Stein. 2015. Sovereign bond issues: Do African countries pay more to borrow? *Journal of African Trade* 2 (2015): 87–109.

Opiyo, Levin. 2019. https://www.insideover.com/economy/monetary-independence-looms-for-west-and-central-africa.

Pritchett, Lant, and Nita Ghei. 1999. The Three Pessimisms: Exchange Rates and Trade Flows in the Franc Zone. In *Exchange Rate Misalignment: Concepts and Measurement for Developing Countries*, ed. L. Hinkle and P. Montiel. A World Bank Research Publication. Oxford: Oxford University Press.

Ranganathan, Rupa, Vivien Foster, and Cecilia Briceno-Garmendia. 2012. CEMAC's Infrastructure Gap: Issues and Policy Options. In *Oil Wealth in Central Africa*, ed. Bernardin Akitoby and Sharmini Coorey. Washington, DC: IMF.

Razafimahefa, Ivohasina. 2012. Exchange Rate Pass-Through in Sub-Saharan African Economies and its Determinants. IMF Working Papers 12/141, International Monetary Fund.

Rodrik, Dani. 2008. The Real Exchange Rate and Economic Growth. *Brookings Papers on Economic Activity* 39 (2): 365–439.

Rogoff, Kenneth. 2002. Managing the World Economy, Economic Counsellor and Director of the Research Department, International Monetary Fund, The Economist, London.

Ross, Michael. 2014. *What Have We Learned about the Resource Curse?* Los Angeles: University of California, (UCLA) Department of Political Science.

Sachs, Jeffrey, and Andrew M. Warner. 1995. Natural Resource Abundance and Economic Growth. NBER Working Papers 5398, National Bureau of Economic Research, Inc.

Sachs, Jeffrey, John McArthur, Guido Schmidt-Traub, Margaret Kruk, Chandrika Bahadur, Michael Faye, and Gordon Cord. 2004. Ending Africa's Poverty Trap. Columbia University and UN Millennium Project.

Schenk, Catherine. 2010. *The Decline of Sterling Managing the Retreat of an International Currency, 1945–1992*. Cambridge University Press.

Schenk, Catherine. 2018. *The Sterling Area 1945–1972, Handbook of the History of Money and Currency*. Singapore: Springer.

Setser, Brad. 2007. The Case for Exchange Rate Flexibility in Oil-Exporting Economies. Policy Briefs PB07-8, Peterson Institute for International Economics.

Stasavage, David. 1997. The CFA Franc Zone and Fiscal Discipline. *Journal of African Economies* 6 (1): 132–167.

Stasavage, David. 2003. When Do States Abandon Monetary Discretion, Lessons from the Evolution of the CFA Franc Zone. In *Monetary Orders: Ambiguous Economics, Ubiquitous Politics*, ed. David Kirshner. Cornell: Cornell University Press.

Stiglitz, Joseph. 2016. The Problem with Europe is the Euro, Interview with *The Guardian*. https://www.theguardian.com/business/2016/aug/10/joseph-stiglitz-the-problem-with-europe-is-the-euro.

Sy, Amadou Nicolas Racine. 2006. Financial Integration in the West African Economic and Monetary Union (September 2006). IMF Working Paper, 1–25

Sylla, Ndongo Samba. 2020. The Franc Zone, a Tool of French Neocolonialism in Africa. https://www.jacobinmag.com/2020/01/franc-zone-french-neocolonialism-africa.

Tabsoba, Rene, and Zorobabel Bicaba. (2014). Low Inflation Luxury. Economic Lindau Nobel Laureate Meetings.

Tchatchouang, Jean Claude. 2015. The CFA Franc Zone: A Biography) in The Oxford Handbook of Africa and Economics: Volume 2: Policies and Practices (edited by Célestin Monga and Justin Yifu Lin).

Tornell, Aaron, and Andres Velasco. 2000. Fixed Versus Flexible Exchange Rates: Which Provides More Fiscal Discipline? Journal of Monetary Economics, Elsevier 45 (2): 399–436.

Tschirley, David Lawrence, Colin Poulton, and Patrick Labaste. 2009. *Organization and Performance of Cotton Sectors in Africa: Learning from Reform Experience*. Washington, DC: World Bank.

UN Intergovernmental Panel on Climate Change (IPCC). 2014. Fifth Assessment Report. New York.

United States Treasury. 2009. Report to Congress on IMF and World Bank Collaboration and IMF Accountability. https://www.treasury.gov/resource-center/international/int-monetary-fund/Documents/(2009-07-22)%20Bank%20Fund%20collaboration%20report%20FINAL.pdf.

Van de Walle, Nicholas. 1991. The Decline of the Franc Zone: Monetary Politics in Francophone Africa. *African Affairs* 90 (360): 383–412.

World Bank. 2016. *Togo Systematic Country Diagnostic*. World Bank: Washington, DC. http://documents1.worldbank.org/curated/en/179631474899157168/pdf/Togo-SCD-Final-2016-09222016.pdf.

World Bank. 2017. Cameroon Country Economic Memorandum: Markets, Government, and Growth. Washington DC.

World Bank. 2018a. The Challenges of Urbanization in West Africa, AFCW3 Economic Update. Washington DC, Spring.

World Bank. 2018b. Groundswell: Preparing for Internal Climate Migration.

World Bank Group. 2019. Profiting from Parity: Unlocking the Potential of Women's Business in Africa. World Bank, Washington, DC. © World Bank. https://openknowledge.worldbank.org/handle/10986/31421.

WBGU (German Advisory Council on Global Change). 2007. *Climate Change as a Security Risk*. London: Earthscan.

Yade, Mbaye, Anne Chohin-Kuper, Valerie Kelly, John M. Staatz, and James Tefft. 1999, The Role of Regional Trade in Agricultural Transformation: The Case of West Africa Following the Devaluation of the CFA Franc, Michigan State University, Lansing, Staff Paper 99-28, June 27–30.

Yilmaz, Serdar, Abdoulaye Ouedraogo, and Mehmet Serkan Tosun. 2016. Cyclicality of Public Investment in Africa. *International Journal of Public Policy* 12 (3/4/5/6): 378–405.

Zafar, Ali. 2004. What Happens When a Country Does Not Adjust to Terms of Trade Shocks? The Case of Oil-Rich Gabon? World Bank Policy Research Working Paper No. 3403, World Bank, Washington, DC.

Zafar, Ali. 2005a. Revenue and the Fiscal Impact of Trade Liberalization: The Case of Niger. World Bank Policy Research Working Paper No. 3500, World Bank, Washington, DC.

Zafar, Ali. 2005b. The Impact of the Strong Euro on the Real Effective Exchange Rates of the Two Francophone African CFA Zones. World Bank Policy Research Working Paper No. 3751, World Bank, Washington, DC.

Zafar, Ali. 2007. The Growing Relationship between China and Sub-Saharan Africa Macroeconomic, Trade, Investment and Aid Links. *The World Bank Research Observer* 22: 103–130.

Zafar, Ali, and Keiko Kubota. 2003. The CEMAC: Regional Integration in Central Africa: Key Issues. The World Bank Working Papers—Africa Region Working Papers 52, Washington, DC.

Index

A. Zafar, *The CFA Franc Zone*,
https://doi.org/10.1007/978-3-030-71006-4

GPSR Compliance
The European Union's (EU) General Product Safety Regulation (GPSR) is a set of rules that requires consumer products to be safe and our obligations to ensure this.

If you have any concerns about our products, you can contact us on

ProductSafety@springernature.com

In case Publisher is established outside the EU, the EU authorized representative is:

Springer Nature Customer Service Center GmbH
Europaplatz 3
69115 Heidelberg, Germany

www.ingramcontent.com/pod-product-compliance
Lightning Source LLC
Chambersburg PA
CBHW060429200525
26896CB00016B/727
9783030710057